Nicholas Royle is the author of three novels – *Counterparts* (Penguin), *Saxophone Dreams* (Penguin) and *The Matter of the Heart* (Abacus) – and around a hundred short stories. He has edited numerous anthologies, including *The Ex Files: New Stories About Old Flames* (Quartet) and *The Time Out Book of New York Short Stories* (Penguin). He is also online editor of *Time Out Net Books* (www.timeout.com).

EDITED BY NICHOLAS ROYLE
NEONLIT

Time Out BOOK OF NEW WRITING VOL.1

QUARTET BOOKS

First published by Quartet Books Limited in 1998
A member of the Namara Group
27 Goodge Street
London W1P 2LD

Introduction copyright © Nicholas Royle 1998

The moral right of Nicholas Royle to be identified as editor of this work has been asserted by him in accordance with the Copyright, Designs and Patent Act 1988.

All rights reserved. No part of this book may be reproduced in any form or by any means without prior permission of the publisher.

A catalogue record for this book is available from the British Library

ISBN 0 7043 8090 0

Typeset by FSH Ltd, London
Printed and bound in Great Britain by Cox & Wyman, Reading, Berks

Introduction copyright © Nicholas Royle 1998, *Thirteen Places of Interest in Kentish Town* copyright © Christopher Fowler 1998, *Spaces* copyright © Cath Skinner 1998, *Head of a Girl* copyright © Brian Howell 1998, *Quaint Honour* copyright © Christopher Burns 1998, *Travelling at Night* copyright © G.A. Pickin 1998, *What the Water Yields* copyright © Mike O'Driscoll 1998, *Clean* copyright © David Rose 1998, *The Precipice* copyright © James Miller 1998, *The Big Picture* copyright © Bonnie Greer 1998, *Me and the Rest of the World* copyright © John O'Connell 1998, *The Dressing Floors* copyright © Tim Nickels 1998, *Huddersfield versus Crewe* copyright © Alan Beard 1998, *The Ball* copyright © Stephen O'Reilly 1998, *Umph* copyright © Hannah Griffiths 1998, *Not That Funny* copyright © Gabriel Brown 1998, *The Beautiful Space* copyright © Jason Gould 1998, *Fishy Tales* copyright © Fred Normandale 1998, *The Gift* copyright © Louise Doughty 1998, *Looking for Jake* copyright © China Miéville 1998, *Daddy's Girl* copyright © Emma Donoghue 1998, *A Higher Agency* copyright © Toby Litt 1998, *Breathing Under Water* copyright © Christopher Kenworthy 1998, *Alice* copyright © Ron Butlin 1998, *Threshold* copyright © Colm O'Gaora 1998, *Lessons in Pleasure* copyright © Hilaire 1998, *eta* copyright © Conrad Williams 1998, *A Designated Space* copyright © Trezza Azzopardi 1998, *Graceland* copyright © John Burnside 1998, *Black and White* copyright © Derek Marlowe 1998, *Framework of Loss* copyright © Art Corriveau 1998

CONTENTS

INTRODUCTION	1
THIRTEEN PLACES OF INTEREST IN KENTISH TOWN – CHRISTOPHER FOWLER	9
SPACES – CATH SKINNER	18
HEAD OF A GIRL – BRIAN HOWELL	24
QUAINT HONOUR – CHRISTOPHER BURNS	30
TRAVELLING AT NIGHT – G.A. PICKIN	48
WHAT THE WATER YIELDS – MIKE O'DRISCOLL	52
CLEAN – DAVID ROSE	73
THE PRECIPICE – JAMES MILLER	80
THE BIG PICTURE – BONNIE GREER	98
ME AND THE REST OF THE WORLD – JOHN O'CONNELL	102
THE DRESSING FLOORS – TIM NICKELS	116
HUDDERSFIELD VERSUS CREWE – ALAN BEARD	126
THE BALL – STEPHEN O'REILLY	137
UMPH – HANNAH GRIFFITHS	145
NOT THAT FUNNY – GABRIEL BROWN	156
THE BEAUTIFUL SPACE – JASON GOULD	159
FISHY TALES – FRED NORMANDALE	177
THE GIFT – LOUISE DOUGHTY	189
LOOKING FOR JAKE – CHINA MIÉVILLE	193
DADDY'S GIRL – EMMA DONOGHUE	208
A HIGHER AGENCY – TOBY LITT	215
BREATHING UNDER WATER – CHRISTOPHER KENWORTHY	228
ALICE – RON BUTLIN	237
THRESHOLD – COLM O'GAORA	241
LESSONS IN PLEASURE – HILAIRE	248
eta – CONRAD WILLIAMS	258
A DESIGNATED SPACE – TREZZA AZZOPARDI	277
GRACELAND – JOHN BURNSIDE	284
BLACK AND WHITE – DEREK MARLOWE	297
FRAMEWORK OF LOSS – ART CORRIVEAU	312
BIOGRAPHICAL NOTES	325
APPENDIX	329

To the memory of
Robert Rubens (1937-98)

INTRODUCTION

Neon was first separated from other inert gases exactly a hundred years ago by British chemists Sir William Ramsay and Morris Travers. It may be a colourless, odourless gaseous element that makes up only a tiny fraction of the Earth's atmosphere, but stick neon in a vacuum electric-discharge tube and it produces the instantly recognizable crimson glow that has become an inseparable part of the urban environment all over the world.

Which is not to suggest that all of the thirty short stories that make up this volume are city-based. Dip into *Neonlit* and you're as likely (in fact, three times as likely) to end up somewhere in rural Ireland as haunting the backstreets of Kentish Town; you've as much chance of finding yourself marooned in a trawler off Scarborough as trapped in an Italian restaurant in Shepherd's Bush. It was never our particular intention to bring you stories set in some of the world's most vibrant and exotic cities, but that is what we appear to have done: Tokyo, Rome, London, Naples and, ahem, Birmingham provide settings for different narratives. If you find the idea of the Greek islands, southern France or coastal resorts in Massachusetts and Western Australia just too exotic, there's always Warrington to come back to.

But setting is not everything. There are stories here about the past, the present and the future, tales of race and sexuality, accounts of seductions and meditations on violent death. If we were to attempt fully to describe the near infinite variety of the work in this book, we'd be up all night. Let's just say that this is a collection of new writing, by a mixture of new/newish writers and established authors. Not one of these pieces has appeared anywhere in any form before. Six contributors (Gabriel Brown, Hannah Griffiths, Fred Normandale, John O'Connell, Stephen O'Reilly and Cath Skinner) are being published here for the first time.

The only item published posthumously is Derek Marlowe's contribution. Marlowe, an English author and screenwriter whose suspenseful, elegiac novels took him to the fringes of a number of genres (espionage, crime, thriller, macabre, historical) while still allowing him to enjoy the benefits of mainstream respectability (today they are all out of print, a lamentable state of affairs that needs to be addressed), died in Los Angeles in November 1996, leaving an unfinished novel-in-progress under the working title *Black and White*. Thanks to the kind co-operation of Marlowe's sisters and his son, Ben, we are able to publish the prologue and first two chapters of that unfinished novel.

Jack Trevor Story Memorial Prize

While we're on the subject of late, great English writers, you know someone's in danger of drifting into obscurity when you search for their name on the Internet and both AltaVista and Excite fail to find it. Jack Trevor Story (1920–91) was the author of *The Trouble with Harry* (filmed by Hitchcock), *Live Now, Pay Later* (also filmed), *The Urban District Lover* and *One Last Mad Embrace*. The Jack Trevor Story Memorial Prize, sponsored and judged by Michael Moorcock, is now being run in conjunction with this volume. When it was organized alongside the London Arts Board's London Short Story Competition, the prize-winner was quite simply the author who, in the judge's opinion, had entered the funniest story. A couple of years down the line, the prize-winner needs to do more than make Michael Moorcock laugh the most. He or she needs to express something in his or her story that is closest to the essence of Jack Trevor Story. One does that either by accident or by going to dig out Story's stories. This year, in this book, since there was no advance warning given about the prize, the winner succeeds via the former route.

The terms of the prize, worth £500, are based on Jack Trevor

Story's famous reply to the bankruptcy judge who asked where his film advance money had gone in such a short time: 'You know how it is, your honour, twenty or twenty thousand, it always lasts a week to a fortnight.' The terms, then, as devised by Michael Moorcock, are that the money be spent within a fortnight and the author should preferably have nothing to show for it.

And the winner is...

'There were about four close contenders,' Moorcock e-mails us from Texas, 'but in the end I picked Fred Normandale's "Fishy Tales" – its authenticity, I suppose, reminds me of Jack's and it had that broader humanity. Not fiction, really, but since the prize is entirely based now on what I like best and what I think reflects Jack's outlook best, I don't have any trouble with that. Moreover, the recipient will be able to spend the dosh like a drunken sailor.'

The three runners-up are John O'Connell, Toby Litt and Alan Beard.

Voices and Outlets

In 1963, Michael Joseph published *Voices*, which it described, accurately, as 'a collection of new short stories'. It included contributions from William Sansom, Christine Brooke-Rose, Terry Southern, Jean Rhys, Doris Lessing and many other interesting writers. Edited by Robert Rubens, a young American living in London, who was also working in an editorial capacity on the very fine *Transatlantic Review*, *Voices* aimed 'not only to include new stories by established writers...but to introduce "discoveries" hitherto unpublished in book form'. In the blurb on the jacket flap the publishers declared, 'Outlets for new short stories have become increasingly scarce and, in this country, are mostly confined to a handful of literary magazines.' Have things changed in the last thirty-five years?

Voices was conceived as the first of a series but doesn't seem to have been followed up. Anthologies of this kind come and go and most of them don't last very long. Penguin has been responsible for some of the most interesting series over the years, with *Penguin New Writing* (published 1940–50), *Penguin Modern Stories* (1969–71, reached double figures; each volume contained three or four authors) and

Firebird (four volumes, 1982–5). John Calder published *New Writers*, which by Volume 13 in the late 1970s became *New Writing & Writers*. Giles Gordon and David Hughes edited several volumes of *Best Short Stories*, starting in 1988, but these consisted of reprints of what the editors considered to be the best short stories published in the previous twelve months. There were also several volumes of the Arts Council anthology *New Stories*, which at first was published by the Arts Council itself (Volume 1, edited by Margaret Drabble and Charles Osborne in 1976, contained a piece by Christopher Burns, a contributor to the volume you hold in your hands, entitled 'The Mummification of Princess Anne', as well as contributions by Elizabeth Baines, who would later edit *Metropolitan*, and Giles Gordon, in those days a writer of experimental fiction); it was later taken on by Hutchinson. PEN, the international writers' association, was also involved in *New Stories* and later two further PEN anthologies appeared under the title *New Fiction*, published by Quartet. Volume 1 (1984), edited by Peter Ackroyd, included the first published short story by Ackroyd's mentor Iain Sinclair; Volume 2 (1987) was helmed by Allan Massie.

Bloomsbury has published a number of volumes in its *Soho Square* series, which became a themed affair (recent volumes have been devoted to Irish and Scottish fiction), and in 1997 published the first of an intended series of anthologies in collaboration with the *Independent on Sunday*, which ran a competition to attract contributions. There has been no sign of a second volume.

Granta Books published a new anthology, *Shorts*, in September 1998. Although a few of the stories had appeared or been broadcast before, most contributions were original. Highlights included stories by Christopher Burns and Philip MacCann. Sadly, there are no plans for a second volume.

Faber and Faber still publishes the annual *Introductions* anthology (now up to volume 14), which showcases a substantial amount of new work by a small number of writers (some of whom, it is then announced, have longer work forthcoming from Faber and Faber). Vintage and the British Council collaborate on *New Writing* (Volume 7 is current); its annually changing editorship may mean that it keeps fresh, but it doesn't help to create any sense of consistency. Flamingo's *New Scottish Writing* has been going, in one form or another, since

1973; and Phoenix House now has a series for Irish fiction. You might well ask where are the anthologies devoted specifically to new English short stories? Whoever finds the courage to instigate one will no doubt cause a minor fracas. Arc Publications does run an annual Northern Short Story Competition and publishes winning entries in *Northern Stories*. The Centre for Creative and Performing Arts at the University of East Anglia, of course, publishes an annual anthology of work by students taking the MA course in creative writing. A new north London-based publisher, Pulp Faction, which published its first anthology, *Skin*, in 1995, already has more than half a dozen subsequent volumes under its belt and appears to be going from strength to strength, having branched out into publishing novels.

If there is one publisher which has done more than any other to keep the short story anthology alive in the last decade it is Serpent's Tail. Its supply of ambitious, high-quality anthologies – usually themed, but intelligently so – shows no sign of drying up. Victor Gollancz and Sceptre (now part of Hodder Headline) have shown a certain amount of interest in – and enjoyed a gratifying degree of success with – original, themed anthologies as well in recent years.

Numerous anthologies are published in the popular genres – horror, science fiction, fantasy and crime. Two titles are outstanding and notable: *Dark Terrors* (Victor Gollancz), edited by Stephen Jones and David Sutton, and *New Worlds* (White Wolf Publishing), edited by David Garnett. Neither is a themed anthology, both publish only the very best new fiction in their respective fields, and it's to their credit that each is constantly blurring the border between genre and mainstream. Much of the best material from these two long-running, award-winning series would be just as at home in some of the supposedly more literary anthologies.

Colonizing the grey area between genre and mainstream, Barrington Books published three significant anthologies, *The Sun Rises Red*, *Sugar Sleep* and *The Science of Sadness*, in the early 1990s before closing. These have not been easy times in which to run small independent presses and publisher Christopher Kenworthy (another *Neonlit* contributor) was left with little time to devote to his own writing. Occupying similar territory, Cambridgeshire-basedTTA Press published an anthology, *Last Rites & Resurrections*, as an offshoot from its award-winning magazine, *The Third Alternative* (see Appendix).

Time Out has made its own contribution to the world of anthologies with *The Time Out Book of London Short Stories* and *The Time Out Book of New York Short Stories* (both Penguin). *The Time Out Book of Paris Short Stories* is forthcoming from Penguin in spring 1999.

Literary magazines, like anthologies, come and go. Some have come (*em writing & music, Entropy, The Edge, This Is*), a few have gone (*Panurge, Metropolitan, Sunk Island Review*) and others have stuck around (*London Magazine, Ambit, The Devil, Main Street Journal, Back Brain Recluse, The Third Alternative, Granta*). Most pay little or nothing for contributions. Ron Butlin, yet another contributor to *Neonlit*, unwittingly provided a *Guardian* reporter with his opening anecdote to a piece about short stories and the markets available for them. 'Ron Butlin, hailed by Irvine Welsh as "one of the best Scottish writers for years", has just sold a 7,200-word short story to a magazine. His rejoicing, however, is muted,' wrote John Ezard. 'The magazine, a reputable one, told him it usually paid £5 per 1,000 words. But his story was so long that it hit its top rate of £20. Mr Butlin accepted. British outlets for short stories are pitifully few. Most magazines no longer publish them. Poor sales have killed two of the main yearly book anthologies for the once-dominant form in the past few years' (*Guardian*, 20 July 1998).

(The article went on to talk about the Travelman, a new concept in short story publishing. Stories are published individually in fold-out form like a map and sold at station bookstalls as well as in bookshops. At the time of writing, the series has just been launched and it's pretty much all reprints by famous names. It would be good to see them do some new stuff by interesting – i.e. not just the most obvious – people.)

Contributors to many of the magazines listed above are often glad of the exposure and any payment is a (small) bonus. If some of these magazines don't pay their contributors, it's not for want of the desire to do so. The magazines are also struggling to survive. As we are about to go to press we hear that *Entropy*, one of the most innovative and exciting of the bunch, is running into the kind of financial troubles that can prove fatal. *Billy Liar*, too, has announced that funding problems lie behind its temporary closure; it hopes to be back by the summer of 1999.

If print journals are having a hard time of it, things are a little easier on the Internet. Links to just a few of the countless online literary magazines can be found in *Time Out Net Books* (www.timeout.com).

Publishing has certainly changed since Robert Rubens edited *Voices* in 1963, but perhaps specifically in relation to short stories it hasn't changed all that much. Rubens, sadly, died in January this year. Living in London again, he had been working on an ambitious ten-volume work of fiction, five books of which he completed. A new novel, *Two on an Island*, is forthcoming from Arcadia Books this autumn.

The above was only ever meant to be a partial (meanings one and two both intended) overview of the recent history of anthologies and the state of play in the literary magazines business. Any errors or inaccuracies are entirely the fault of the editor and he offers his apologies to any editor or publisher who feels they have been overlooked. Glaring omissions can be rectified in *Neonlit 2*, provided it gets the go-ahead, which is entirely dependent, of course, on the performance of the current volume.

Nicholas Royle
Time Out, London
August 1998

THIRTEEN PLACES OF INTEREST IN KENTISH TOWN
CHRISTOPHER FOWLER

These places of interest in Kentish Town may be enjoyed in a single pleasant stroll through the area. You should allow a time of approximately two hours. Unlike most walks, which take in only buildings of local historical interest, this walk is designed to give a flavour of daily life in the neighbourhood.

If you would prefer to take a shorter route, may we suggest commencing from Camden Parkway Cinema, walking up to the base of Parliament Hill near the Gospel Oak Lido, then down to Burghley Road in time for tea. This shorter journey should take no more than forty minutes, or less if you are walking briskly with a companion. If you are walking at dusk, be careful crossing the base of Parliament Hill, as the ground is often muddy and it is easy to slip over.

1. Bentinck's Grocery Store, Angler's Lane

This unassuming one-storey house once stood on the bank of a tributary of the River Fleet. When the river was enclosed and connected to the Grand Union Canal at Camden, it became part of north London's new sewer system and a roadway was constructed above it. At that time the building was converted into a vegetable store, and has remained so to this day.

The store stocks a wide variety of traditional market produce, mostly grown in Kent, although some non-seasonal items are imported from the Canary Islands and certain fashionable fruits are shipped in from the West Indies. At Christmas Bentinck's extends its range to include nuts, dried fruit, floral wreaths and table centrepieces. The store is used mainly by housewives living in the immediate streets to the south and west of Angler's Lane.

A typical visitor to the store would have been Mrs Kathleen Atherton. Every week for thirty years she purchased the family's fruit and vegetables here. A native of Kentish Town and the last surviving member of one of the area's oldest families, the strong-willed Mrs Atherton was always careful to balance her family's dietary needs with the availability of fresh farm produce. She continued to patronize the shop after growing infirmities limited her mobility, and refused all offers of help from staff, preferring to select produce personally. A lifelong Conservative, she found it difficult to express emotion, and preferred to take action, however inappropriate.

Since the opening of two hypermarkets in the vicinity, custom has declined at Bentinck's Grocery Store. The little shop could not compete with low prices brought about by the bulk-purchasing power of the superstores, and is now closing its shutters for the last time.

2. Kentish Town Baths, Prince of Wales Road

This elegant Edwardian building with art-nouveau flourishes started life as the St Pancras Baths and Wash-houses. It was provided with four swimming pools, a hundred and twenty-nine slipper-baths and a public laundry which is still in use to this day. Like many housewives in the neighbourhood, Mrs Atherton preferred to pay someone to do her laundry twice a week, and disliked the idea of owning her own washing machine.

On the first floor of the baths a state-of-the-art gymnasium now caters for the area's young professionals, and its apparatus provides much-needed physical stimulation for local men and women of all ages.

In charge of the exercise classes is Ms Pauline Metcalf. Thirty-two-year-old Pauline hails from Derby and moved to London with her young son Neville, on whom she doted, to escape unhappy memories of a difficult divorce. Twice winner of the National Physical Prowess Certificate, Pauline took step-classes and aerobics every day except Sunday, enjoyed swimming and liked to keep herself in shape.

In November 1986 she gave up her classes following a painful personal tragedy and moved back to Derby in February of the following year. Like many young women, Ms Metcalf grew lonely on cold winter nights, and sought solace in the arms of married men.

3. Number 236, Kentish Town Road

Formerly the headquarters of EH Olive & Company, Tailors and Outfitters, who inhabited the building from just after the turn of the century, this property is now occupied by Abba Electronics, which sells reconditioned televisions, radios and all manner of electrical household equipment, available on easy terms of payment.

It is odd to think that in 1903 an overcoat purchased in EH Olive & Co. cost just eight shillings and eleven pence, which in today's decimal currency is just under forty-five pence and would not buy a light bulb in Abba Electronics.

The stables at the rear of the shops on Kentish Town Road were constructed to house the horses from nearby Highgate Racetrack, and after the Second World War were converted into warehouses for use by the high street's various stores, including Abba Electronics.

The former manager of the establishment, Mr William Atherton, worked here and at two other branches located in Camden Town and Belsize Park until 1987, when he was forced into sudden retirement on grounds of ill-health. Mr Atherton would describe himself as a good but essentially weak man.

4. Bus Shelter, Fortess Road

This small, unprepossessing concrete shelter was built in 1946 when the new bus routes to Highgate via Archway came into use, and has been twice featured in the national news.

In March 1953 a coach full of nuns visiting the Richard Stanhope Catholic School in Prince of Wales Road mounted the kerb and ploughed into a party of Agnostics waiting at the bus stop, killing two and injuring seven. Father O'Hanlon, the driver of the bus, was subsequently found to be drunk, and was jailed for four years.

Then, on 11 November 1986, the shelter was photographed and described as the site where a young schoolboy, Neville Metcalf, aged nine, was last seen alive. Witnesses recalled spotting him on one of the red plastic seats, dangling his legs and studying a comic in the late afternoon drizzle while he waited for a bus to take him in the direction of Camden Town.

Neville Metcalf was a shy, quiet pupil at Richard Stanhope who had learning difficulties, and was usually supervised on outings because of his willingness to be led by strangers. He was, however, a member of the school cinema club, and enjoyed swimming and football. He was an Arsenal supporter and an avid fan of the James Bond series, and would see each 007 film several times.

Despite an extensive police search lasting for several months, little Neville's whereabouts were never ascertained, and his disappearance remains one of the area's most enduring mysteries. Shortly after the disappearance his distraught mother made an emotional appeal on national television, but the resulting leads all proved to be dead-ends.

5. Number 24, Burghley Road

This is an Edwardian terraced house of a type typically found to the north of Kentish Town's main thoroughfare. The high-ceilinged, well-proportioned rooms were created for well-off middle-class families at a time when Kentish Town was still considered to be a leafy suburb of London, long before it gained its present reputation of being 'inner city'. The house, within walking distance of Parliament Hill Fields, was for many years the home of Mr and Mrs William Atherton, typical residents of Kentish Town.

The airy, pleasant rooms of the houses were intended for families who could afford several children, but shortly after their marriage Mrs Atherton discovered that she would never be able to bear a child, and the upstairs rooms she had planned as a nursery and live-in nurse's quarters remained empty for many years.

In early November 1986, Mrs Atherton suffered a nervous attack and disappeared overnight, returning the next day only to lock herself inside her back bedroom. She refused to come out for two days, and then only agreed to do so after her husband had left the house. Subsequent to this she converted to the Catholic religion, and redecorated the upper floor of the house for her own habitation, leaving it only to cook her husband's meals and to care for him after his retirement.

Mr Atherton died nine years later in 1995, after a tragically prolonged illness, at which time the house was sold and divided into four flats.

6. Number 5, Cathcart Street

This modest home, typical of the area, was rented by Pauline Metcalf, who lived there with her son, Neville, for a number of years. The street takes its name from one of the generals of the Crimean War, which was fought just before these houses were built. Many of the surrounding area's street-names recall battles from that glorious folly in the Valley of Death. The residential properties were originally constructed to provide homes for immigrant Irish workers, who were employed by the council to build railroads extending from the north of the city in 1860, and many of these houses are still occupied by their descendants.

Today the original cobbled street remains much as it appeared in the previous century. The Crimea public house, which stood on the corner of Cathcart Street and Alma Street, once acted as a secret rendezvous-point for public-school spies Burgess and Maclean, and was a focus for much of the street's social life. It has recently been converted into apartments for young professionals.

Ms Metcalf's house, rented from the council, typically suffered from condensation and occasional flooding, being situated close to the underground river beneath Angler's Lane, but, like the other dwellings in this overlooked area, offered a small oasis of calm in an inner-city neighbourhood. Ms Metcalf eventually vacated her home following the tragic loss of her son.

7. The Vulture's Perch, corner of Islip Road and Kentish Town Road

This popular public house, while not as famous as its nearby neighbour the Assembly Rooms, which still boasts one of the finest collections of Victorian etched glass in England, began life as the Oxford Vaults. Many fine brewery products are available on tap, including London Bitter and Kronenberg. Its Saturday night discos, a throwback to 1970s entertainment, are extremely popular and attract a mixed local crowd of all ages.

One such typical customer would have been Pauline Metcalf, who often came here after she finished conducting exercise classes at the Kentish Town Baths. Ms Metcalf started attending the Saturday night discos in October 1984, and continued to enjoy drinking and dancing there for the next two years.

Just before Christmas of that year, Mr William Atherton also began visiting the pub on Saturday nights while Mrs Atherton was visiting relatives in Belsize Park, and subsequently took up weight-training at the gymnasium in Kentish Town Baths in order to lose the stomach he had gained through drinking.

8. Holmes Road Police Station, Holmes Road

If you stand outside this fine late Victorian building, built in 1895, you will see the old arch of the stables to your right, and a sympathetically constructed modern extension to your left. Many Victorian police stations still retain their original architectural features and compete in the maintenance of their summer flowerbeds, and Holmes Road is no exception. In the basement of the building are four overnight holding cells, still with original Victorian fittings, and at the back of the ground floor is the interview room where Pauline Metcalf was first questioned about the disappearance of her only child, Neville, in November 1986.

After a highly emotional series of interviews Ms Metcalf was released pending her availability for further questioning. She was particularly upset that a two-month sentence for shoplifting seven years earlier appeared to be prejudicing the course of the investigation, and later sued the police, winning her case.

During the course of her penultimate interview she admitted that her involvement with a married man had begun over two years earlier and continued to the present time. Although she officially refused to name him, it is believed that Ms Metcalf later revealed her lover's identity to the officer in charge, and that the gentleman was subsequently brought in for questioning.

The unnamed man explained that he had been drinking in the Vulture's Perch, Kentish Town Road, on the evening of Neville Metcalf's disappearance, and his alibi was confirmed by the bar staff and several customers. Visibly distraught, he was released without charge. Shortly after this time, Mr Atherton's health began to deteriorate, and he was forced to retire.

9. The Old Post Office, Leighton Road

This attractive red-brick postal sorting office, which finally shut its doors to the public in 1994, was built during the reign of King Edward VII, and the initials ER (Edwardus Rex) may still be seen on the building and the adjacent railings. In the decades of its public service it saw the style of its staff change from smartly uniformed courteous post officials to louts in trainers. At this building a letter could be collected if for some reason it proved impossible for the postmen to deliver it.

Taken at random, a typical letter might have been the one posted to Mr Atherton on 9 November 1986. The recent heavy rainfall had rusted the spring of the letter box at Abba Electronics, a popular high street shop, and the postman was unable to deliver the mail that morning.

Responding to a Royal Mail form she found in the breast pocket of her husband's shirt as she took it to the laundry, Mrs Atherton was able to go to the post office that evening and collect the letter, which bore a handwritten return address in Cathcart Street, Kentish Town.

10. Parliament Hill Fields, Upper Kentish Town

There is much confusion as to where exact boundary lines fall between Parliament Hill, Kentish Town and Gospel Oak, but it is a fact that the rolling green hills bordering all three areas are enjoyed by residents from every part of the borough. At the foot of the main hill are numerous tennis courts, a bowling green and refreshment rooms incorporating a special play area for children. The nearby heath is particularly popular with gentlemen who prefer to take their constitutionals at around two in the morning.

The grass at the base of the fields was wet on the evening of 11 November 1986, and shone a livid green even in the sickly winter light. A lost item, such as a boy's red and white Arsenal scarf, would have stood out quite clearly, even at a distance.

Later that night, the year's fiercest storm broke out above the town, blackening the sky over Parliament Hill, where several oak and beech trees were rent asunder by lightning, and the downpour soaked the ground so thoroughly that all footprints were washed back into the soil.

11. Gospel Oak Lido

This charming open-air swimming pool was constructed in 1934 in an art-deco style, complete with curve-fronted cafeteria and sapphire-blue moulded fountains, and has played host to thousands of local children and parents who have braved the chill waters of its Olympic-sized pool. In June 1996 Camden Council completed an extensive refurbishment programme on the lido, improving its sixty-year-old facilities for a new generation of bathers.

During the excavation to the west of the car park, below Parliament Hill Fields, a gruesome discovery was made when the body of a small child was dug from the upturned earth by a passing dog. The skeleton lay in builders' rubble which had been used as landfill for the shallow ditches that had lined this quiet corner during the previous decade.

Unfortunately, lime from builders' bags had soaked through to the skeleton, damaging it so badly that identification was rendered impossible. In an area as rich and diverse in population as this, great personal tragedies are certain to unfold, and we might only ever glimpse small parts of these interesting human stories.

12. Odeon Cinema, Camden Parkway

This popular venue was constructed in the 1930s and featured an elegant interior design typical of such cinemas built in central London before the war. During the box-office slump of the 1970s the auditorium was divided into two screens, and the foyer featured a stylish bar where nightly live entertainment could be enjoyed by patrons between film performances. No more than 500 yards away, another cinema, the Camden Plaza, showed continental and art films. In the late 1980s both cinemas were closed down, although the public protest that accompanied the closure of the Camden Parkway eventually resulted in it reopening as a bland modern multiplex reeking of overpriced stale popcorn.

A typical bill of fare on a random date, say an early evening performance on 11 November 1986, would have featured the new James Bond film, *From a View to a Kill*, in its main auditorium, and a typical audience at this time would include local schoolboys, and housewives from Kentish Town filling in the angry, empty hours before their husbands' return from work.

13. Raglan Road Day-care Centre, Raglan Road

This day-care centre run by Camden Social Services is a second home to local elderly ladies, many of them widowed, alone and barking mad, who attend during weekdays and enjoy a chance to socialize with others of their own age. On Tuesdays there is a sing-along with Mrs Birch, a local schoolteacher, at the piano, and a wide variety of other pursuits are available for the enjoyment of those attending.

There are a limited number of permanent residents who, through bereavement and ill-fortune, have found themselves destitute and alone in their twilight years.

One such resident is Mrs Kathleen Atherton, who came to the centre in late 1995 and stayed on until her hospitalization and subsequent death three years later. This colourful character outlived her husband after nursing him through the course of a crippling wasting disease, for which doctors could find no cure, or indeed cause.

Mrs Atherton was a familiar sight who touched the hearts of everyone passing the centre on their way to and from Bentinck's Grocery Store in Angler's Lane. On most summer days she could be seen seated at the open window, framed by the dingy net curtains, draped in an old Arsenal football scarf, and she would tell anyone who listened fanciful stories of infidelity, rage and retribution.

SPACES
CATH SKINNER

The First Space

The first thing that happened was that Angela saw her hand as if through a magnifying glass (the weak, bulby kind you get in Christmas crackers) – more perfectly lined but smaller and somehow isolated. And a space of about three inches was created between her and the hand.

To begin with, the extra space was rather awkward. It got between bus doors and tins of carrots in the supermarket and deflected water from the tap. But Angela got used to it and it became more amenable.

Then it began to fill up. At first Angela noticed only a gnat, rather squashed; it simply appeared in a corner and vanished at the edge of the space. Over the next few days spiders and butterflies and wasps came to inhabit the space. It got quite crowded. Angela hung yellow flypapers from the living-room ceiling and took to constantly dusting and brushing the house, though of course none of this had any effect on the space.

The Second Space

arrived on Tuesday. It had a local postmark and was delivered through the letter box with the rest of the post and a flyer for a leather-jacket sale. It made the post look like it was hovering above the doormat.

Angela felt this second intrusion was too much. She tried to brush it out with a newspaper – she didn't want to touch it (it was oozing a bit at the edges), just in case – but it wouldn't budge. She managed to flick the other letters off the top of it and opened them with washing-up gloves on. When she'd finished, she took the envelopes out to the wheelie bin, unrolled the gloves very carefully so the outsides rolled back on themselves into a ball and dropped them into the bin too. Then she went back inside and opened all the downstairs windows and the front and back doors, hoping for a breeze to blow the space out on to the street.

The Third and Fourth Spaces

appeared under the swing in the garden. They were deep transparent columns and glittered like ice on a June day. Angela got used to taking a wide berth when she went to water the wallflowers. She worried about letting the kids play on the swing, but the spaces didn't seem to bother them. They were young, after all.

Proliferation

It was a hot summer. Angela spent most mornings indoors, reading the paper or doing the children's ironing or watching daytime telly. Sometimes she popped across the road to Gill's for coffee. Or Marion and Sue stopped round on their way into town.

Angela usually had the radio on in the kitchen – she liked to have a bit of a dance when she was doing the washing-up. But one morning when she came in to put the kettle on she was horrified to find spaces pouring from the radio. For every note, every beat, a space wobbled out; they drifted up, then sank down and melted like drops of wax. She slammed the radio off, but it was too late. The kitchen floor was a mess. She tried to scrape the spaces off with a knife, but they had set. Spaces caked the curtains, the cooker and the work surfaces. The kitchen looked like the inside of a monkey cage. Tears began to roll down Angela's cheeks.

After that, Angela decided to try to outwit the spaces. She knew that if any more appeared without warning, she would instinctively react. And, although no one had seen her so far, she worried that it was only a matter of time before they might. She thought that if she found the spaces first, she could avoid the consequences of any more surprise appearances. She began to keep an eye out for them. Cautiously at first, out of the corner of her eye, then more boldly, challenging them, daring them to reveal themselves in whatever tints and solidity they took. And it was amazing how many more spaces there were that she hadn't even noticed before: one under the drain grid outside the bank; a space like a lunch box under the bench at the bus stop, filled with old keys (she wondered who'd lost them all); and a long rectangular space like a metal ventilation shaft, with air blowing through, sometimes hot, sometimes cold, suspended around the outside of the DMG offices.

It became a battle. She embarked upon a regime of meticulously checking all the places where she knew from past experience that they were likely to appear. And very quickly she had honed the art of tracking them down. The larger ones, she knew, were partly bounded by buildings, man-made and particularly angular: predictable. The miniature ones were more imaginative: they rattled in cans, showered from roadwork steam and inserted themselves in between teenagers holding hands.

Angela tried to put them in classes: by size, by shape, by whether they appeared on a warm or a breezy day. And, when it became hard to remember each one individually, to recall its particular character, she began to keep a notebook. She bought a cheap watercolour kit from the art shop in town and took to creating an impression of each space next to the information she had recorded about it. Of course she had her favourites, and, when she could, tried to pass by them. She smiled to herself when Sue at the corner shop talked about going to learn Spanish at the college in the evenings – she already had a hobby, and a most interesting one. She could get her notebooks out in the morning when the kids had gone to school and look at the spaces she had catalogued.

But the more there were, the more difficult it became to remember them all, and sometimes she would be surprised by a space she had forgotten about. Increasingly, it became trying, even dangerous, and she felt constantly under strain. She worried about what would happen if her memory deteriorated and she was swamped by the familiar spaces around which she currently planned her movements. This alarmed her and she bought a bottle of iron tablets to improve her memory.

She tried to halt the spread of the spaces while she could still cope with their numbers. She began to see the useful parts of her days as those in which she successfully checked out for spaces and didn't find any. Before she went to sleep each night she would go over in her mind how long it was since she had found the last space. This seemed to work: their rate of multiplication seemed to be slowing.

But some of the larger ones were becoming unmanageable. Particularly the huge, empty expanse that had opened up between the road and the island on Queen Street, which made getting to the NatWest so difficult that Angela had to persuade her husband to change their account over to Lloyd's, which was, so far, space-free.

Outmanoeuvred

Angela had been looking forward to Sheila from work's birthday do: it was at the new Indian that had opened up next to Tesco's. And she wasn't disappointed — the food was excellent and they'd got a discount because Rupa's son was assistant chef. Maybe she'd had one too many glasses of wine — she didn't get to go out much after the kids — but she only lived two streets away and the others were getting a taxi in the opposite direction out to Letchworth. It seemed silly to ring for another taxi when she could be home before it arrived. And she felt a bit guilty spending even more money on top of the meal.

She got half-way across Queen Street roundabout before she realized she couldn't cross the wasteland-space. She turned to go back, but, to her horror, the tarmac began to heave and roll like a bad Channel crossing, and finally splintered apart in a jagged rift behind her, cutting her off on the roundabout island. Her legs started to wobble and she lurched down into a sitting position. She put her head between her knees and was sick. She got some tissues out of her handbag and tried to wipe some of the red wine and red-coloured bits of chicken off her shoes. Fortunately none had gone on her dress. She crawled away from the small heap of ex-chicken tikka and lay still for a while, feeling a lot better for having been sick.

When her head had cleared a bit, she began to think about how she could get out of her encirclement. She risked a quick peek down over the edge of the island. Sharp black rock and the rusty carcasses of metal birds. And she thought she could hear the distant clanking of wings far, far beneath. She threw up again.

Rescue

It was the roadsweeper who found her. Stopping off for a fag at one of the entrance roads, he thought he could see a body on the roundabout. He tossed the fag out the cab window and went over to see if there'd been an accident or something. He tapped her on the shoulder. She felt icy. He tapped harder. Angela came to and started to cry. 'Been out here all night, love?' Angela nodded. 'Fall over last night or something?' She tried to shake her head, but the muscles for moving her neck sideways had seized up. 'Looks like you got a spot of hypothermia, like. Better get down the Lister, get it checked out. Stay here, right. I'll call an ambulance, get you taken in.' She tried to shake her head again, but it hurt too much. And by then, the roadsweeper had put his coat over her and gone off to find a phone box.

The ambulance took a long time to come. Angela felt terrible, but she managed to talk to the roadsweeper for a while about the state of the ambulance service and about his two young daughters before she passed out again. The ambulance siren woke her. As it drew up, she felt her body being swamped in a haze of comfort and had an overpowering yearning to be wrapped up in cotton wool and put in a nice warm bed. But when the back doors opened and the paramedics came towards her she had a sudden flashback to the scene in *ET* where the NASA people in spacesuits come down the plastic tunnel to try to get ET. They seemed to be dragging her down a long white tube towards the back of the ambulance. And the ambulance doors were opening on to a cupboard-like space. She couldn't see what was inside. A picture of an autopsy slab flashed up in front of her eyes and she began to struggle. The more she kicked, the more the paramedics seemed to tighten their grip and propel her forwards. They were talking to her, maybe laughing, but she couldn't hear what they were saying. As she approached the door she suddenly saw that the cupboard was a school kiln with children's pottery lined up inside, but the pieces of pottery were all Medusa heads and wild animals with gore dripping out of their mouths. Even after a sedative, it took two paramedics to get her in, screaming not to be thrown into the kiln.

Recovery

She spent a long time on the ward. It blurred a lot. That must have been the medication. In the blur nurses whisked by with syringes and food trays. They had grey uniforms, grey caps and grey faces. And her childhood aunts hovered just outside her field of vision, talking German to each other.

After a month, the drug aunts went away and the doctors sent Angela home. They put her on pills. She got a little plastic pill cabinet with a drawer for every day of the month. Like an advent calendar. By the time Christmas Day came, everything was grey. So she started the advent calendar again.

HEAD OF A GIRL
BRIAN HOWELL

When Kimura got back to the dump about ten minutes later, it was still there, wrapped in plastic like most of the piled rubbish. You could not see through the bag, however, as with most of the others tonight; it was a night for unburnables, when you were supposed to use transparent bags.

Between the dump and his flat there was a small car park, mostly empty, where he often stood on clear nights looking up at the sky. He felt secretly ashamed that, even at his age of fifty-nine, he still could not identify constellations. Yukiko had known a few, but he had never found the time. He knew it would simply be a question of buying a book. But perhaps he had been saving that particular pleasure for his old age.

The question occurred to him: had his old age begun? And if so, what had he done in his life to justify this heavy mantle? Perhaps it had begun when Yukiko had died. But why meditate on it? It would not serve him any good now.

He picked it up. He had not been prepared for how heavy it would feel. A shock of true excitement went through his body. Now he knew why he was doing this.

On the way back to his flat he thought about this ironic end to his day.

He had been bored with the exhibition. He found his attention wandering from the paintings to the legs of the many women moving quietly and respectfully around the gallery. He did not often go to exhibitions such as these; for that matter he did not go into central Tokyo that often, so perhaps he should *not* be surprised by the predominance of female patrons. They were mostly around twenty-five and, if they were in pairs, they often subsided into an unexpectedly casual posture, not the kind he was used to seeing from so many young women on the JR and subway lines.

He felt increasingly nowadays a sense of repugnance at so many aspects of modern female fashion, particularly a look common to many eighteen-year-olds, of brown, sometimes goldeny hair, metallic pink lipstick and overdone suntans which did not sit well on skin already blessed with a dark pigmentation.

Perhaps he dreamed that one of these young women would lapse so much into her pensive pose that her thoughts would wander, and gradually she would become aware of the sight of this older man so knowledgeable about the arts. Strange that he should have such thoughts now after so many years teaching when he had hardly noticed the young women in his charge.

Yet it was not, finally, the sight of these uniformly inviting features or indeed the sudden realization of their appearance in his life that gripped him now. It was rather the sight of one particular face, in a portrait, of a young woman, of perhaps seventeen or eighteen years, which had come into his view. The painting was entitled, simply, *Head of a Girl*.

One impression it made more than any other, except for her wide-open eyes and half-open mouth like a tiny waterfall, which captivated him equally, was how the head seemed to hover in the black background, as if it were not part of that awkwardly shaped, turning shoulder. *Head of a Girl* was indeed an apt title, though he knew that such paintings at the time had no official titles. They were, rather, descriptions.

This painting, he thought suddenly, will drive me crazy if I look at it much longer. Was it his imagination that the head moved very slightly if one stared too long at any one point or contour not in the centre of the composition? An optical illusion, of course. Yes, he had seen the painting in reproductions countless times, and had never till now been able to see it. Strangest of all was that he had forgotten it was in this show, as it had been used to advertise it on the exhibition poster. But he put that down to his meandering state of mind and the sheer uninspiring nature of the exhibition as a whole.

He must come back, again, nevertheless, when his mind had had time to settle.

He did not remember descending twenty-five floors in the lift and coming out into the heart of Shinjuku, but he found himself walking up a flight of steps into the station. The sight of a schoolgirl holding her palm to the back of her pleated tartan skirt he found rather endearing, until he put himself in the position of the anonymous voyeur she was trying to frustrate. He even thought for a moment that he had seen that unmistakable white material, angled like a beautiful calligraphic figure. But these indulgences were washed from his mind once he was on the platform staring over the shoulders of various commuters reading about the disappearance of a fifteen-year-old girl.

He was looking at the head in his lap. The bed of plastic was holding, but only just, as he could see a pocket of the darkest blood he had ever seen collecting at the bottom. For a moment he had almost jumped up, thinking it had somehow escaped through on to his trousers.

She must have been about thirteen, fourteen, but her features, especially her eyebrows, which formed questioning, intelligent arcs, fixed him, making him the more immobile of the two. And as he gazed upon her there, against the deep umber of the side of his bureau, she seemed to be not just floating, but the very axis of his being. Then, the folded plastic, with its narrow choker, in fact the cotton belt from his *hakama*, and its various folds reflecting globules of light from his table lamp, looked for all the world itself like the top of a robe.

He could have held her there all night but for the cold she gave off. He did not know how long he could keep her, in any case.

He carried her into the kitchen, passing the small framed photograph of Yukiko on the wall. (How *long* he had debated with himself over the right size and colour of such a frame, and, of course, the position.)

She only just fitted into the fridge, and even then he had to lay her on her side. As he did so, the blood surged up the side of her cheek, as if the artist had gone insane. He thought about placing a large dish below the head, but it surely would not be necessary, as he intended to take her back tonight. He just had to choose the right moment.

But first he would look at the news. It was a perverse pleasure, but there was a chance here to be connected with a special event, one that, though nobody would ever know it, would raise him above the masses, above the faceless crowds of commuters, teachers and schoolchildren that the world seemed to be made of these days.

He was flicking through the channels in a constant cycle, but he couldn't find any news. It must already be late, which was confirmed by a glance at the clock. Where had the evening gone?

He was looking at various semi-nude teenagers taking part in a ridiculous unknown sport that, as the culmination of the scoring of a point, involved one of them spreading her legs, whereupon the camera zoomed in for an unsubtle examination; a change of channel delivered a fly-on-the-wall camera eavesdropping on a group of schoolgirls talking some nonsense about dress code, which they meant literally. A flower of a certain kind or colour worn in the hair, for example, might signify that the girl either had already, or was looking for, a boyfriend. My God, why are things so trivial these days? he asked himself. Another channel ushered him into a sex soap opera that took place in...a school.

He looked up at Yukiko's photograph and from there to the fridge, as if expecting an answer. Perhaps it flashed across his mind, because he made a nervous movement to get up, as if decided on a course of action, but just as quickly it was gone, and he was back in his chair.

Was he aware of his head lolling to the side like a train commuter's, supported by another's shoulder? Flashes filled the room, strange creatures speaking in Japanese advertised the most unnecessary products, short scenes with the oddest music and dialogue of no consequence, proceeded into his head like trains into a station. But nothing was leaving. Everyone was sleeping. Everything was suddenly dark.

The thunderous banging on the metal door startled him awake. He presumed it was the Jehovah's Witnesses on their regular recruiting mission. But the banging went on, so he found himself at the door apparently in conversation with two policemen. They were not in uniform but he knew instantly they were the police.

'Mr Kimura,' the older of the two, and seemingly in charge, said. 'We would like to look at the head – if you wouldn't mind.'

'The head? Oh...yes, of course. Please come in. It's, er, this way.'

They were looking at it, lit up in a ghostly way by the solitary light deep inside the fridge. Curiously the head was in an upright position.

'Ah,' the two policemen gasped almost simultaneously, more, Kimura thought, out of aesthetic admiration than out of relief that they had succeeded in locating the object of their search.

'The lighting here really doesn't do it justice,' Kimura said, as if his only crime were this failure to present it in a suitable fashion.

'Let's take it out,' said the detective. It was not, however, the world-weary, routine direction one might have expected, but more an expression of childlike excitement.

'If you think we should,' Kimura replied, deferring to authority, yet feeling that in some way the mask had not yet been drawn away from their play-acting.

The detectives set it on top of the fridge on his white cutting board, a surface inlaid with countless striations.

'Well, it's her, certainly,' the detective said.

'Yes, certainly, it is,' his colleague agreed.

'And there can't be too many fifteen-year-old heads around, and so pretty too,' the older detective said, winking at Kimura, but without actually committing himself. Then, to Kimura, 'Would you have a bag, by any chance?'

'A b-bag?' Kimura stammered.

'Yes, we didn't turn up very well equipped, I'm afraid.'

'Yes, I think so.'

Kimura reached into the cupboard under the sink and produced a bag that should be adequate.

'Here you are.'

Whereupon, the two detectives silently eased the head, without spilling a drop of liquid, into the bag.

'Well, we'll be off now,' the older of the two said, almost as if he were an old friend who had turned up after many years, only now to leave early. 'Goodbye.'

'Goodbye.'

Kimura's sense of loss was quite profound. Where was he? The television was still on, but it was beginning to get light outside.

His neck ached and his whole body was stiff. How could he let them do such a thing?

With trepidation, he approached the fridge and opened the door.

It was still there, lying on its side, the blood along the cheek now noticeably congealed. The image came to him of a beautiful luxury ocean liner beached on dark exotic sand, the hull now beginning to rust, the orange-red sun of dawn beginning to fall on to its deck and many portholes. But no object of beauty could last for ever, surely.

It was time now. The dream had been a warning.

After returning from the exhibition, then, he had passed by the local dump. It was his habit to cast an eye over the rubbish, even if it wasn't a night for things that couldn't be burned, such as old CD players or rice cookers that might still be usable. Perhaps if he hadn't seen the exhibition, if he hadn't returned at the time he did, with his mind particularly focused on incidental detail, he would not have noticed what he at first took to be an optical illusion.

It was the only white bag, turned on its side, with something of its contents showing. It had obviously not been tied up well, or perhaps a stray dog had unravelled it.

What he thought he saw on coming closer he could not give credence to, but he would have to investigate. He opened the bag fully, without moving it, closed it almost immediately, and scuttled quickly off to his flat, the hidden cameras of his mind tracking and reproducing his shadowed path.

But is it criminal, what I have done? he asked himself, as he replaced the bag and its confounding contents on the rubbish pile.

He was wearing gloves and he was certain, as certain as one could be in such a situation, that no one had seen him make his third and final trip.

He could not see an answer to the question coming for a long time. Until he realized what he was doing, standing in the middle of the car park staring up at a star. A star or a planet? It could be a dead celestial body or one that still had a strong influence on us struggling creatures down here, he speculated. And suddenly he realized he was not afraid. Tomorrow he would spend the whole day in the library, he was sure.

QUAINT HONOUR
CHRISTOPHER BURNS

At first it seems that an early autumn gale has blown scraps of paper into the foliage, but as Simon approaches he sees that the terebinth is festooned with clothing — shirts, brassières, dresses, handkerchiefs. Many are torn and faded, and must have been knotted around the branches years ago. Near to the trunk there is a faint odour of turpentine.

He stoops beneath the offerings and locates a flight of stone steps that have been hollowed by visitors. The catacomb entrance could be a well, its sides are so steep, its depths so gloomy. Only the upper rim is still in daylight. Tree roots snake and twist down the walls and disappear into cracks.

Fifty feet down and the steps end in a roofless chamber whose uneven floor is covered with empty bottles. Simon picks one up and sniffs. A smell of red wine clings heavily to the glass.

All around the chamber there are ledges, crevices, pegs. Hanging on the pegs are wax heads, dolls, and thin metal plates stamped with reliefs of limbs. Tiny effigies crowd the ledges, staring from the stonework with eyes of cloth or porcelain. And every fissure is jammed with folded papers.

At random, Simon extracts a few of the papers; he has enough Greek to read them. They are pleas, oaths, prayers. One begs for a sickness to be healed, another for a lost relative to be found, a third for good luck to be visited upon a poor family. Many supplicants have inserted photographs into the apertures. Simon finds one of a severe but handsome woman of about thirty, black-haired, with a gold necklace. Someone, a rejected lover perhaps, or a betrayed husband, has torn it in two before thrusting it into the crevice. Simon even finds love letters, complete with addresses and dates. These, he reasons, can never have been posted. Instead they have been left there to absorb the catacomb's magic, and perhaps cause it to be manifested in the workings of the outside world.

When he returns to the surface an unexpectedly cool breeze shakes the terebinth boughs so that the clothing sways. The sun broadens as it disappears into the sea. Simon eases the rucksack on his shoulders so that it sits more comfortably and walks into town.

An hour later and he has found a room on a street leading up the hillside from the harbour. He spreads out his clothes, puts the rucksack on top of the wooden wardrobe, and places his six books, which include his complete works of Rochester, on top of the cupboard by the bed. After hesitating a moment, he chooses a selection from Cavafy and puts it into his pocket before he leaves.

This will be his second winter away. Despite all his travelling, all his disappointments, Simon is still a believer in the possibility of rapture.

The tourist season is ending and there is little chance of finding work. The information bureau is closed, so he asks at bars and restaurants, but there is no interest. Perhaps he will stay for only a few days, returning in the spring.

Choosing a table overlooking the sea, Simon eats at the last restaurant along the front. While he waits he opens the Cavafy and reads. A line of coloured lights strung above the balustrade tints the paper a delicate rose.

Soon the owner notices Simon's book and strikes up a forced conversation. Simon confesses that he likes poetry and knows some Greek, but that his degree is in English. Left alone to eat his feta and olive salad, he loses himself in the text. The sea laps below the balcony.

Someone speaks to him in lightly accented English. 'I hope you are not waiting for the barbarians.' It is an allusion to one of Cavafy's best-known poems.

A thin man in his early fifties, with an unfashionably narrow moustache and slicked-back hair, stands beside the table.

Simon picks up the quotation. 'Night has fallen and they still haven't arrived.'

Without asking permission the man sits down.

'Some think they are here already,' he says, and studies Simon's face like a buyer unwilling to commit himself before he has conducted a close examination. 'Spiliadis. Call me Theo. You have been talking to my brother. He may not know much about literature, but he had the presence of mind to telephone me.'

Simon waits for the proposition.

'You have a degree in English — when? Last year? And from an English university?'

'Two years ago. Oxford.' He does not mention his college; he guesses it will mean nothing to Spiliadis.

'And you are spending time drifting around the islands. Why is this? Are you following the footsteps of Byron? Durrell?'

Simon smiles.

Theo clears his throat with a dry, rustling cough. 'I believe you must be a poet yourself.'

Simon's moment of indecision is enough.

'I understand,' Theo goes on. 'You do not wish to talk about it.'

Theo's consideration clasps the insight and seals it. Simon knows he cannot deny it now.

For a long time he has done nothing of any worth. Recently he has written descriptions of places, moments, people. Last year, he worked for months in a coarse demotic, coming to terms with the loss of a girlfriend who he felt had betrayed him. Always Simon tries to give weight to the lines so that they embody something more universal than his own experience.

For a few days he judges the work a success. The turn of a phrase, the delicacy and fibre of his words fire him with a belief in his own talent, perhaps in his genius. Then, later, the poem unravels in his hands. He sees that its structure is crude, its symbolism pedestrian, and that the movement of the language is lumbering, graceless, derivative.

'You must know all the important English poets,' Theo suggests.

'Some.'

'Browning? My wife translated some Browning very recently.'

'Robert or Elizabeth?'

Simon's cleverness is too sharp. Theo's lips tighten in a false smile and he nods.

'I mean the better poet. The one who wrote of how he missed England. Do you miss your home country?'

'Not yet.'

'You will not return for the winter?'

'No. I still have miles to go. And promises to keep.'

'An American writer, yes? But I do not know who.'

It is enough for Simon to gain an edge of superiority. He is only ever really comfortable when he can feel this.

'Robert Frost.'

'And your promise is to yourself. Is that so?'

When he receives no answer Theo laughs and claps Simon's shoulder with excessive familiarity.

For several minutes, perhaps as long as ten, they quote lines at each other from some of the best-known poetry in the English language. Sometimes Theo speaks them in Greek. At the end of this time he shakes Simon's hand again, and gives him an instruction.

'Be here tomorrow morning. I will pick you up at ten. And I suggest you are a little more presentable. To begin with, you need a shave.'

When Theo has left, Simon rubs his bristles and tries to decide whether or not he should forget what has happened. Theo has been both mysterious and inquisitive, a combination that he dislikes. But then the restaurant owner approaches his table again. His brother has suggested that the young Englishman may wish to eat more than a mere salad. A meal and a bottle of local wine have been paid for. It's too good an offer for Simon to refuse.

As he eats he stares at the quiet sea beneath him. Its shallows are made pallid by the lights, and on the rocks dozens of anemones have gathered together in black, tarry stars.

A washed and newly shaved Simon sits next to Theo and is driven out of town, past villas, cactus, the laden terebinth. Theo drives with a dainty, unMediterranean precision, not even complaining when a tractor driven down the middle of the road delays them for several minutes. Simon wonders if this is a man who believes himself too civilized for anger.

He asks about the catacomb. Theo tells him that the cavern has been used for at least three thousand years, and that it was probably a shrine from the time when men first came to the island. He speculates that trees and shrubs growing round it would always have had offerings tied to them.

'The Christians of today are no less superstitious,' he adds.

'I can understand leaving the prayers,' Simon tells him. 'The rest is more primitive. Like the mannequins and the wax images of body parts. They're like fetishes; images of a disease that needs to be cured.'

'Not only disease. All kinds of afflictions.'

'Accidents?'

'And emotions.'

'Love, you mean?'

'Those who have lost a lover tie a piece of his shirt to the tree. Men driven mad with desire place a photograph of their girl in cracks in the stone. Sometimes they do this to win her, sometimes to forget her.'

'There are bottles of wine down there. Recently emptied ones.'

'Poured out as a libation to secure the magic. Holy water is neither powerful nor pagan enough.'

'Their prayers won't be answered. The dead can't return. Lovers never come back.'

'Most people recognize that. It is not the point. What they leave is a sign. A demonstration. A proof that passion once existed. Perhaps still exists.'

'A way of coming to terms, do you think?'

'A way of letting go. And an educated man like you will realize the symbolism of a deep cave surrounded by shrubs.'

Until this moment, Simon has never thought of such symbolism.

Five minutes later and they pull up outside a villa. It overlooks olive groves, terraces, the town tucked into its bay, a sea wide as the horizon but for the next mistily blue island. A black cat watches their arrival. Late bougainvillaea trails down stark white walls and there is a smell of jasmine. A large satellite dish catches the sunlight. The swimming pool is tiled a Californian blue.

'Tell me,' Simon asks, 'is this an interview?'

'In a way. My wife will ask the questions. Her name is Hortensia. Call her Sia.'

Inside the house there are paintings, floors of polished wood, paintings, expensive ornaments, full bookshelves. Simon sits on a sofa draped with a covering from somewhere in the Near East. Once he has introduced Simon, Theo unexpectedly absents himself, closing the door quietly as he leaves.

Sia is a plump, wide-hipped woman, only a little younger than her husband. Her hair is dyed a glossy black to mirror what it must have been in her youth. She wears gold – a broad necklace, and a bracelet that slides between wrist and forearm whenever she moves her hand. There is a sense of concentration about her, and of ripeness, as if she anticipates the cruelty of further years. Simon has the worrying suspicion, which he knows must be false, that he has met her somewhere before.

Sia speaks in careful, well-modulated English. 'I'm told you like Cavafy. A great poet, but such an unhappy man. He was homosexual – did you know that?'

Simon, who has read Forster and Durrell, knows it, but nods as if a suspicion has been confirmed.

'And he lived most of his life as a government clerk. Poor man, he was no Byron. He was not even a Browning.'

Browning, Simon thinks sourly, was such an innocent that he thought the word *twat* referred to an item of nun's clothing; he wrote as much in *Pippa Passes*. Simon wonders if, as an adolescent, Sia watched a version of *The Barretts of Wimpole Street*. Perhaps she is romantic, unworldly, literary.

'Your husband told me you've translated Browning,' he says.

'A selection, yes. I read about his life. He was a fascinating man. Such careful phrasing, and in his private life, such passion. *Who knows but that the world may end tonight.* You know that line?'

'*The Last Ride Together.* Your husband has already tested me, Mrs Spiliadis.'

'Poets often set themselves too far apart from the world. Do you not agree? They feel they are observers, commentators, mandarins. They even distance themselves from their pleasures. Browning, Byron – these are exceptions.'

Simon thinks of Rochester, struggling in his nets of rapture and loathing, loyalty and deceit.

'I don't think your generalization is particularly apt,' he comments.

Sia shakes her head. 'Wordsworth did not write of his French lover or their child. Eliot says nothing of his life; he is too dry, too academic. His appeal is to the mind, not the heart. But you know all about this. You have an excellent degree.'

As she speaks Sia puts her fingers on Simon's arm and lets them rest there. He finds her familiarity even more unsettling than her husband's.

'I specialized in Restoration poetry,' he explains. 'Rochester. You may not know his work.'

Sia nods slowly, like a mathematician absorbing a new formula. 'I've heard of it but have not read it. It's very – ' She searches for the right word.

'Explicit,' Simon offers.

'Yes.'

Quite suddenly Simon believes that he is with the woman whose photograph, ripped in half, he found wedged in the wall of the catacomb. And then, swift as the recoil on a gun, he convinces himself that this cannot be true. Twenty years or more must separate the images.

Aware that if he looks at Sia he will study her face too closely, Simon looks out through the French windows. Theo is pacing the far side of the pool, one thoughtful hand on his chin. Reflections from the water play across his face. Simon imagines him, possessed by anger, scourged by humiliation, taking an old photograph of his wife, ripping it in half, pushing it into the stonework. And then he realizes that a man such as Theo would never do such a thing.

'I need help with my new translations,' Sia tells him. 'A young countryman of yours assisted with the Browning. He has moved on now, just as you will do. He was interesting, but his knowledge of literature was not great. You, on the other hand, are highly educated. And Theo told me of your ambition.'

'What ambition?'

'You want to be a poet.'

'I didn't say that.'

'You did not have to. Come; let us discuss literature a little more.'

As she talks, Sia's eyes begin to shine. Simon wonders if it is only literary excitement that makes them do this.

She tells him she wants to produce an anthology of English love poetry. In addition to translating the works, she will also choose them. She has given herself until next spring to complete the selection.

'But there's no end to love poetry,' Simon protests.

'Of course not. How could there be?'

'Have you started on this?'

'I have several chosen already. *Shall I compare thee to a summer's day. Had we but world enough.* That is poetry which I know I must do, even if it is difficult to turn into Greek. But it would be better to include works which are not so well known. You see all those shelves, all those books? Many are English. If I began to read them now, and did nothing else, I would still not have read a quarter by the time my life had ended. Someone like you will be able to guide me. I have not world enough. Or time.'

Simon looks for Theo, but he has vanished from the poolside.

'My husband is working in another room,' Sia tells him. 'He will not disturb us. Already it has been decided that you are the right man. When we have finished, he will drive you back to where you are staying. I shall pay you at the end of each week. In cash. It will not be much money, but there is no money in poetry. You have studied the lives of the poets; you know that is true. Some of them could not compromise and died too young. Others, the best of them, lived their life to the full. They took whatever was offered.'

'It's true,' Simon agrees, 'there's no money in poetry.'

Sia nods and moves an inch closer to him.

'No,' she says, 'the money is not what matters. The words are what matter. They are like a wine.'

He wants to scoff at such an exhausted simile, but he says nothing. Sensing that he is not convinced, Sia continues.

'Do you not agree? But many say that poetry is like wine. Words can make the reader drunk. The author, too.'

Simon shrugs. 'Whatever you say.'

During the rest of that day she and Simon discuss much poetry and many poets. They deliberate on stresses, clarify phrases, bandy competing translations. A light lunch has been prepared in the kitchen. They sit on opposite sides of a table and turn their attention to the Romantics. Theo is still nowhere to be seen. He only reappears late in the afternoon, when he tells Simon he will drive him back to town.

Simon expects him to ask about their progress, but instead Theo is self-absorbed, perhaps even depressed. He shows no interest in the task for which he had been so eager to recruit a clever Englishman. Whenever a subject is raised, Theo nods as if his mind is elsewhere. He does not even look at the tree of offerings as they drive past.

When Simon steps from the car Theo says: 'I'm leaving for several days in Athens. It has happened quite quickly. Tomorrow you must take a taxi to our house. Sia will pay if you are really so poor. And you must consider what you will do next.'

Simon wonders if he is talking about their selection of poems, or if something else is on his mind.

'You are a young man,' Theo continues. 'You are expected to take the decisions of a young man.'

He accelerates away before Simon can ask him what he means.

Jealousy, he decides later as he lies in his narrow bed; he's jealous of me because I'm young.

And then, as if from nowhere, a few half-formed phrases come into Simon's mind. Excited, he waits for them to dissolve, but they do not. He knows that they are vivid yet malleable; concise, yet capable of expansion; resonant, referential, yet unquestionably his own.

He has the beginnings of a poem.

On the next day Simon walks all the way from town. The journey takes him almost an hour.

Sia is waiting for him. Poetry books, two dictionaries and a thesaurus lie waiting on top of the long table they have grown used to sharing. They sit together, and for the next hour they labour over *To His Coy Mistress*.

At first they are a few feet from each other. Whenever they discuss a point this distance is increased because Simon leans further away. But some points need to be argued closely, and both Simon and Sia emphasize their arguments by taking the books from each other's hands. Simon even commandeers Sia's notepad to scribble suggestions on it.

Gradually they move closer together. They both know it is happening, but neither does anything to stop it. Soon their shoulders touch, and then their bare arms. Sia's handwriting, as it records Greek correspondences to Marvell, becomes jagged, then sprawls. When she pauses she does not loosen her grip on the pen but eases the ball of her thumb along its cylinder.

She tells him that *turn to dust* is easy to translate, but that *quaint honour* is difficult. Her voice trembles above huskiness like a diver above a pool.

He agrees. Their gazes lock. Simon feels that any further words will slip and collide. Sia's mouth parts slightly. She flicks her tongue across her lips. Its sharp tip glistens. He can smell closeness, perfume, musk.

Because he knows it is expected of him, or perhaps because he really wants to, Simon leans forward, half expecting her to move away. She comes to meet him. Her saliva tastes of heat.

When they draw apart he places the fingers of one hand on her skin, just below the gold necklace. They stare at each other, wordless among the books. Simon feels that their hearts have begun to follow the same beat. Sia's skin is flushed; sweat glosses it with a thin film. When Simon moves his fingers further down her body she takes hold of his wrist and grasps it tightly.

'Wait,' she says, and stands up.

He imagines that she will take off her clothes. Instead, she begins to remove all the books from the table.

As he watches Sia stack the books on a chair, Simon decides that not until afterwards will he explain that *quaint honour* is, in fact, an obscene pun.

For the next three weeks, as autumn tightens, Simon works on translations during the day, and at night he writes his own poetry. At the best moments of writing he feels a kind of controlled delirium, and knows that what he writes is good.

The meetings with Sia develop their own momentum. Detailed textual analysis, listings of synonyms, testings of rhythm and rhyme alternate with rapid and intense lovemaking. Lexically and sexually, they deal in varieties of exhaustion. By the end of their time together, Simon thinks, they will have left no possibilities unexplored.

Theo is almost always absent from the house, but his occasional presence in another room sometimes gives a dangerous edge to their pleasure. One day he floats on an airbed in the pool, riding its buoyancy as he catches a weakening sun. Sia leans across the table and Simon enters her from behind. They can both look out of the window and see Theo dreaming, eyes closed, in his azure isolation.

When he visits them ten minutes later they are demure and industrious, but Simon has seen Theo's nostrils widen like a tracker's, and is convinced that he has detected a scent of rut that reeks in the still air.

Once, too, they conduct a brief, scrabbling liaison while Theo listens to music upstairs. As they strain after fulfilment they also listen intently, waiting for the music to end. When it does, and Theo comes wandering idly into the room, Sia is asking Simon about the Restoration poets. She knows little of them, she confesses; would something by Rochester perhaps be suitable for the anthology?

Theo looks directly at his wife and the English stranger. Simon looks down, but Sia is unperturbed. The black cat moves stealthily by the pool.

At this moment Simon begins to wonder if their deception is in itself a sham. Perhaps Theo approves of his wife's affair. Perhaps he has even helped to arrange it. After all it was he, not Sia, who did the recruiting.

The more he thinks about this, the more likely it seems. And more likely, too, that it has happened before. Gradually, with a rising sense of unease, Simon begins to wonder about his predecessor.

At the same time, during an examination of the bookshelves, he finds some copies of Sia's translations of Browning. The appearance of the binding immediately arouses his suspicions. It does not appear to be a volume which has been properly published.

When he opens the book at the title page he finds that Sia's name is prominent, almost as prominent as Browning's. Nothing else is mentioned – no publisher, no colophon. He turns the page. There is no reference to either publisher, copyright or ISBN. Only the printer's name is shown at the foot of the page. He closes the book abruptly. Every indication is that Sia's Browning is a vanity publication.

Simon replaces the copy among its fellows and leans against the shelf. His fingers reach upwards so they touch the spines of some of the other volumes.

Theo and Sia have allowed him to conclude that she is a professional translator. Now he realizes that she is not. Her work is an indulgence, a game, a plaything, a dream, nothing more. So is his part in it.

Theo is away. They have worked on an unsatisfactory translation of Christina Rossetti for an hour. Simon is unimpressed. Anger frays at his nerves. Sia has slipped the fingers of one hand beneath the belt of his jeans.

'The young man who helped you before,' he asks, 'was he unsatisfactory?'

Sia smiles as if the question is not worthy of an answer, and moves her thumb and index finger to the zip of his fly.

'I mean: was he not as good as me?'

She slides the zip open an inch, teasingly. The metal teeth separate with a quiet rasp.

'I have had helpers for some years now. What does it matter? None have translated as well as you.'

'That isn't what I asked.'

She parts the fly and slips her hand inside. Her mouth moves closer to his ear. He can feel her breath on his skin. 'Why is it that each man wants to be the best?'

'That's not an answer.'

'Then I shall tell you that you are the best. Is that enough?'

Her hand encloses Simon. A reflex stiffens him; he had meant to resist. He takes her wrist and tugs her hand away, but she snakes past his grip and encloses him again. The texture of her fingers is dry and papery.

'I'd like you to tell me.'

She shrugs, pulls a face, but does not withdraw.

'His name – ' And Sia hesitates for a moment, as if she has difficulty remembering what her helper was called. 'Adam,' she announces.

'Was your arrangement the same as ours?'

'He translated, yes. Browning. He was only here for a few days.'

Simon's mouth has dried. 'And were you lovers?'

'What does it matter?'

'Perhaps it doesn't. I'd just like to know.'

She tightens her grip and begins to move her hand around him. 'How can you think of other people, when we are together like this? I think of no one else. Not even Theo.'

'How did you meet Adam?'

Sia shakes her head in puzzlement.

'Did Theo find him for you?'

She says nothing but increases the pressure and swiftness of her hand. Simon knows that she expects this will make him forget. But he has been taking less and less pleasure from these encounters. He feels himself to be a pattern of reflexes, nothing more.

'Sia, was Adam recruited by your husband, just like I was recruited?'

'Be quiet,' she says throatily.

There is a pause of a few seconds, as if she is about to say something else, and then Sia moves her mouth towards his crotch. As she does so Simon wonders if she has temporarily forgotten his name, too.

Afterwards, physically satisfied but emotionally frustrated, he will not, cannot stop asking about his predecessor. Sia shrugs and pouts like someone much younger than her years, unwilling to answer. But perhaps there are no answers to his questions.

Perhaps, to Sia, neither he nor Adam is distinctive. Perhaps they are mere physiologies, automata, men without characters. Perhaps, for her, only literature is real, and the world never able to match the high levels of the imagination.

That evening Simon examines the poetry he has written over the last few days. His room is tiny, airless, dim. Invaded by a mounting desperation, he reads his own words over and over again.

He is like a man examining banknotes who knows, with each additional one that he handles, that they must all be counterfeit.

Today it is different. Simon is confident, instructive, efficient as a practised teacher. A beast, call it revenge, sharpens its claws beneath each sentence.

'John Wilmot, second earl of Rochester,' he tells Sia. 'An Oxford man, like me. Not only a poet, but a courtier. Not only a family man, but a libertine. A soldier, a philosopher, a hedonist. A man who was very much part of the world he lived in. A man who never distanced himself from his pleasures. Or his hatreds.'

Sia looks at him. One hand is extended on the table top. As Simon talks she flexes her fingers, exercising them.

'And his poetry?' she asks.

'Vivid and direct, but censored and suppressed for three hundred years. I have the Yale edition of his complete works. Vieth, 1968.'

'You think we should translate one of them?'

'I have the very one.'

He smiles coldly, and sits opposite her. Her fingers stretch for his hand but Simon keeps it out of reach.

'Let's get to work,' he says, and draws three sheets of photocopy paper from his bag.

That morning Simon has walked into town, booked his ticket for the evening ferry, and copied one of Rochester's poems. Now he clasps the copies between thumb and index finger, holding them vertically, flexing them like sails filling with wind.

'Rochester saw that this life was all there is. He followed Lucretius, Seneca, Hobbes. The soul is a function of the physical body, that's all. There is no purpose other than earthly purpose. Straight, unflinching materialism underpins all his writing, most notably in his portrayal of sexuality. No one saw more clearly the weaknesses and corruptions of what we call love. He was as obsessed by coition as Swift was by excretion.'

If she sees anything suspicious in the yoking of these functions, Sia gives no sign. Simon continues.

'In this poem, here, a London park is seen as a vessel of teeming, rapacious sexuality. What goes on, what Rochester sees, is the hinge on which all of society turns.'

He places the photocopies on the table, but spreads his hand across them, pinning them down. Sia takes one of his fingers and tries to lift it, but Simon leans forward so that he presses even more firmly on the sheets.

'You are teasing me,' she accuses.

'Am I?'

'Of course you are. Here is an English poet like Aretino. You have the work of a man who relishes love, and you pretend to keep him from me.'

Sia gives a smiling, convulsive little shiver, partly mocking her own excitement. Simon picks up the poet's name, as he had picked up poets' names with Theo.

'Each imitative branch does twine / In some loved fold of Aretine.'

Sia is puzzled. 'Aretine,' he repeats with emphasis.

'Ah, Aretino. Of course.'

'I thought you'd get that easily. Other names, words, phrases I'll have to explain. They're too much of their time. You can't be expected to know who the Mother of the Maids was, or Sir Edward Sutton.'

'Simon, are you sure this poem is for me? Is it perhaps too English?'

'It's universal.'

'But difficult. Full of strange names that will mean nothing to my public.'

'Ah yes, your public. All those thousands that bought your earlier translations, you mean?'

He is so eager to press his point that his guard relaxes, and she snatches the photocopies from beneath his hand. At the same time he realizes that she has ignored the sarcasm in his voice.

Sia glances at the poem, skipping over the verse like a stone over water, touching it only briefly until at last she pauses, and sinks beneath its surface.

Simon raises his eyebrows in mock expectancy.

'You are right,' she says, 'it is very – '

He waits for her to complete the sentence, but she cannot.

'What part in particular?'

'This,' she says. '*So a proud bitch does lead about / Of humble curs the amorous rout*... Aretino celebrated the act of love. This poet does not. I do not think I wish to translate him.'

'Ah, but you must,' Simon counters smoothly. He is about to continue the verse when Sia shakes her head.

'Why does he hate women so much? No woman would want to read him.'

'Rochester was in advance of his time on women's rights.'

'It does not read as if he was.'

'I'm an expert. I can assure you he was. That doesn't mean he didn't sometimes loathe women. Of course he did. But he loathed men, too. And often he loathed the equipment and the action of pleasure.'

Sia pushes the poem back at him. On each of her cheeks a large red area is growing, like an allergic reaction. He does not know if this is anger or embarrassment.

'You are insulting me,' she says. 'You insult all lovers. This man despises passion.'

'Not so,' Simon objects. 'This is one of the most important poets that England has produced, one whose view of love is detailed and unique. You owe it to your readers to translate him.'

He lets his tongue rest, like an unwanted caress, on the word *readers*.

'What do I care about my readers?' she asks, stung into attack. She points a half-open fist at her heart. 'This is what I care about. This is what is important.'

'Read on,' Simon tells her.

She shakes her head.

'Listen to this,' he says, and quotes from memory. '*Why this treachery / To humble, fond, believing me –* '

'You know all of this poem?'

'By heart.'

'Why spend so much time learning it? There are better works you could have learned.'

'But perhaps none so appropriate.'

Simon leans forward and speaks the lines softly. They open on the table like unwrapped knives.

'*When your lewd cunt came spewing home / Drenched with the seed of half the town –* '

'Enough,' Sia says, and stands up. 'I will have nothing to do with such hatred.'

'*Full gorged at another time / With a vast meal of nasty slime / which your devouring cunt had drawn / From porters' backs and footmen's brawn*,' Simon recites. He lingers over the words, a gourmet of his own disgust.

Sia stands by the window. Through the glass, the deserted swimming pool is wintry, and a sluggish breeze chops at the water.

'You are insulting me,' Sia repeats.

'Believe me, I haven't even started.'

'I will not stand here and listen to your hatred.'

'The words aren't mine. They're Rochester's.'

'I want you to leave my house, Simon. I want you to leave it now.'

Simon leans back in the chair, pushing its balance to the edge.

'*May your depraved appetite / That could in whiffling fools delight / Beget such frenzies in your mind / You may go mad for the north wind –* '

The door opens. Theo enters. He surveys them, his fingers resting lightly on the door handle.

For a moment everything is silent. Then, melodramatically, Sia begins to weep, or pretend to weep. Simon cannot see any tears because she places her hands across her face.

Theo, thin and emotionless, stares at him. Suddenly he looks far older than his years.

Simon stands up. Once on his feet, he finds that his limbs are trembling with rage and self-pity.

'I'm going,' he says.

Theo stands aside to let him leave. All is quiet but for Sia's weeping.

The mucus in Simon's mouth has thickened and it is no longer easy for him to speak. So he is unable to offer a last few lines from Rochester to seal his own humiliation, his own misery, and he leaves without another word.

'Do you understand nothing?' Theo asks as Simon brushes past him.

Simon looks down, unable to answer, incapable of meeting Theo's eyes.

Clouds mass in the square of sky and the branches heave in a rising wind. Light withdraws from the bottom of the shaft, seeping upwards over the walls.

Simon stood here weeks ago. He is sure he is standing on exactly the same spot, facing the same section of wall, picking offerings from the same crevices, but each time he is disappointed.

He only finds prayers, gratitude, photographs of people he has never seen before. Twice he thinks that this must be the one; twice he thinks this is the image of the thirty-year-old woman he had drawn so casually from its fissure. But the faces he finds in the gloom are not her. They have not even been torn in half.

Darkness accumulates. Life dies in the porcelain eyes of the effigies. Soon Simon cannot even see the catacomb floor. He knows, now, that he will never find the woman's photograph, and that he will never be sure if it was Sia. When he steps back his heel touches one of the wine bottles. It gives a faint clink but does not fall over. He looks up. The terebinth branches are slowly thrashing.

Simon reaches forward again. He touches the stone like a man going blind. It is smooth, cold, crossed by a thin film of slipperiness – snails, perhaps, or algae. Each fissure seems already to have a blade of paper hidden within it, and it takes him several minutes to find one that is empty. Unable to gauge width in the gloom, he runs his finger up and down its vertical cleft. Satisfied that it will be wide enough, he takes several sheets of paper from his pocket and folds them. He eases them carefully into the gap, pushing them as far as they will go, packing them down until they are lost within the crevice and can only just be touched by his fingers. Then he turns and walks up the steps.

Simon tries to hope that he will forget every word he has written. At the same time he cannot help but think that, if he had been serious, he would have torn the poems into scraps before forcing them into the wall. If he had done, and if someone else were to pick out the fragments, they would be unreadable.

At sea the swell is queasily heavy. A weak phosphorescence heaves and slides in the dark wake. The ferry rises, tilts, plunges. Ahead there is only night.

Simon sits alone on the upper deck, his rucksack on the empty bench next to him. He leans slightly forward to counter the motion, his hands grasping the underside of the slats so that he will not fall. Only after a while does he become aware of how hard he has to grip.

A north wind rips the crests from the waves. Water breaks continually over the rail, spattering on the planking in a pattern of slaps. An empty wine bottle careens back and forth across the deck, slewing with each pitch and roll as the ferry heads out to sea.

TRAVELLING AT NIGHT
G. A. PICKIN

There's something about travelling at night that is a universe away from daytime touring. The dark presses right up against the windows of the car, cocooning you against the world. Everything outside remains a mystery, or ceases to exist at all, with the exception of the freeze-frame images illuminated by a streetlamp or a shop sign.

If it's late enough, these snapshots consist of empty scenes, unfamiliar places without a human scale to give them definition. Sometimes, though, the circle of light will define a mini-drama; overtime workers hurrying home to a dried-up dinner, gangs of lads looking for good-time trouble, lovers slipping out of the limelight and into the embracing anonymity of the dark.

Embellishing these glimpses of street tableaux is entertaining; a game of 'what happened next' can fill between-town miles better than the raciest radio programme. Take, for instance, the overtime workers I mentioned.

'My wife's gonna give me five kinds of hell when I get home. I promised to leave on time today so I could attend the open evening at the school, but you know what Hartington thinks about "family commitments" – '

'Yeah, I'd rather face the music at home than listen to one of his lectures on "corporate loyalty" and "we're only as strong as the weakest link".'

'We're this late anyway, what say we nip into the King's Arms for a swift half before facing martyrdom?'

The gang of lads is more predictable, and 'what happens next' has only two outcomes, I've found: either they become maudlin, swear their undying love for each other and start singing, usually leaving a trail of empties and late-night chip papers (and perhaps something more unpleasant) for the pub's neighbours to clear away the next day, or they get aggressive, meet up with other tribes on the warpath, and end up in Casualty at two in the morning.

The lovers are better. There are so many ways the story can go, depending on whether this is their first meeting or their twenty-first, if one or both of them have other attachments, their ages, where they're from, what they do for a living, if they share the same intensity of feeling – the permutations are endless.

It's a good game, and I have whiled away countless hundreds of miles indulging its various twists and turns, but it hasn't got a patch on my favourite. When you've been on the road as long as I have, the rented room you call home becomes just another impermanent stop. The fridge is empty, the sheets are cold, the post piled behind the door is mostly rubbish. It is indifferent to your arrival, noncommittal about your departure, an inanimate space for the practical necessities of shelter, nothing more. It makes you long for something you can hold on to, something to look forward to after weeks or months of travelling, a thread to tie you to the place, a reason for returning.

So the most satisfying way to pass the midnight miles is this. It has to happen by chance, which makes it all the better, because the element of unpredictability makes it all the sweeter when it does occur.

You're making your way through some nameless hamlet in the wee hours, the amber glow of the streetlamps letting the inhabitants sleep undisturbed in their vague, two-dimensional houses when, from beyond a shadowy garden, someone switches on a light. In this one stranger's house a light goes on, and the undrawn curtains frame the drowsy, unfamiliar figure. This is someone's home.

By the time I've registered what I've seen, the car has accelerated away on to the open road once more, but already in my mind the stranger is glancing up out of the window, his eyes meeting mine and, seeing my face pressed against the cold glass of the car window, he smiles in recognition. His hand comes up in a friendly wave, and he turns briefly, calling silently into the dark interior of the house to rouse the sleeping family, tell them of my arrival.

I pull at the door handle eagerly, and by the time I have extricated myself from the seat, the man is coming down the path to me, hastily pulling his dressing gown around him against the pre-dawn chill. Behind him, the open door allows a welcome mat of golden light to fall across the front steps, blocked now by another tousled figure, sleepily leaning against the frame, hugging herself.

I can feel my face mirroring his grin, and whisper a greeting, not wishing to disturb the neighbours. I pull my bags from the boot, and he pins my laden arms against my body with a quick, warm embrace before prising the heaviest for himself and leading the way up the path. I use my free hand to wave a greeting to the woman, and she unwinds one skinny arm for a quick wave before turning back inside to put the kettle on. He has already gained the hallway and placed the battered case against the wall before joining her in the kitchen, busying himself with preparing a feast.

I step into the square of light and enter the house, placing my bag beside the other. I close the door, shutting out the cold, letting the warm groggy air caress my tired body. The man motions me in, and the woman gives me a hug, using the contact to guide me to a chair. I warm my hands on the mug of tea between bites of toast and jam, and the couple sit opposite, pressing me for tales of my travels, but all I want to hear about is home. Who won the angling competition, has the house on the corner been sold yet, did the little one do well in her piano exam, has the drought affected the garden?

They laugh at my eagerness for the mundane gossip of the hamlet, thinking my interest a feigned politeness after the wonders of my travels. She finally notices the tired bruises round my eyes, the weary set of my limbs, and gives him a pointed nudge. He apologizes for their nattering on, but I won't have it. Their stories ease the miles off better than a hot bath.

He shows me upstairs, although I could find the room in my sleep. Everything is as it should be. The desk is still scattered with brochures and abandoned itineraries, the wardrobe hides the clothing unsuitable for life in a case, the cabinet with its tiny lamp sports a half-read paperback I borrowed and forgot to return before I went away; all are comfortably unchanged.

I shed my clothes lazily, enjoying the ache of the tired muscles in anticipation of the healing warmth of the bed. I lower myself slowly on to the mattress, pulling the covers round me in soporific ecstasy.

I am already half asleep and am drifting into oblivion, when someone shines a torch on my eyelids, and I blink awake, confused and upset by this cruel interruption of my rest. No one here would disturb me now, I know they would put themselves to great inconvenience to see that I am left undisturbed until I surface in my own time, rested and ready to face the day.

I put my hand up to shield my eyes from the glare, muttering in irritation. My mind starts to function, and I wonder if it is an intruder, a burglar come to rob me of my precious ephemera. Reluctant to let go of oblivion, I try to think of how to deal with this invader, this despoiler. To take the right action I must identify the source of the merciless, sleep-destroying light.

I shake my mind fully awake, and focus my eyes beyond the piercing brightness. Now I can see the culprit. It is an oncoming car, flashing its high beams in annoyance at my failure to dip my own lights. Too late I flick the lever to take them down; he is passed, another solitary night traveller trying to get somewhere, like me, wanting only to reach the end of the journey, to arrive.

I roll the window down and let the cold air bring me fully back to the road. I never worry about the lack of concentration. There is a separate part of my brain that can drive the car, avoid obstacles, deal with traffic, change gears, obey road signs, watch for the right exits, without disturbing my game. It is rare for this automatic pilot to forget to dip the lights, but it has never made any more serious error, I can rely on it to contact me if I am needed, as it did just now.

Ahead, a damp grey dawn seeps over the horizon, banishing the intimate insulation the darkness provides. I must rejoin the world as interloper, become once more a visitor who is just passing through.

But there are many miles yet to travel, and the nature of my journey means that many must be travelled by night. There is always the chance when I'm driving by a stranger's house, the lights will go on inside, revealing someone's home, and I'll know in my heart's bones that it's my own.

WHAT THE WATER YIELDS
MIKE O'DRISCOLL

In a rare space above the cold ocean, hard choices bore down on Nancy Kelly, choices attendant with fears and uncertainties she had never, even in her more despairing moments, imagined she would have to face.

Beside her, oblivious to her confusion, Kieran slumped in the driver's seat, trousers open and bunched around his hips. His flaccid cock no longer seemed impressive. She leaned over and stroked it, figuring the odds on a resurrection. Feeling guilty, she withdrew her hand and pulled her knickers on instead. Hardly worth bothering taking them off in the first place. Was she too easy? Is that why he didn't seem to make much of an effort? Or, like most of them, did he think there was nothing in it for a girl to enjoy? Sometimes, she wished that the lovely things he said to her, just once, he'd say them sober. So many fellas relied on drink to loosen their tongues; was it really so hard for them to say the things they felt? Or, as bitter experience had taught her, did they simply say what they thought you wanted to hear?

Not that Kieran was like that. He did care about her, she was sure; it was just that he found it hard to articulate his feelings without a drink. Which was surprising, him being an intelligent and sensitive fella, half-way through his final year at university. Not like most fellas she'd been with, whose idea of emotional commitment seemed to be to get inside your drawers as quick as possible and then tell their pals what a great ride you were.

Earlier, after driving from Tallamount to Toe Head, they'd walked along the cliff-top path. She'd wanted to say things to him but had been struck dumb by the beauty of the full moon as it silvered the black ocean. It was a beauty that the cold impressed on her mind like a mental tattoo. She lit a cigarette and flicked the match out over the cliff, wishing she could dance on the ocean. It burned for one brief moment before gravity sucked the life from the flame.

Mildly drunk, Kieran said, 'Let's sit awhile.' She heard frosty grass crunch beneath him as he lowered himself to the ground. Then he opened one side of his coat to create a space into which she might fit. 'I've been thinking,' he said, when she was huddled next to him. 'About when I graduate.'

'Letters after your name, is it?' Nancy said, laughing. 'Doesn't the future ever scare you?'

Kieran shook his head, then pulled a bottle of Jameson's from his coat, took a long swig and passed the bottle to her. 'Warm you up.'

'You don't have to get me drunk to make love to me.' She was only half joking.

'The secret of success in anything, Nancy, is to plan ahead.'

'Tell that to the sea. You think the tides are planned?'

'The tides? Sometimes you say the weirdest things.'

She felt disappointed at that but didn't show it. 'I only mean you have to allow for chance. Like the first time we met.'

'Perhaps,' he said. 'Listen, I want you to promise me something.'

In two days it would be Christmas; a week after that, he would be back in Dublin. Make the most of it, she told herself. 'What is it?'

'That you'll wait for me, till I graduate.'

Say yes, it's not that hard. 'Won't I see you till then?'

'It'll be a busy time for me,' he explained. He wasn't looking at her as he spoke, but at the sea, absorbed in his plans for the future. She admired such confidence, such determination. Most fellas she'd known were nothing but wasters but Kieran would be something real, an engineer. 'But I'll be home for Easter, Nancy. We'll talk about London then. You won't have to spend any more time in that damn bloody hat factory. No girl of mine will have to go out to work.'

The factory wasn't so bad, she had friends there. But he was asking for a commitment she wasn't certain she felt. 'I'll wait,' she said. 'As long as I can.'

'I knew you would,' Kieran said, and, after another swig from the bottle, he kissed her on the lips.

Had she said the right thing? Was she ready to make plans for what she would do with the rest of her life? Don't think about it, she told herself. For God's sake, he's a fella that respects you, unlike most of the idiots you've called boyfriends. He doesn't think you're a tramp even though you had sex the third time you went out. He was different, she was certain. Then why was she afraid?

Saliva dribbled from one corner of his mouth. She wondered what he dreamed about and whether she was a different girl in his dreams. She retrieved the half-empty bottle of Jameson's from the back seat and took a swig, drawing strength from the burning liquid. You've said you'll wait and there's an end to it. Look at your future: nice husband, nice house, nice children; what every girl wants. Panic rose in her and she felt a momentary compulsion to smash the bottle over his head. Instead, she lit a cigarette and got out of the car. She walked twenty or thirty yards along the path, trying to discover the source of her uncertainty.

Did she really love him? She thought so. Then what more do you want? What more was there? Her vision blurred with unwanted tears. They confused her when what she needed was certainty. In the summer he would probably ask her to marry him. What would her parents say? Would Momma be OK with it, or would she question Kieran's motives, accuse him of getting her daughter up the pole? Momma wouldn't put it that way, but she saw only sin in the minds of the young. Especially in Nancy. A hot, bitter wave of anger swept through her as she remembered that her mother had been the first one to ever call her a bad name. Slut. It had been so unjust, but Momma had brooked no arguments.

The moon fell slowly from its zenith towards the glassy sea. Neither wind nor current disturbed the air or water, no sound was born anywhere in the world. The universe paused, waiting for her to decide. The cold stillness frightened her, its awesome totality making her feel small and insignificant. She wanted to scream but ice clogged her throat and lungs, smothering her resistance. It was nothing short of dying; nothing she could do or say would ever change that fact.

Water. A faint splash, a ripple on the surface of the distant ocean, clearly visible, clearly audible. Then another, moving in towards the shore. Something sleek and indefinable breaking the surface then submerging. She wondered if it might be something never before seen, and in that wondering, the world sighed and moved on. She sat down heavily, the dead cigarette slipping from her fingers. Her breath came hard and fast and beads of sweat froze on her face.

So.

That was the way of it. She would wait, till Easter anyway. That was four months, time enough to decide, time enough to find certainty. By then she might have forgotten how he came in her fist; by then perhaps, she would have the memory of being inside his head, inside his dreams.

In the world that she imagined, dreams had a real and startling power; even those creatures you'd forgotten you'd dreamed about could sneak up and surprise you. And then there was the world where power resided in prayer. Momma's world — Mass, Rosaries, Stations of the Cross, Benedictions — her defence against sin. Momma maintained a severe vigilance against it, invoking Jesus as her constant saviour. But what Nancy dreamed was more real to her than a Jesus she'd never seen.

But here it was, Holy Thursday, and neither dreams nor prayers had brought him home, merely a letter saying it could not be so. Her friends offered tepid consolation and failed to hide the relief that dwelt in their eyes. 'Lying bastards,' said Dolores Brown at lunch break. 'Tell you anything to get what they want.'

'He isn't like that,' Nancy said, trying to make her best friend understand. But maybe Dolores and the others resented the fact that she'd got herself a decent fella who wasn't out for just the one thing. Or so she'd thought. But all she had now were his paper excuses, not him. 'Ah Jesus, Kieran, why didn't you just come home?'

'Forget it, Nance,' Dolores said. 'Come to the dance with us tonight.'

'Kate's got her eye on a fella over from London,' Gail Regan said.

'I have not,' Katy Delaney said, blushing. 'But he's cute as fuck.'

'I bet he's got a prick like a donkey,' said Dolores, teasing. 'If you're not careful, Katy, he'll introduce you to it.'

Katy glared at Dolores. 'He'd be better off introducing it to you. Everybody knows you'd give him a place to put it.'

'Hark at Mother bloody Teresa,' Dolores came back. 'At least he'd be more than happy to put it there. Put it in you and 'twould most likely drop off.'

Katy was stunned into silence. Nancy was confused, not knowing who they were talking about. She wrapped a half-eaten sandwich in tissue and left it on the table. 'Who's this fella that's got ye all riled?'

'Katy met him last night in Tallamount,' Gail explained. 'His name's Roland and we're all going for a gawp tonight.'

'Hold your horses,' Dolores said. 'Nance's in mourning.'

True enough, Nancy thought, but too much of mourning was a bad thing.

Roland Bright was tall and thin with spiked black hair, dark eyes and pale bony cheeks. He said he was twenty but he looked younger. The fact that he played in a punk rock band in London gave him an exotic air in Nancy's eyes, even though he admitted his day job was as a hospital porter. 'One day we'll be big,' Roland told them. 'If we can get our act together.'

Giving him her best smile, Nancy leaned across the table and said, 'If you wrote a song for me, I bet it'd get to number one.'

Dolores and Gail burst into laughter but Katy stared daggers at her. 'I'd need to know you a whole lot better first,' Roland said.

'That can be arranged,' said Nancy.

Later, they danced together while the others consoled Katy. He held her close as he danced her gracefully round the floor, showing her off. Later still, she rode behind him on his motorbike to the guesthouse where he was staying outside Tallamount. She waited outside while he let himself in the front door and a few minutes later a light came on in a room at the side of the house. The window opened and he called softly to her.

'Welcome to my house, Miss Harker,' he said in some fake accent she didn't recognize. 'You can go anywhere in the house except of course where the doors are locked.' She snuck up to the window. 'And of course, you won't want to go there,' he said, before helping her climb through into his room.

'What was that all about?' she said. She was nervous, unsure whether or not she wanted to be there. She hardly knew anything about him and here she was in his bedroom. One small part of her urged the larger part to run. Before she could do anything, he'd turned the light out and was standing before her in the darkness.

'Nothing important,' he said in his own voice. He touched her breast through the corduroy jacket. She started to say something but he said, 'Don't say anything yet.' He undid the buttons of the jacket, and then her blouse. She caught her breath as a cold hand slid beneath the cup of her bra. She was caught between the fear that he might want more and that he might stop. She thought for a moment of Kieran and a small wave of guilt passed quickly through her. She shuddered, or imagined that she did. Roland kneeled in front of her, his head pressed against her crotch, and she wondered if what she felt was what poets meant by swooning.

'Wait,' she cried, scared by the intensity of her desire. 'I don't know if I can do this. If I should, I mean.'

Roland stood up and held her face between his palms. 'Why?'

She tried to turn away but he held her firm. 'I don't know anything about you,' she said. 'I don't usually sleep with fellas I've just met.'

'That's OK,' he said. 'Neither do I.'

'You know what I mean.'

He sighed, softly, and said, 'Never mind.' His hands dropped to his sides and a small panic exploded in her stomach. Then she saw that he was smiling and that it was OK. She leaned forward and kissed him, grateful for not having to explain. She felt the skin that covered his vertebrae through his T-shirt, felt how cold it was.

'I'll go soon,' she said.

'Yeah,' he said, and she realized they were moving, almost imperceptibly, towards the bed. No, she thought, you don't want to do this. But her body moved of its own volition, as did Roland's, and within seconds they were laying side by side on the soft blankets.

'Jesus Christ,' Nancy whispered, her voice not sounding at all like her own. 'Jesus Christ.'

They groped and tore at each other's clothes in the dark, and without knowing how it had got there, she felt her hand clasp his stiffening cock and once again she thought of Kieran. But when Roland put a hand over her uncovered cunt, and pressed firmly there, she squeezed her eyes shut and Kieran vanished for that night and more besides.

They had two weeks together, during which time Dolores and the others gave them a wide berth. She supposed she should feel guilty about having taken him from Katy but the fact of the matter was he had never been Katy's to begin with. She had not forced herself on him, no matter what they might assume, and so she would not punish herself to satisfy their envy. Katy would survive.

They got drunk together in O'Mahoney's on his final night and swapped lists of favourite films and songs. She told him his lists were pretentious but laughed to show she didn't mean it. When he asked her why she'd chosen *Saturday Night Fever* as her favourite film, she said it was because Travolta's dancing made her go weak at the knees.

'Ballerina,' Roland said. 'I wish I could make you go like that.'

'You already do,' she told him. She was silent for a while, thinking about the time to come, after he had gone. 'When you get back to London,' she said, 'will you tell your friends about the good Catholic girl you screwed on holiday?'

Roland was puzzled. 'Why?'

'Because it's what fellas do.'

He took a sip from his pint. 'You think I'm like that?'

Nancy felt on the verge of tears, but she suppressed them. This was all coming out wrong. 'No, I don't think so. I just wanted to hear you say it.'

'Listen to me, Nancy, you mean more to me than that. I don't think any the less of you because we've slept together. If other people think that way, fuck 'em. It doesn't matter.'

His words touched her deeply, but they didn't stop her imagining the words that every girl feared might be used behind her back, words like slut and whore, words they'd use to define and cage her in a prison of their own fears.

It was easy for Roland to say it didn't matter; he came from another world. Even as they rode his motorcycle through the midnight rain, part of her wanted to chastise him for failing to set her free. He parked just down the road from her house, so as to avoid bringing Momma down on them at that hour of the night. They held each other as the rain soaked through their clothes. When he stepped back she saw his eyes were full, but she knew it wasn't tears. Tomorrow he would be back in London with the Mutilated Babies singing about riots and urban deprivation and there would be no song for Nancy Kelly.

'Nancy,' he said, his voice choked. That would be the cold.

'Don't say anything,' it was her turn to say. Watching the black watery shapes crawl down his face like tiny monsters. Just dirt. False Gods in liquid graves. 'I can't bear it when people lie to me.'

'I just want to promise – '

'And I hate promises,' she said. 'Especially when someone's leaving me.'

'OK, girl,' Roland said, gently. 'I won't promise a damn thing.'

She respected that, even though it hurt like Hell. After he'd gone, she stood for a long time staring at the place where his tail-lights had been, watching the way the rain washed away what he had meant to her, leaving just a hollow space that would soon fill up with all the bile that Drumassan saw as her due.

The sky was a blue rarely seen in the West, and it spoke of good things to come and not at all of pain. But pain and heartache were all the day had to offer her. She felt as if she were dancing without music, offering explanations where none would suffice. 'I never meant – ' she tried again, but Kieran cut her off.

'You've said enough,' he said, gazing up at Rook Mountain, as if calling on it to bear witness to his pain. 'You've said nothing.'

Nancy leaned against the car. 'Then why'd you bring me here?' She'd seen it in his eyes when he called for her, that he already knew. That was Katy, she guessed, getting her revenge. She'd wanted to explain how it had happened and how it changed nothing, but whatever she said, it would all sound wrong.

'I – I don't know,' he said, unable to articulate his feelings. 'I wanted to hear you deny it. You should've thought about – '

'Don't lecture me,' Nancy snapped, sick of trying to make him understand. She'd already been tried and found guilty.

'Lecture you? Jesus Christ.'

'You always do.'

'But not enough to make you wait for me.'

'You should've come home at Easter,' she said, reaching in her bag for a cigarette. To her annoyance, she found she had none.

'I wrote and told you why I couldn't come.'

'Your bloody exams, yes. It didn't matter that I was missing you.' Kieran grabbed her by the arms. 'I couldn't just drop everything because you were lonely. I was trying to think ahead.'

'You're always thinking ahead,' Nancy cried, pulling free of his grip. 'Why don't you ever think about what's happening now?'

'God Almighty! It's only been six months. You promised you'd wait for me.'

'And you fucking promised you'd be here,' she said, furious at his attempted emotional blackmail. After all, if he had been home for Easter, none of this would have happened. 'You think you're the only one who counts? You say we'll go to London, but you never think to ask me, never think I might have an opinion.'

'That's fucking shit. You couldn't wait cos you don't feel the same way I do. All you want is…' He left the words unspoken.

'Want what? Why don't you just say it?'

'What are you talking about?'

'What you're thinking – that I'm a cheap tramp.'

'I never said that.'

'But you believe it, don't you?' And would believe it even more, she felt, if she were to tell him her real fear.

Kieran smashed a fist against the bonnet. 'OK, did you have sex with him?'

'Sex?' Nancy raged. 'Why don't you just say what you all say to each other; did you shift her? Did you get your hole?'

His fist caught the side of her mouth, pulping her lips, loosening some teeth. She spun round and went down on her knees. Blood filled her mouth and her stomach churned with nauseous pain. All the sounds of the world ceased, as if shocked by the sudden violence; the pale sun tainted the day with its sick, watery light. She spat blood and wiped her lips, watching him, numb with disbelief.

Anger and self-loathing moved across his face. He took a tentative step towards her. 'I'm sorry, I never meant – '

'Don't touch me,' she said, afraid, not just of him, but of the realization of what it meant to be more than a month late and the raw wound that left on her heart. 'Just go.' And he did, leaving her there beneath the mountain, the peaty scent of ancient, primitive days drifting up from the bog to cloud her mind.

A week later, she received a letter from London. In it, Kieran tried to explain how he felt and said he blamed himself, not her. Much as he wished he could turn the clock back, much as he wanted things to be the way they were, he couldn't get it out of his head that she'd been with someone else. Maybe in time his bitterness would fade and they could be friends at least. She'd always hold a special place in his heart and he hoped that she could find it in her heart not to hate him.

She read it alone in her room, hating him for trying to be reasonable. She didn't feel like being reasonable; what she felt was anger and contempt. The truth was, she was lucky to be rid of him. Then why didn't she feel that way?

There was a knock at the door, then Oonagh, her sister, came in. 'Is it from himself?'

Nancy lit a cigarette then put the lighted match to the letter.

Oonagh watched it burn, fascinated. 'You oughtn't have done that, Nancy. Momma will smell the smoke.'

'Blast Momma,' Nancy said. 'I'm not a child.'

'Well, maybe it's for the best, though we all liked him, even Momma.' Oonagh could be so sanctimonious sometimes, a proper Holy Mary. Give her another couple of years though, and she'd change her tune. She pointed at the flames and said, 'Did he forgive you?'

Nancy let the burning paper fall in the bin. She looked at her younger sister with a mixture of pity and despair. 'Momma can kiss my arse, Oonagh, and so can he.'

Shocked, Oonagh fled the room. Nancy laid down on the bed, shut her eyes, and put one hand on her breasts and the other on her cunt. She tried to imagine she was still Kieran's girl, to see how that would feel, but her hurt wouldn't let it be so. And when she thought of Roland, she found his face was already fading in her mind. She cried hot, angry tears then, and when she was all cried out she wrote a letter to Kieran. It was short but it said what she wanted it to say. It said, 'Dear Kieran, go fuck yourself, regards, Nancy.' She put one kiss on the bottom of the page, for old times' sake.

She stood in her underwear and wiped steam from the wall mirror, hating the colour in her cheeks. Music moved towards her though she was alone in the house. What did that mean? She lingered on the edge of doubt, hoping for a reason to step back from the precipice. She scrutinized her body and found no reasons there. Five months gone, her already tender breasts would swell even more; her stomach would balloon, she'd need new clothes, she'd walk differently. No longer a dancer's body. The music grew closer, more distinct. She looked out the window. A donkey and cart plodded by the house, old Jackie Hannigan propped up against a churn on the cart, sleeping, and behind him, on a transistor radio, Kris Kristofferson singing about it being Sunday morning and him wishing to God he was stoned.

But it wasn't Sunday and all she had was gin. That was the usual method, though she had something extra, just in case. She opened the bottle and drank, wincing at the bitter taste. Cheers, Jackie, sleep well. Kieran would call you an anachronism, would say that the country was full of them. What she intended was as much one as that donkey and cart. She took off her underwear and stepped into the bath. She eased herself down into the hot water, holding her breath till her legs, stomach and breasts were submerged. How does this bring it on? Don't think about that, just drink. So she did, three or four mouthfuls in quick succession. She watched her nipples swell and imagined a mouth on them, not a child's. But imagination wasn't called for now; imagination led to mistakes and she'd already made too many.

Momma had told her fellas were only after the one thing, even before Nancy knew what that one thing was. But it wasn't long before she found out. She remembered the time she saw her brother, John, wanking in the barn. When he'd shot the white stuff on to his stomach, she'd remembered Dolores saying that it was called spunk and it was what fellas put inside you to make babies. She'd wondered then, if John would go to Hell for wasting it. When she did it to herself, the first time, it had felt so sweet, almost profound, and so too was the sense of shame. But weighing one against the other, trying to measure the sin, she came to realize that it was no sin at all. How could it be a sin to make yourself feel that way?

Doing it, though, was the worst. She sighed and drank some more, feeling the gin dribble down her chin. Her body slid further into the water, making islands of her nipples and toes, small fragments of herself fighting for breath beneath a sea of lies and rumour. She touched both nipples in turn, as if to check that they were still part of her. Choosing was scary, but if she had the power to choose, she had a duty to live with whatever choice she made. Guilt, she had learned to live with, though it had taken her a long time to do so, a long time not to feel that her desires were wrong. And there was always the fear of what people would say if they knew.

She remembered a time four years back, fetching home the messages from the Co-op, singing Donna Summer's 'Love to Love You, Baby', like she was signalling her intentions to whoever might hear them, which she was. One moment she was alone on the road, the next a shadow fell across her face. Without looking up she said, 'So you're here, after all.'

'I said I would be,' Danny Riordan said, leaping down into the road. 'And I meant it.'

'So you did,' said Nancy, putting her shopping bags down. 'You had something you wanted to show me?'

Danny shrugged, scratched his head and kicked a stone in the road.

'Didn't know you were shy, Danny.'

'I'm not. Just I ...'

'Just ...' she prompted. When he didn't take the hint, she said, 'Do you fancy me?'

'I ...' Danny began, then faltered and finally he nodded.

'Dolores told me,' Nancy said. The warm summer sun intoxicated her, making her light-headed. 'Said you fancied me for ages.'

'Did she now? You know you're sweating?'

'So are you. You gonna show me whatever it is you have to show?'

'It's in there,' Danny said, nodding towards the ditch.

'Is it now? You want me to go in there with you?'

'Sure, why not?'

'Right so,' she said, shinning up the ditch. 'Be a gentleman then, and fetch me messages up with you.' She watched as he grabbed the two bags and followed her up. So, he fancied her, did he? Well, he was a handsome fella, with his shoulder-length blond hair and eyes like green jewels. The girls all said he had a bit of a head on him, always showing off, but sure, that only made him more of a prize. She followed him along a winding path through a sea of furze, till finally they came to a small clearing.

She looked around, hands on her hips. 'So, where is it?' He put down the bags and offered her a cigarette. Lighted, she said, 'What do you get up to in here?'

Danny lit a cigarette for himself then sat on the dewy grass. 'Black magic,' he said, grinning mysteriously. 'I cast spells.'

Nancy sat, cross-legged, a few feet away. 'What sort of spells?'

'All sorts.'

For a while they smoked in silence, each slyly surveying the other. Feeling the sweat on her back, she began to sense why she had come here. A delicious panic rumbled just below the surface of her calm, prompting her to ask, 'Love spells?'

Danny cleared his throat and gazed directly at her. 'Could be, depending on who I was thinking about.'

'Who're you thinking about now?'

'You,' Danny said, and Nancy felt some bonds loosen inside her.

'What happens when you cast a spell?'

Danny stubbed his cigarette out and edged closer. 'All sorts.'

'Tell me,' she said in a voice that seemed unconnected to her.

'Girls want to kiss me.'

'I see.' Her voice had fallen to a near-whisper.

'Like this,' he said, and kissed her, delicately, on the lips. He pulled back and said, 'Is the spell working?'

'That was you kissing me,' she said. 'You meant this.' This time she leaned forward and put her lips on his and held them there for a longer time. When their mouths parted, she said, 'Ah, sweet Jesus.'

'Did you like that?'

'It was grand.'

'I can make the magic stronger,' he said. 'If you want me to.'

Her heart was beating deliriously inside her chest and she felt a momentary panic that he might hear it thumping away. What should she do? What if she went ahead and did it? Oh God, would he talk about it, and what would her friends say? Dolores was always talking about it, but had she ever actually done it? Who'd ever know? It was too late now. No, there was still time to stop. Her throat was dry and she had difficulty forming the words. 'Stronger how?'

'Like this,' Danny said. He touched her breasts through her cotton dress. A tremor of fear and delight ran through her body.

'Don't,' she sighed.

He opened the top two buttons of her dress. 'Magic,' he said.

His fingers were warm and rough and she felt the heat rise in her face. Part of her wanted him to stop but this last vestige of fear was overwhelmed by a desire to let it happen. The top of her dress was open and he'd pushed her bra up to reveal her small, white breasts.

'They're lovely,' he said, gazing at them like he was the one who was spellbound.

'You can touch them if you want,' she said, hardly aware that she had spoken. Her insides were melting like wax in the heat of the sun. She closed her eyes as he placed a hand on each breast, holding them gently, as if afraid of hurting her. Her tongue felt thick and swollen and she wondered if he could decipher the words she spoke. They were, 'Show me it, your magic wand.'

He sat back and unzipped his jeans. His face was flushed as he pulled his cock out; it quivered, long and thin in the shimmering haze. Something ferocious burned between her legs. Don't, she thought, but she did, reaching out to stroke him. Danny gasped and clenched his teeth. 'Abracadabra,' Nancy whispered, and lay back on the grass.

Danny slid a hand between her legs and pushed his fingers up against her knickers. She gripped his wrist and held it just away from her. 'I'm scared,' she said.

'So am I,' Danny said.

She loosened her grip, felt him touch her again, felt how good it made her feel. 'Fuck's sake, Danny,' she said. 'Don't tell anyone.'

'I won't,' he gasped. 'I swear to Christ.'

Then he was on top of her, hoisting the dress up round her hips, pulling her knickers down below her knees and his cock prodding against her while his breath roared in her ears and her breath in his, a hand beneath her buttocks, pulling her up against him and feeling the pressure as he entered her and she resisting but knowing there was no going back, then gritting her teeth as a sharp pain assaulted her and was gone and feeling embarrassed at the noise they made and scared in case someone should hear and, after a final shudder, realizing he was still, knowing it was over, wondering was that all there was?

But it hadn't been, not then, because afterwards there had been the awful guilt, and the fear that people, that Momma, would know by her face what she had done. And though Danny Riordan had been as good as his word, those emotions had stayed with her for a longer time than Danny himself had stayed. Until finally she'd come to realize that, although that first time had been nothing special, sex wasn't just something you put up with for the sake of making babies. And if it was OK at fifteen for a girl to feel desire, then how could it be wrong now, at nineteen?

So how had she come to this, a near empty bottle of gin in one hand, a number-three knitting needle in the other? Anger and disgust welled up inside her. She drowned it with the last of the gin and let the bottle fall over the side of the bath. Tears fell from her eyes, tears for all that had gone wrong over the last six months. She wanted to be strong at this moment, not crying like a child. She wanted to believe that she'd do it again, that she wouldn't change anything, but she was no longer sure. The thought of the rumours and accusations she'd have to endure frightened her.

Far out beyond the fleshy rocks, something sleek and metallic slid through the water, gliding towards the shore. She shuddered as Momma's instrument swooped and dived, coming for her like a vengeful angel. She braced herself but there was no defence. It plunged into her and tore the scream from her lips. Pain, and the names of her lovers, boiled from her lips as she cursed them, and herself, for giving in. She kept on screaming and cursing as brutal waves crashed against the shore of her flesh, tossing ships and mountains above the foam, then sucking them down again to leave the flotsam of bones and clothes with no occupants to disintegrate on the crimson surface; ballerinas bound hand and foot, drowned babies, spiders; a red tide ebbing and flowing, carrying her past away, everything she'd wanted to be, everything that was her.

Everything except what was inside, which was inside her still.

Oonagh came to see her on Saturdays, bringing money from Pop to help pay the rent on her one-bedroom flat. She was the only one of the family who came, the only one who tried to understand. Momma hadn't seen or spoken to her for four months. Nor had she seen her grandchild.

'I've some news,' Oonagh said. 'You'll never guess who's home.'

'Who?' Nancy said, feeding the baby in her lap.

'Kieran McCarthy.'

'Oh.' The news unsettled her, stirred up old emotions.

'He called round to see you,' Oonagh elaborated. 'Pop told him you'd moved out, didn't tell him why.'

'Good.'

'I haven't finished. Momma'd been out, but he was still there when she got home. We thought she'd lose the head, but sure, she was as good as gold, made him stay for supper and all. Eventually, didn't she ask him was he the father.'

'Lord,' Nancy said. 'Why can't she mind her own business?'

'There's no point blaming her, Nance. You brought it all on yourself.'

Nancy wanted to tell Oonagh to leave. Instead, she glanced down at her sleeping son, then laid him down on the bed behind her. 'So what is she up to?'

'Look,' Oonagh said, her voice rising. 'Forget Momma, think about Robert. You really want to bring him up alone in this dump? Without a father?'

'I can manage,' Nancy said, defiantly.

'Kieran's in town. He gave me a lift here. He wants to see you.'

Anger flared in Nancy, but so, too, did other feelings, emotions that confused and excited her. It should have been simple to say that she wanted nothing to do with him, but the words refused to take shape on her lips.

'I think he still has a soft spot for you,' Oonagh went on.

It was too late, she told herself. He'd had his chance. But, what if it were true? A soft spot? Think of Robert. What did she feel? 'I...don't think I can see him.'

'He's in Cassidy's, waiting for you. I'll stay with Robert.'

And so she went, through streets crowded with New Year shoppers undeterred by the icy rain. The sky above Tallamount was darkening and smoke and steam billowed from pub doorways, trailing mournful folk songs in their wake. She remembered Christmas a year ago, with Kieran, singing those same songs in those same pubs. It seemed a lifetime away.

Cassidy's was an old, dark café on North Street. She saw him through the window, his head stuck in a newspaper. Glancing up, he saw her and waved. She took a deep breath and went inside.

'Nancy, you're looking well,' he said, getting up and holding a chair out for her. 'I'm glad you came.'

She didn't try to speak, not yet. She was too uncertain as to what to say.

He ordered two cups of coffee, seeming nervous and on edge, but then so was she. His hair was shorter; otherwise, he hadn't changed much. But, she wondered, what about his heart? When the coffee arrived she lit a cigarette and waited for him to moan. He didn't. He said, 'I've done a lot of thinking since June, especially since I heard about the... your being pregnant.'

'Yes,' was all she could bring herself to say.

'I acted like an arsehole, Nancy. The exams made me lose sight of the things that really mattered.'

If he was expecting her to contradict him, he was wrong. 'What did you want to see me for?' she said.

He shook his head, avoiding her gaze. 'I... I thought about you a lot while I was away.' She sensed how difficult it must have been for him to come here, and sensing that, she felt some hardness give way inside her.

'You mean you thought about someone else apart from yourself?'

'I missed you, Nancy. I wanted to...' He faltered, then said, 'Let's go somewhere we can talk.'

'We can talk here,' Nancy said.

'I can't say the things I need to say, not here.'

'I can't be away from Robert too long.'

'That's his name, Robert?'

'You like it?'

'It's a grand name. How old is he?'

'Three weeks.'

The rain fell heavier as he drove through the crowded streets, hurrying the night down. He put a tape of the Bee Gees in the cassette player, a concession he'd rarely made before, and as she listened to 'Jive Talkin'', Nancy wondered where her panic had gone. She felt surprisingly calm, willing to admit she didn't hate him. He drove to the lake where, in the early days of their courtship, they used to go picnicking. The trees were all naked now, their shapes blurred by the rain that drummed on the roof and the windscreen. She felt caught between hope and doubt, and was confused about what it was she really wanted from him.

'I made a big mistake, Nancy, treating you the way I did.'

Had she heard those words before, or merely dreamed them?

'I should've come home at Easter. If I'd been there, then maybe things might've been different.'

'But they're not.'

'It doesn't matter any more. You're all I really care about.'

'That isn't enough.'

The smile faltered on Kieran's face. 'I... I don't understand.'

'I have a child now, remember?'

'Yes, yes, of course. I meant the both of you.'

The rain fell harder, making it impossible to see the world through the windscreen. She felt as if she were in a bubble, isolated from a reality which dissolved around her. Was this a dream of Kieran? And how did it connect with her? 'You care about us,' she said, testing the dream. 'What does that mean?'

'It means I want us to try again,' he said, opening the glove compartment. He brought out a small bottle of Jameson's, offered it to her and, when she declined, took a long swig himself.

Her heart sank but she said nothing. Perhaps it gave him insight; maybe it had even given him the strength to come back for her. He'd finally said it, that he wanted her; so did she have the strength to forgive him and say yes? Take away what had happened between them back in the summer, and wasn't it what she'd wanted all along? But it didn't feel that simple, it wasn't just a question of betrayal and rejection. There were other factors to consider.

Before she could respond, Kieran continued, 'I want you both to come back to London with me. I've a job with a petrochemical company, a real chance to make something of myself. But I want you with me. I know it won't be easy, but I think we should give it a try.'

'I... I don't know,' she said. 'I need time to think.'

'We'll get a flat together and, if things work out, then maybe we'll get married.'

What did he mean? He'd have her on condition? Did his love involve conditions? 'What do you mean,' she said, '"if things work out"?'

He wasn't looking at her, but out at the liquid world. He held the bottle in one hand and gesticulated with the other as he spoke, making plans for the future, mapping it out in his head. 'Sure, there's plenty time to sort out the details, and – '

'What details?' Nancy said, her voice rising.

Kieran turned towards her, smiling. 'Don't worry, Nancy. I'll take care of everything. And think of the boy, he'll be getting a name.'

'He has a name already.'

'What, that English eejit's?'

'He has my name.'

'Of course, cos that fella never offered to do the decent thing.'

She felt claustrophobic suddenly, and a little nauseous too. He didn't know who she was; and worse, she was no longer sure herself. 'I – I have to go now,' she said, fighting to control her voice.

'For fuck's sake,' he said, the smile crumbling on his face. 'What the Christ did I say?'

'I don't know you at all,' Nancy said, pulling on the door handle. 'I never did.' She threw her shoulder against the door, opening it, then stumbled out of the car. The headlights flicked on and dazzled her, and she heard him shouting, 'Damn it, Nancy, get back in the fucking car.'

The rain iced her flesh. It wasn't that he'd changed, she realized, it was her. She saw now what he really was, what he'd always been, and knew that she didn't want to be with him. She imagined his conditions, saw herself choking on them. She turned, trying to run, but mud sucked at her feet, holding her. She felt a hand on her arm and turned, saw him there, waving the bottle at her, but talking calmly, rationally, trying to make her see the sense of it. But in his eyes she saw the unquenched flames of rage, and saw herself in them, metamorphosed, become plastic, face all shiny and bright, as beautiful and compliant as a doll, his doll. He embraced her and smothered her frozen cheeks with kisses. She felt herself disintegrating in the rain, identity slipping from her like a shedded skin. His lips moved as if he were speaking in a badly dubbed film, having no connection to the sounds they made. She knew that what he was really saying was how he'd gather the pieces of her into himself, shape her anew so that people could say he'd done the right thing, letting her live through him, giving her child a name.

'No!' she screamed. 'I won't do it!'

His animated face became still, his arms dropped to his sides. 'You don't realize,' he said, 'what I've gone through for you.'

'I'm sorry,' she said, crying. 'But I didn't ask you.'

His features twisted as he tried to get to grips with what she was saying. 'You're saying no to me?'

'I'm sorry,' she repeated. 'I don't love you.'

'You think anyone else will have you?' His voice was cold and emotionless.

'It isn't a question of anyone having me.'

'I don't fucking care what it is,' he screamed, lurching towards her. She tried to run but the mud didn't want her to go. She threw her arms up to protect herself but Kieran lost his balance and slipped. The mud embraced him with a loud, sucking kiss. 'Fucking bitch,' he screamed, as a hand shot out and grabbed her by the ankle. The Earth let go her other foot and she kicked him in the face. He loosed her ankle and tried to push himself up, but before he could get to his knees, she'd grabbed the fallen bottle and smashed it against the back of his head. He crumpled like a slaughtered beast and sank back down to the ground. He lay there groaning as she hovered over him with a foot raised above his head to crush his skull. She balanced like that, on one leg for a minute or more, teetering on the edge of madness, seeing how long she could exist in that place. But when she saw that his dissolution was complete, she lowered her foot and left that place to walk back to Tallamount in a rain that no longer had anything to wash away.

She read Momma's letter once more, then tore it into pieces and let the wind carry it out over Toe Head and down to the sea. It was no use ever trying to explain or justify her choices, not to Momma. All she saw was sin and shame.

Robert was strapped to her chest in a sling, his head peeking up above the V of her coat. He was nearly three months old. She wondered who he looked like, her or his father? She wondered what her own father would think of him, but since Kieran had returned to London alone, even Oonagh had stopped visiting. He might have said, 'Sure he's the spit of his father,' but he'd never known him. Where was Roland now, and would she ever see him again? She didn't think so. That thought might have saddened her but it didn't. What did, was that he didn't even know of Robert's existence. What he might do with that knowledge was something else entirely, but she wished she could have told him.

'I'm sorry, Bobby,' she said, nuzzling his face. 'I never meant to hurt you.' Pop had found her in the bath, passed out in the red water. In hospital he'd tried to persuade her to have the baby and give it up for adoption. Dolores offered to lend her money to go to England for an abortion. Momma said nothing at all. But when she came home from hospital, five months gone, her mother called her a whore, and told her never again to darken her door. Pop tried to make her see reason but Momma's word was final. He helped Nancy find the flat, while she prayed her daughter's shame out of existence.

'I could make it easy for them,' she whispered to her son. 'It would make things complete.' She stepped nearer the edge of the cliff, unafraid of the gusting winds. 'They might even thank me for it.' Not only that, not only would it make life so much simpler for everyone else, it would be an end to all her loneliness and fear.

One step would be enough. A hundred feet. Two or three seconds and it would all be over. She turned sideways to the edge and hoisted Robert further up her chest. Out on the ocean, sunlight danced on the heavy swell, and below her the white foam roared in appreciation. Dazzled, she pointed it out to her son, whose lively eyes seemed drawn towards the spectacle. Waves peeled off from the swell and threw themselves forward to assault the cliff-face. Her heart beat faster as they pounded the roots of her world. Robert grew excited in the sling, kicking and bucking his tiny body. People might find honour in what she did. Kieran might grieve for a week or a month, and then he would rationalize her actions and take pride in the knowledge that he at least had acted honourably.

So easy to make everything right. She raised one leg and held it out over the drop, where the wind tugged at it as if urging her to join its game. But before she could, a giant wave fell out of the sky and christened them with its spray. My child, she thought, as she put her foot down on solid ground and took one step back.

CLEAN
DAVID ROSE

It hadn't seemed so pressing then, though it's hard to remember. I do remember the match though, keep remembering, every time I shave.

They had hired a wide-screen set for it, hung from a gantry on the wall opposite the bar. The blue rosettes and red were evenly scattered, but the Irish enclave had adopted Manchester for the day, as nearest to home.

Twig pulled out his *Sporting Life*. He said, 'What are we going, score or straight win?' Max said, 'Score, you'll get no odds on win.' 'So what'll it be?'

Jerry and Galway looked at me. 'Four–nil,' I said casually. 'Who to?' 'United, of course.' You don't mix it with Micks.

Twig scanned the print. 'They're giving 33 to 1 on four–nil.' Jerry said, 'OK then, tenner each?' They seemed impressed by my chill assurance.

'I'm broke,' I said, 'bar the price of a pint.' Max said, 'You've got to back your own tip.' 'All right,' I said, 'lend me a tenner, I'll give it back out of my winnings.' I meant it as a joke.

Galway crossed to the bookies while we got in the drinks.

I nursed my Guinness through the first half while Chelsea controlled the game.

When Peacock hit the bar, Galway cracked his glass, had to gulp the last third before it trickled away.

At half-time Jerry said, 'It's gonna be a fucking no-score draw.' Max said, 'Yeah, the FA Cup.' Galway pocketed his splintered glass while Twig cleared the rest. Cantona's first penalty damped their hostility. When he banged in the second six minutes later, they began to perk up.

Galway said, 'They won't get four fucking penalties though.' But the mood had turned.

When Hughes hit United's third goal in ten minutes, I knew it was all over. I kept thinking of Peacock hitting the bar, willing it in.

Spencer nearly did it for me in a late attack. Jerry and Twig each grabbed one of my sleeves. Not a drop had been swallowed in fifteen minutes. The clock in the corner of the screen ticked down.

In the last minute the fourth goal came, scored, as if to rub it in, by a substitute. Max whispered, 'The bugger's done it.'

Galway pulled off his wig, poured the last of his Guinness over his head. Jerry offered him a chaser. Max said, 'That's sixteen hundred and fifty fucking quid you've rolled us in today.' They were hugging, squeezing or patting me, depending on their proximity. Twig called for champagne. Galway said, 'Make it Black Velvets, give it some body.' Hughie shouted over that the first round was on the house. Jerry said to Galway, 'If you've lost those fucking slips – '

I followed them to the bookies.

I peeled off a ten from my wad and handed it to Max. 'Keep it,' he said, 'frame the fucker like those French writers do.'

We went back for another round of Black Velvets while they made a list of clubs, planned the night's itinerary.

Galway said, 'Whose turn to drive tonight?' Max said, 'We're not taking the bloody van. We'll do it in style, dress up, take the bus in.'

Jerry said, 'Bollocks to the bus, we'll get a cab.'

I said, 'Why waste money? We can get a cab home. But we won't all get in it.'

We arranged to meet at eight. They drank up and left.

Red and white scarves were being waved in the street. Maybe it was the reflection of that in my glass, distorted by the bubbles – a convex close-up of a swerving bus.

As I walked home for a shave, I kept thinking of Peacock hitting the bar. I stopped on the way, bought some clean socks.

In the event, it was Max who was taken. Hit and run job. I was sorry. Can one say that?

It had repercussions for me too. I had acquired a reputation. My name was passed up the command.

The following month I was taken to meet the regional Intendant. He seemed to take to me. Wanted to know my motivation, my plans, my job. I told him all I could.

It's been a grey, wet day, the traffic was bad. Not just heavy but moody, no open windows and stereos, no carnival buzz. Summer's over.

The bike kept fading on me. It's an odd sensation to suddenly feel yourself coasting powerless through the urban drizzle, but familiar enough. I used to feel that way all the time, waiting for some convulsion to kick-start my life, weld it together. Later I could tell myself, this is just a cover, ordinary life is just a cover.

Now I'm beginning to feel the same even when I'm on active. I delivered some graphics to a Euston Road address, grabbed a burger and spent my lunch flying tracts on windscreens in a multi-storey. I watched myself in the convex mirrors on the pillars.

The afternoon was hectic, five rush jobs and two tickets, but the radio cackle lifted me and the bike was sweeter. The last drop was a film can to the Hayward. I left the bike locked and sat on the Embankment. Just me and a few alcos and the gulls. The light brightened a little and bounced off the mottled water. I wanted to get below that, to the silken silt where there are no reflections, to the reality of the fish.

It seemed easy – strap myself to the tank, rev up one of the ramps the skateboarders use and wheelie over the parapet.

Once the strap had snapped I'd be carried by the tide to the open sea and the underwater lightning.

They'll be gathered round a grave with an empty coffin, quiet set faces, a quiet set speech. *We are again depleted in our fight, by the loss of one of our gifts in men, lost or taken, in strange circumstances. For we may not forget that they are thickly around us, the enemies of the vision, their machinations beyond our reach, inspired in the highest office. Yet will they know that we will not give up or compromise our cause, and in honouring this our comrade, redouble our zeal and serve notice on governments, rivals and the powers of darkness...*

★

Besides, there's Randolph to consider.

Stupid name for a dog. Only a politician would call a dog Randolph. Cowardly too. Refused to come across. Sent an official driver with a note saying 'You keep him', wrapped round a tin of dogmeat. What sort of hard-hearted bastard would let his dog die to save his own skin?

I couldn't see him butchered. I just sent his collar back with a few bloodstains on it. We're good friends now. Couldn't be without him.

I fed him and took him round the park.

I settled him for the night and went on to the meeting. A devotional meeting, but an informal one, so Kirk had brought his button accordion and we finished with some of the old songs, 'Apples in Winter', 'Johnny When You Die' – they're some of my favourites, but I found myself miming.

I keep seeing a white wooden headstone amid bloodrusted bracken.

Wednesday's my service night for the Intendant. I have to shave carefully, up and down, against the grain. I usually shave quickly, for the face I see in the mirror I neither like nor recognize. Like my name, I've never felt it fitted.

His wife was waiting for me in the conservatory. She took me straight up to her room. He, I assumed, was already in his, the other side of the connecting bathroom, so I went ahead.

She was wearing a new perfume which I told her I liked but I didn't catch the name.

She was clawing my spine when I heard the bathroom door click shut. I guessed he'd been called away to a summary convocation, and wondered if it was a disciplinary and if so whose. It was too late to stop then so I carried on, then we lay together sharing a cigarette.

I sent his money back next morning.

I keep dreaming a woman with red hair and freckled breasts. We were close once. Maybe she'll put a claim on me too, assume it was because I couldn't live without her.

I could leave the usual note. But that's always struck me as ludicrous, it's like cancelling the milk. And what to say, how to explain? Explanations only widen the gap.

A Mission and Vision meeting at eight. It was an educational meeting, so we used the boarded-up school by Union Hall. Randolph wouldn't settle, so they'd started without me. We discussed spirituality, speaking in turn on how freedom of spirit depends on freedom of space, freedom of land – this was a man who owned a Sussex estate and twenty thousand acres of conifers in Scotland with nothing to show but newspaper. Some of the others got a little zealous with their razors, but I calmed them.

We sang some hymns to Kirk's accordion, and he joined in. He had guts, and a good voice, I'll say that.

After the meeting I stopped for a drink on the way home, alone. I took my glass into the pool room. There was a mixed crowd round the table and a game on. I watched, waiting for my head to settle. The player was midway through a break. He was oblivious to the banter, absorbed in his shots, his soul lasered down the cue. Then he missed a shot and relaxed into the crowd, laughing and looking for his drink, which someone had hidden. I envied him that easy unreflection.

I drank up and walked home. In the neon shimmer of the puddles I saw a swerving bus, and a white headstone.

There was a sealed note waiting for me on the mat, informing me I'll be on active alert the first weekend in November. I was also to contact the Intendant next day.

His wife opened the door, took my arm, but led me to the study, where he was waiting. It's an ambitious job, a visiting Foreign Minister. He asked me to visualize the route to Burnham, suggest where to stage the diversion. I told him they would use a helicopter, so it would have to be between Denham Aerodrome and Dorneywood, but couldn't help any further. He went back to the maps. I came away, letting myself out.

I saw a burst under cover of a firework display, but it's out of my hands now.

And what if I were wrong? What if the mission failed? Would they think it deliberate? What if it were?

It has to be on my terms. That's the whole objective. The only way would be to resign, formally dissociate, do it before they find me. There's precious little privacy in this country. Eventually a newspaper cutting, a radio clip.

No coffin but the same still faces and a symbolic grave.

He who was once a brother is now buried in a potter's field. We the living still owe him compassion, imagining the agony of his betrayal, not of us but of himself, and his desolation. Indeed we owe him this final debt, as each looks into his heart and strengthens his resolve...

The terms will still be theirs.

Next morning I took Randolph out early, then put in a full day. The sun was warm – we seem to be in for an Indian summer.

The bike was running better in the drier weather. The haze still lay over the city but was slowly lifting. As I crossed Vauxhall Bridge I realized that above me there's a mile of blue and beyond that an eternity of black, a furnace of ice.

I'd accepted an out-of-town job – to Shepperton Studios – that no one else was keen on, but I was glad then. Once clear of the city traffic I stoked the bike and leaned into its keening.

I stopped by Chertsey Bridge to look at the Thames. It changes completely out of the city. I wished I could trace it back to its source, to where it first bubbles out unreflective and eager.

On the way home I saw Galway. He told me some of the boys, those that were left, were joining up for a drink, wanted me to come.

I washed and shaved. I shaved slowly, wiping a porthole in the steam, reading each wrinkle and pore. I put on a clean shirt, then called Randolph.

He stopped to explore a hedge. I slipped his lead, went on ahead over the crossing then called him. There was a bus. Someone had an arm out to request it, but maybe the driver didn't see it, maybe it wasn't on his route. He didn't stop, or slow, until he saw Randolph, then he swerved, too late.

I held his slowly stiffening body in my arms, carried him home, wrapped him in his blanket. It was late by then, and I had to find a working cash dispenser.

Galway, Jerry and a couple of others were there, a round ahead of me. I bought the next two.

Jerry said, 'You flush?' I said, 'Flushed, maybe it's the weather. Anyway, what the hell?'

Galway said, 'What about a tip?'

I said, 'You know I'm not supposed to use my gift for mundane and personal uses.' He said, 'True enough. But a little literary conversation couldn't be frowned on. We'll have a tickle on the Booker.'

I said, 'Not the ghost of a chance.' Patted his wallet. It hardly matters now.

Jerry spotted a bloodstain on my sleeve. He said, 'You on active?' I told him about Randolph. Galway said, 'Poor little bugger.' He offered to carve up the driver.

I said, 'Life's a bitch, but it's all to plan. Besides, I didn't get his number.'

They all left ahead of me. I finished my drink and went to the convenience. It was empty. I wrenched the wooden toilet lid from one of the stalls and went out the back exit.

I worked into the night, cutting and carving a headstone for Randolph, burning his name on with a poker, whitewashing it. Then I went down to the local sorting office, borrowed a van, loaded it up.

I hope I haven't forgotten anything. Randolph, headstone, shovel, two washing-up bowls, two flasks of boiling water, spare razor.

There's a spot I've always loved on Chobham Common. Away from the footpaths, across a bog, a clearing of bracken amid the pines.

The red van will show up but by then I'll be gone, welded by the blue arc of sky.

What sort of stupid tosser would top himself over a dog?

THE PRECIPICE
JAMES MILLER

He left the girl sitting on the bench and went over to the pay phone. As he reached for the receiver he glanced back to give the girl a quick smile that was supposed to be reassuring. The phone was answered on the fifth ring.

'Hello?'

'Mum? It's me.'

'Robert... where are you?'

'I'm in Rome. I'm OK, really.'

The line crackled as she inhaled sharply.

'Rome! Robert, Jesus! When will you give this up? Is...?'

'She's still with me. Yes. She's fine,' he continued, hurriedly trying to anticipate her questions.

'Well...' He could sense her exasperation as she struggled to find another way of emphasizing her disapproval while at the same time trying to be helpful. 'Are you sure you should do this, Robert? I wish you'd come home, your father's going absolutely... and Jessica misses you and... I mean, how are you holding out for money?'

'I'm OK... it's expensive but we're managing.'

'We can always send...'

'No. It's OK, honestly.'

'Have you phoned John?'

'Yes, yes, it's fine, absolutely fine, the job's there, he has a hut for us on the beach and Lucy will be able to get something and we'll be fine.' He spoke quickly, hoping she wouldn't be able to sense the fears behind his confident façade. He hadn't been able to get through to John. But there would be a job, if not with John then somewhere else on the island, or on another. Everything would be fine.

'How...how was your birthday?' his mother continued, following the unconvinced, even critical pause with which she punctuated his last statement.

'Fine. We were on a train. Lucy made me a card...it was really sweet actually, I don't know when she did it, but, I mean, it was lovely. That was all I wanted, it was perfect, really.' He'd hardly thought of it as his twentieth birthday, spent for the most part on a night train from Paris. Lucy had slept most of the time, slumped against his shoulder, his lips pressed against the top of her head, tasting the sweet, soft smell of her bright brown hair. He couldn't think when she'd been able to draw the card, a psychedelic blue cat with sunglasses waving at him while clouds above the cat wrote HAPPY BIRTHDAY in woolly letters. 'Look, Mum, I think I should go...we're just going to rest here for a couple of days then head down to Greece as quick as possible...I'll phone in a few days, OK?'

'Well...'

'I've got to go, I'll call soon.' Robert hung up quickly, not waiting to hear if she said goodbye. He stood by the phone for a moment looking at Lucy, where she had been waiting for him to finish, staring into space. He hoped the reassurance of her beauty would soothe his uncertainties. She smiled weakly back at him before hanging her head down in a sweeping, fatigued gesture, like a bright flower yearning for water. She was leaning forward over her crossed legs, her left arm balanced by the wrist over her knee, her right hand steadily moving a cigarette up to her lips. Then she sat back, uncrossing her legs and tugging at the hem of the short, flower-printed dress she was wearing, fingers gliding over the tanned swell of her thighs before reaching back, returning cigarette to lips. Morning sun shone through her hair, striking the white gravel path around them and dissolving upwards like a fine spray of dusty gold, bathing her in a halo of pure warm light, and yet again Robert wanted to imagine she was something too precious and beautiful, like a stranded butterfly, to survive alone in the outside world. And, as soon as he thought this, he felt the pain of trying to draw such an ideal from a situation that was so painfully real, like a fresh wound still bleeding and at the same time so strange, filled with all the exhilaration and uneasy solitude of a dream. And sometimes, when Lucy seemed to slide into her own world of tiny gestures and invisible expressions, and nothing he might say or do would mark the still pool of her indifference or touch the impenetrable sadness that, at times, emanated from her like a distant, cool haze, then Robert wondered if he was the precious one. In those eerie, broken aporias that lurked between them like a stain on the bedsheets Robert realized how much he needed her to love him, needed her to be *in* love with him; even that seemed impossible, like a jigsaw puzzle missing half its pieces, with nothing left to do but guess at the pattern already lost.

'Was it OK?' she asked, standing up as Robert approached.

Quickly, he pressed her against him, a tangle of hair caressing his cheek. 'Yeah.'

'Does she still not like me?'

'I don't know. It doesn't matter, you know I don't care what she thinks.'

'I know.'

They kissed quickly. He could taste the tobacco on her lips.

'Rome. What do you want to do?'

She shrugged. Her eyes, luminous with the blue of the Italian sky, mapped his face as if his question was a test, the answer to be divined from his expression. 'I don't know. Anything. What's here?'

'You didn't look in the guidebook?'

'Only a bit... I was tired. Where's the Vatican?'

'We can see it from here.' They were in the Villa Borghese, above the Spanish Steps. Robert pointed to the marble dome of St Peter's, hanging like a serene cloud over the russet tangle of tiled rooftops before them. 'There.'

Lucy nodded, looking at him again. 'Can we go later?' She wove her fingers around his. 'It's so hot. I'm tired... I want to lie down for a bit.'

'OK... it'll take us a little while to get back to the hotel anyway.' The humid August heat was exhausting, the soupy city air stinging his eyes. He took a swig from a lukewarm bottle of water and shuddered. The memory of the early morning was still inviting: Lucy's cool, wet hair drying on his chest, the two of them lying motionless, arms reached back, fingers entwined, shrouded by the press of their mutual exhaustion. They arrived in Rome at midnight, the city thick and sweaty under a restless, cloud-black sky sucking up air and light; a weight collapsing above the rooftops. They dragged around the cheap hotels by the station, trying to find a vacancy. Lucy, who had hardly eaten or slept for a couple of days, made Robert almost frantic as he carried both their bags while she slunk behind him, head bowed, biting feverishly at her nails because she'd run out of cigarettes, and he'd sensed in the girlish curve of her pale body an almost vampiric weariness. But he'd pressed on, eventually paying over the odds for a tiny double in a hotel located on the single floor of a massive, sienna-hued block. A thunderstorm had awoken them near dawn, shutters banging loudly, the drone of rain eventually fading into the hum of morning traffic, clouds replaced by a fresh glaze of sunlight, an identikit blue sky.

'Is the money OK?' Lucy asked as they walked down the Spanish Steps.

'We'll manage,' Robert muttered. He couldn't bear to let her know how fast it was going. He wasn't even sure himself as he tried to keep control of the diminishing wrap of traveller's cheques in his moneybelt. But he didn't want her to worry about it. It wasn't as if she was expensive, hardly eating anything some days, just smoking, drinking coffee with a restless intensity, talking for a long time in a distracted way about the beaches near where she lived, about camping in the summer. And in these glimpses, snatched from her conversation, of a private, scarcely tenable utopia Lucy herself hardly seemed to know she was expressing, Robert felt disappointed that money should even concern them, that its wretched necessities should taint them, should taint her, at all. He knew they needed to stop for a couple of days to rest and get a better perspective on their situation. A necessary objective distance, he called it. But it was so difficult, as the necessities entailed in trying to achieve that distance – that privileged moment of clear vision – continually threatened to engulf the very distance they paid so much for. One hundred and forty thousand lire a night. That moment, an elusive hotel-room epiphany, the promised peace of a park, long contemplative hours on a train or ferry, when they could talk and understand, seemed always ahead of them, conflated with the expansive beaches of Amorgos. The island was something Lucy and Robert could only talk about, but incessantly, as if mere words might bring them closer. Their vision of Amorgos became a shared thing. Lucy would ask vague, often contradictory questions about the place and Robert found his often arbitrary answers shaped his own idea of the island. He didn't let her know his fears about John's reliability and so this anxiety was absent from the image created; spoken by Lucy but taken from Robert's own answers. 'Think about all that blue sky,' she would say, 'and the sea, the twinkling sea, with little fishing boats. And it will be warm, not too hot, just lovely. And I'll swim in the sea each morning and buy food from the town market. What's it called again?' 'Chora.' 'Chora. A pretty little town. Little white houses like boxes, like ice cubes that can't melt, jumbled all over the hill. Amorgos.' 'In the Cyclades.' 'In the Cyclades.' So their vision would grow from these quiet moments where Robert felt their love was its most intense. He hoped their private vision could be built into reality, a private life of secret love and disclosure, their emotional landscape spread before a simmering Greek sky.

As they walked away from the park Robert couldn't help noticing how many of the Italian men turned to watch Lucy; and he would wonder if she noticed at all, with her over-bitten nails and inexplicable small bruises on her ankles and legs, the blim burns on her dress, the sunflower painted on the toe of her right Doc Marten. He reached down and his arm circled her waist, his hand fitting perfectly against the sudden curve of her hip. She didn't flinch from her customary loping stride, effortlessly accommodating his arm. Robert could never tell if his gesture signified possession or tenderness.

They hardly talked as they walked back through the city. Opinions exchanged at street corners or squares whether it was the same way they came. Something might catch Lucy's attention – expensive women in designer clothes, stray cats stretched out in the sun by a café, a gaggle of fat Americans, *carabinieri* with machine guns guarding an unspecified building – and she would gesture and Robert would nod in response and they would smile, quickly, and their moment of silent contact would subside again.

It was easy, Robert realized, to lose himself. Each day that passed with Lucy increased the sense that he was erasing his past, as if each touch of her hand crossed out who he was, or what he used to do and think; and when he awoke with her sweat still drying on his skin, he would see in each new day a forgetting, as if he could cast off and destroy his old self. When he caught his reflection in dirty hotel mirrors he would pause, trying to notice a subtle change in the tone of his skin, the colour of his eyes. He wondered if he could reach a point when all the people he knew at university would cease to recognize him, when his experience would have outstripped everything they would be able to understand. Then Robert knew he would be closer to the freedom he so wanted. He hoped they wouldn't miss him for long when he failed to come back next term. He was doing it all for Lucy. She was the only one who mattered. He wasn't trying to impress anyone, didn't want to upset his family. They just wouldn't understand. He wanted to take his midnight whispers and build a new world from the remains: apart, different, better.

He met Lucy trying to hitch back from Glastonbury: she'd been standing by the side of the world, a tall girl in a scruffy tie-dyed dress, long hair spun by the wind, eyes squinting into the sun, taking heavy tokes from an elegantly rolled spliff. She'd seemed to him beautiful, poised, confident, impossibly cool and something else: an aura of vulnerability surrounded her, in the way she held herself or seemed to perceive the world. She made Robert think of flowers, spider's webs laced with morning dew, icicles, clouds threatening rain. They started talking in a strange, fragmented way: fits and starts, bits and pieces. Robert tried to persuade her to rest at a friend's house near Wells, where he was staying. She agreed. She had a perfect smile, a nervous brightness to her eyes. She was awkward. Her awkwardness was charming. She was open. He didn't need to say anything to impress her. They had nothing to prove.

The same moody receptionist who greeted them last night was still at his desk. 'You must check out by ten o'clock, si? Ten o'clock,' he called after them. Robert remembered the distasteful way he'd glanced at him as he copied down Lucy's passport details.

'That man does my head in,' Robert said, closing the door.

Lucy was frowning at the unmade bed. 'I don't like him. He looks at me funny.'

'Are you OK?' he said, sitting down, putting his arm around her. 'Don't worry about him. Everything will be OK. We're only staying here for a couple of days, to rest and stuff, you know.'

'I know. I don't mind.'

'Soon we'll be in Greece. Amorgos, the beach, the sun. Think about it.'

'Is the ferry journey a long one?'

'Where?'

'What do you mean?' She pinched at her nose, sniffed.

'Which one?' Robert took his hand away. 'Which ferry journey?'

She hesitated, as if unaware what Robert was referring to. 'The ferry to Greece or the ferry to Amorgos?'

'To Greece, of course.' She shook her head, eyelids flickering down, fingering the silver ring on her hand.

'About eighteen hours, something like that.'

'Can we get a cabin?'

'I don't know... it's expensive, but we can sleep on deck, like most travellers do.'

'Hmm.' She sat back, smiling to herself. Robert wondered what she was thinking, if she was toying with images of the ferry, of where they might sleep, what it might be like. 'That could be fun. I always used to go camping with my dad down in Cornwall.'

'Where? Newquay?'

'Oh, I don't know. I guess Newquay. I always used to meet loads of surfers. My first boyfriend was a surfer.'

'Did you just go for a couple of weeks or...'

'No, it was like the whole summer, you know, with my dad's truck, and Lisa and everybody would come and it would be mad. We'd sit out on the beach and Blue – that's my half-brother, remember? – he'd sing songs and play the guitar, he could do Bob Dylan and all sorts. We'd all just lunch out together. I think I first heard Bob Dylan with Blue singing it.'

When Lucy told him about her past it was usually through long monologues, extended reveries broken with sudden digressions and thoughtful pauses, as if the telling was a way she discovered something unknown to herself. His questions, usually designed to focus on a specific point, would be brushed away. She would drop the names of family, friends, people Robert had never heard of, so casually it was as if she was trying to say he'd grown up with her, shared her experiences. Sometimes, if he asked her who was who or when exactly something had happened she would seem annoyed, as if she'd told him before and he hadn't been listening.

'What's he doing now?'

'Well, I don't know. I think he's still living with his girlfriend and their baby in Bristol. I've never met Lori…I really wish I could though, I want to bond with her, she's my niece or something.'

'How old is she?'

'Nearly one, I suppose. It's really important to bond with babies when they're really young though, so they get used to you…'

'Like they can sense who you are?' Robert told her about his past at odd moments: it was something he said to fill in the glazed boredom of a delayed train, while waiting for his food to arrive at a restaurant, or in the first few minutes after sex, when the desire to reveal something more of himself was suddenly overwhelming.

'What? Like with Evan. I mainly had to look after him because Dad had so much on and was drinking loads at the time and Lisa was so ill, so I had to look after him. We used to sleep in the same bed in the truck. I was the only one who could stop him crying. I really miss him sometimes…not that I want a baby or kids, maybe not ever.'

'I think you'd make a good mum.' Robert felt Lucy possessed privileged information, or a special insight; that it was innate and secretive, lurking in the taste of her blood or the colour of her eyes. That it was something he could never share, maybe never even understand.

'Do you? My friend Anna got pregnant and her dad made her have an abortion. She didn't want to, she wanted to have it adopted, but her dad, he's such a cunt, he actually made her.'

'Was she OK?' Either way, these moments of half-born comprehension, the afterbirth of their different worlds, could only brighten the depth of his love for her. He felt they could strip away the stale longings of their respective histories and create a new body between them, a new tapestry of identity.

'I don't know. I last saw her before Glastonbury. She's just getting fucked all the time now, all sorts of stuff, but where she lives there's nothing else to do. I went to school down there for a bit before we moved away again and it was horrible. Blue never wants to go back. Don't you think it's kind of strange how you pay so much less for a coffee around here if you stand up at the bar and don't sit down?' Lucy stood up now, brushing her hair with tugging, downward strokes. The shutters had been closed to keep the heat out, but a single golden bar of light invaded the room, cutting Lucy in half.

'Yeah, but they know how much you need to sit down.' Robert lay back on the bed, closing his eyes. He felt tired.

'Oh God yeah. It's so hectic, you *do* need to sit down. I just think it's a bit of a con.'

'Well, you're paying for... floor space, or service, I suppose.'

'Yes.' She put down her hairbrush and paced about the room, going over to fiddle with the shutters.

'What is it?' Robert opened one eye, his arm curled over his forehead. 'Is something wrong? I thought you were tired.'

'It is beautiful.' She stopped, pressing her hands together. She pulled one of the straps of her dress back up around her shoulder. 'I love the colours and everything. Did I tell you about the Mother Earth festivals I used to go to when my parents were still together?'

'Did you get into trouble?'

'Yeah... like anything, it was great. Oh, I wish we had a radio and some music.'

Since the first day they met, nine, ten weeks ago, when Lucy told him she had nothing to go home for, Robert had found it hard to accept that she had a past. He would struggle to put the things she told him about herself into context, into understanding how they affected and created her. Her moodiness after calling her dad when they were in Paris. He used to get drunk and abuse her mum, so she left. He treated his girlfriend the same way. But then Lucy would talk about what a great dad he was and how he understood everything about her, never criticized her, that it was only Lisa, his girlfriend, who gave her a hard time. She told Robert this frequently, daily, as if there was a hidden third party somewhere in the room who needed to be convinced. Robert imagined her days before they met to have been lonely and listless, spent in cold rooms, in empty old houses. A life kept in boxes and bags, sealed with the strange melancholy that seemed to haunt the back of her words, the underside of her gestures. That was the Lucy he knew: coming to collect her, stopping his car in the small village, hurrying into her house from the rain. Blue and grey light, rain on black stones. She left a note while he carried her stuff to the car.

Two bags and a plant pot, all she had. Then they were gone, heading east again. That was the Lucy he knew. It was hard to reconcile those moments with her other past, the one she told him about, showed him occasionally, with a sudden gesture or insight he didn't recognize, couldn't place. A happier past of surfer boyfriends and camping in fields, cheap acid and wise old hippies. That was how he saw it, after everything she said to him. It was difficult.

'You know, I was so glad when you came along after Glastonbury and just, like, sorted me out and everything.' She climbed on the bed towards him. Robert sat up, lifting his right arm. She turned around and let his arm fit over her shoulder. He lived for these moments, wanted them burnt into his memory, so even after she was gone he would bear the scar of her beauty, bringing her back through the shape of his wounds, the understanding of what they meant.

'I know, it was weird, wasn't it?' He shifted closer to her, trying to get more comfortable. 'And we both saw – '

'I know, and didn't see each other. But then I was tripping and why would we have anyway? Oh, but this guy, you know – '

'Who you told me about.'

'I know, and like we'd finished going out ages ago and I didn't fancy him any more or anything, and he was coming on to me and I was tripping and then I lost all my money and you know, like, oh my God, all over the place...'

He put his face against the back of her neck where he could smell her skin and sweat, her own strange aroma, and through that the other smells, cigarettes, shampoo, deodorant. He thought about the hotel behind the Gare du Nord, three nights ago. 'It doesn't feel right,' she'd said, 'I'm not comfortable, I'm sorry,' and she rolled away, her naked body escaping from his hands. She pulled the sheets tight around her like a barrier. 'Why? What is it? What's wrong?' But she wouldn't say anything, wouldn't even turn to face him. She put the light out and they lay apart from each other in the dark. He'd stared at another shuttered window, the bare walls of another cheap hotel. The sounds of traffic never stopped for a moment. He was too anxious to sleep properly, pulling his legs up to his chest, facing her back, wishing she would only turn around and hold his hand. All he ever wanted to do was hold her, feel the warmth of her breath against his face, the movements of her body as she inhaled, the faint tremor of her heartbeat. He was weak in these moments, the precious one; frayed, disabled. He dreamed of the night before, the wet vibration of her tongue over his penis, and woke up somewhere near dawn ejaculating suddenly, gasping, his hair fuzzy with sweat, weak in a feverish haze of desire. Confused, wondering where Lucy was, thinking for one instant she was gone before plunging back to sleep. When he woke up again he lay for a long time looking at Lucy, at the top of her head above the sheets, wondering if she was sleeping or waiting. A little later she rolled over so he could just see her forehead and eyes, the rest of her face hidden by blankets. They didn't say anything. There was a stillness to the morning. He found one of her hands and held it gently, his fingers squeezing her palm, his thumbs lightly caressing her fingers. Her eyes were wide open, the pupils huge and black. He could still feel the memory of his dream, a distasteful wetness on his thighs. He moved his hand up to her face, running his fingers over her cheek, across the dry skin, the infant tan, along the firm curve of her jawbone then down over the softness of her throat. His fingers traced the heartbeat there. He shifted up slightly so they faced each other, brushing her hair away from her face, smoothing it back. She didn't blink. When they kissed, his lips barely moved over hers, mouths creeping open, the hint of her tongue, the faint gasp of each kiss in the quiet room, the sound of engines in the street. Later she would get up, shower.

Robert hurried over to the pay phone. A steel rush of traffic circled the modern slit of the central station opposite. The early evening heat was heavy on his face, the low sun spread across the sky like golden paste.

The phone was answered on the tenth ring.

'Hello, Caroline Mills speaking.'

'It's Robert.'

'Robert? Oh my God, fancy hearing from you, you old dark horse. What have you been up to? You sound far away.'

'That's because I'm in Rome.'

'No way. Oh, it's absolutely *gorgeous* there... Have you been to Venice? Or Siena, I know this wonderful restaurant where...' Robert watched a police car nosing through the evening traffic, siren wailing. 'But, what exactly are you doing there?' Caroline added.

'I'm going down to Greece. A friend should have a job for me on one of the islands, Amorgos.'

'Amorgos? Why? I mean, is it a holiday job, are you on your own? I don't understand...'

'Do you remember the girl I told you about. The one I met in Glastonbury?'

'Yes... Oh God, are you..?'

'I'm with her, yes. She was getting loads of grief at home and like...'

'What? You're in love and running away?' Typical Caroline, Robert thought, she would hit the mark then deride it.

'I know it sounds silly... but...'

'I don't believe it, Robert. What is this, some kind of eighteenth-century elopement?'

'No. It's not like that.'

'You can't just run away. You can't. What about her parents?'

'They're cool about it,' Robert realized he didn't know if that was true. He remembered her moodiness in Paris after calling home.

'They're cool about it, are they? Really? What's that supposed to mean? Robert, are you listening?'

'Yes... look, it's OK, it's just a bit complicated...'

'You're mad.'

'Don't say that. Why?'

'What about university? You are going back next term, aren't you?'

'You know I hate it there.'

'You don't hate it.'

'Well, I didn't like it, did I? It wasn't what I really wanted to be doing with my time. I thought you knew that. I mean, we talked about it enough... Look, it's hard talking to her about it, she can't even imagine going to university. I say it's all a load of shit and she just thinks I'm trying to be cool. I mean, she'll agree with me but it isn't like she *knows*.'

'Have you actually thought about what you're doing?'

'Yes.'

'Have you?'

'It... it just feels like the right thing.' Robert paused, wishing he knew the words that would explain how he felt, make Caroline realize. He needed her support. 'It's an adventure, isn't it? A real adventure, I mean, this is real, I'm living this, you know... I remember you talking about wanting to have an adventure. "I want to have an adventure," that's exactly what you said. "There are no dress rehearsals in life," you said that as well, remember?'

'But, oh honey, what if... I mean, when you get there, you know... you might not get on. Something might go wrong.'

'Yeah, I know... but that can happen anywhere, can't it? You might go out with somebody and it might all go wrong but it wouldn't stop you, would it?'

'Yes, of course, but... oh God, what's the point in arguing. Aren't the stakes a bit high?'

'Only because the prize is so worth it.'

'Are you sure?'

'Carrie, she's the most beautiful girl I've ever seen. No one says that about anyone they know any more, do they? But I said it. I mean it. I look at her and no one else comes close... I don't know if that means love or what but... don't you understand?'

'No. No, Robert, I really don't, not a thing. I'm trying but – '

'Look, I'm running out of credits.'

'Well, don't do anything stupid – '

Caroline was gone, decapitated by the dialling tone. Robert felt suddenly very lonely, wishing he'd never called. He was sure Caroline would have understood. After all the things they used to talk about, the little 'adventures' they would take together. Maybe that was the problem; they were too close. They'd snogged a couple of times, at the drunken end of a party, stoned in a parked car at midnight. Nothing consequential, nothing spoken about. Maybe he was just flattering himself. Maybe she'd never been the person he'd always believed her to be. It was too hot for six o'clock in the evening. Lucy was resting in the room. He didn't want to go back yet. He went to a bar and drank two coffees and a glass of water. Standing up.

The sunset lingered in the room, spread against the back wall like a pink rash. But fading, cured as the soft grey caress of the dusk brought out the blank wall behind, omnipresent despite the light, and closing in. Robert kissed the top of Lucy's head where she lay wrapped around his arms. He closed his eyes and thought of nothing but the weight of her body against his, a heat and a coolness at once, impossible to decipher. This was the limit, he felt, the end of everything: lying in bed with her, naked and soporific, two faint ripples in a pool. These sudden moments out of time: the numb exhaustion after an orgasm when he would blindly kiss the beads of sweat running between her breasts and his hands would shake as they stroked her back, the pillows wet from their bodies and the long, blank moments with nothing but the feeling of his body, a contraction, her wetness smeared over his groin and down her thighs; the press of her body, a collapse, a withering. He lived for these moments, beyond communication, outside identity: there was a silence about them, a weakness that grew in the twinges of his memory to a perfection, a diamond-bright symmetry.

Lucy sat up and lit a cigarette. She smoked nervously, making sudden, stabbing inhalations, the cigarette popping in and out of her mouth, the ash flicked on to the floor. 'You'd think they might clean the room,' she muttered.

Robert didn't say anything. He looked at the arc of her back, the way her spine pressed against her skin. Her hair, turning blonde as if the sun was dissolving into it, caressed the top of her shoulders. He remembered pushing it forward over her face so he could kiss the slender oasis between skull and backbone, feeling her shivering through his mouth. Her body was a nexus of possibilities.

She sighed, tapped at her cigarette.

'Are you OK?' Robert quickly ran his hand down her back, unsure if the gesture would soothe or annoy her. 'This is an adventure, isn't it? Don't you think?'

'An adventure?' She turned around, frowning.

'Wouldn't you say it had that quality? I mean, it's just the two of us, travelling, going to somewhere we've never been. Anything could happen. Isn't it exciting? I mean, don't you feel alive, really alive?'

As soon as he'd spoken Robert wondered if he'd said too much. Lucy seemed to be waiting for him to say something else, something to which she could reply with a dismissive 'yes' or 'no'.

'I don't know,' she murmured, blushing. 'I don't feel any different... really...'

'Oh, come on.' He was sure she'd understand. Where he thought Caroline would, Lucy *must*. 'It's an adventure.' His hand traced the ridge of her spine. 'They're necessary... life would be boring without them, don't you think?'

'There's never been any routine to my life, not ever that I can think of. I've never known what might happen or where I might be from one week to the next, not since I can remember at least.' Lucy pushed the sheet away, annoyed. She bent down and wriggled into her T-shirt. Then she reached down, picking up her panties, stepping into them. She resumed her cigarette. 'Are we going for a walk soon?'

'Do you want to?'

'In a bit.'

'OK.'

They looked away from each other. Neither said anything for a while.

'You know,' she spoke quietly, 'if things do go wrong, it'll be OK.'

'I know that. We look after each other, as long as we're together...'

'Yes, whatever. I mean, I can still go back and get my GCSEs. Only if I really needed them for something, though. My attitude towards school might have improved by then.' She bent round and kissed him. Robert kept his eyes open, trying to see the way their mouths went together, the way her tongue curled up, touched his.

The steps led down from the busy main road to an overgrown footpath that ran alongside the Tiber. 'I want to walk down there,' she said, tugging at his arm. 'Come on.'

'Shouldn't we stick to the road?'

'Oh, *come on*, Robert, don't be so boring. It looks beautiful.' She walked forward, deftly climbing over a small, rusted gate at the top of the stairs. 'Come on,' she called again from the other side, coaxing with her hands.

She was animated tonight, full of the strange energy that so attracted him when they first met, an innocent wildness emanating from every curve of her body. In these instants Robert was certain she was like this for him alone. Her lassitude and moodiness appeared among other people, a defence against the raw shapes of the world, as if she could seal herself with sadness, with her melancholy talismans. Other people brought disintegration. She made him think of cobwebs in dark cellars, flooded wells, a windswept precipice.

'I'm coming, hold on,' he muttered, climbing after her. Night had almost taken the day, a dark lid sealing the afternoon heat. The moon was a yellow halo behind the tall trees that flanked the Tiber, a distant coolness rippled against the wet black heat. Rome's ancient monuments drew people away from the dark swipe of the Tiber, a green artery weaving between the marble bridges and pink mansions. The trees that followed the river were taller than any of the buildings around it, their leaves hiding the city's frayed edges, turning the river into a hinterland, a dark transport from the splendid churches and designer shops to something older and unspoken. Secret canals and sewers used to wash corpses from the Colosseum into the river. It was typical Lucy should find this place, occult and overgrown, hidden from the urbane eyes of the city yet cutting deep through its heart.

'God! Disgusting! Careful, there's loads of dog shit here,' she called back to him. Robert was at the top of the stairs, Lucy half-way down. Patches of light filtered through the trees around them, bringing out the shine of Lucy's hair, the movement of her dress.

'What is this? It's hard to see.'

'It's better on the path.' Lucy was already at the bottom. She waited for Robert to catch up then took his hand again, leading the way along the narrow path between the river and the thick brambles and grass around it. They felt as if they were beneath the city, stone walls of the river bank closing in on either side, an ancient bridge, half cloaked in scaffolding, ahead of them. A sharp insect hiss masked the perpetual whine of traffic. 'This is beautiful,' she whispered, turning back to check he was OK. 'I've been having dreams about a place like this since we started travelling.' The river ran with colour, deep blue and pale orange, a molten echo of the city's lights. 'Let's keep walking along here until we get to some more steps,' she said, smiling. The undergrowth clawed against her dress, tiny insects whirling out of the grass around them. Robert flinched as he followed her, the grass scratching his legs.

'When I was a kid this was the sort of place where I'd play trolls, or monsters,' he called out. 'That bridge was the sort of place trolls would live under.'

She laughed. 'I know, isn't it funny? Boys would play monsters, I'd play fairies. I'd take Shandy for walks here and he'd chase fairies.'

They approached the bridge. Robert thought he could see shapes, maybe piles of rubbish, in the shadow of its arches. The river beyond was a tiny square of blue and yellow. The bridge shone in the moonlight like a huge bone trapped in a spider's-web lattice of scaffolding.

Robert paused, tugging at her hand. 'I don't think there's any way back up to the road from there,' he said.

'Maybe we should go back then?' she suggested, noticing his expression, sensing his sudden anxiety.

'Wait...'

'No, I think...' she gasped, stepping behind him, eyes wide as the moon, hair spinning around her neck and over her shoulders, twisting with the arch of her body, the sweep of her dress. Robert saw dark spots, eight, nine, a horde of shadows erupting from underneath the bridge, tall grass trampled down, then the dogs were upon them.

Robert grabbed her hand, pulled himself behind her.

'Run,' he shouted. 'Lucy, *run*!'

They were everywhere, huge dogs, the size of wolves. One leapt up, barking at him: white eyes, white fangs, black gums pulled back, ragged ears down, rigid tails. Holes in their coats, a rank smell, like dead meat and sour urine. Dogs, bursting out of the undergrowth, leaping out of the blackness. The distant city above them, hidden by sheer stone walls, iron railings, summer-heavy trees.

'Run!' he shouted again. He still held her hand, lifting it as high as their faces, away from the dogs. His heart was racing, a blind, sweaty panicked feeling.

'No!' she shouted back. Her eyes were huge, wired, almost glowing in the dark. 'Don't run, they'll chase us down, just walk.' She tugged him forward.

Four dogs behind them, two more on either side. More back, in the darkness. All huge, black, brown and grey, snarling, following at their heels. Robert realized he was flinching, his whole body coiled tight, bracing himself against the instant when they'd leap up, biting his back, his bare legs, his hands. So many dogs, huge, angry. No one would hear them screaming down here, he thought. This is why no one ever comes down here, he thought. 'I hate dogs, I fucking hate dogs,' he repeated, over and over, teeth clenched tight, his hand sweating in Lucy's grip.

'It's OK, come on.' She walked with him, her long legs striding forward, pressing down the undergrowth with her DMs.

They could see the staircase ahead of them, against the side of the river bank. Several dogs had fallen away but three still followed, like security guards escorting them from the premises.

'I don't think they're going to attack us.' He felt sick, his legs too weak to run or fight or anything.

'I know that,' she spoke briskly. 'They just don't want us here.'

They were at the steps.

'Don't run,' she said again, leading the way. 'Walk slowly. It's OK, they're just dogs.'

'I fucking hate dogs. I've always hated them.' Robert glanced back. Two dogs remained at the foot of the steps, one still barking at them. When he looked back again, near the top of the steps, they were all gone. The river bank seemed deserted: tall grass and weeds, nothing else.

'Jesus, oh Jesus...' Robert gasped, turning away from the wall and sliding down to rest on his calves, rubbing his eyes with his hands.

'Are you OK?' Lucy knelt over him. She kissed the top of his head, put her arm around his shoulder, pulled him to her breast.

'Yeah... I guess. Just spun out a bit by that. You know?' He laughed weakly. 'God, I'm tired. I hate dogs. I got bit by one when I was five. Since then they've always shitted me up. That was horrible.'

'I know, that was scary... but it's OK now, it's OK.' Her fingers toyed spirals out of his short dark hair. She kissed his forehead, feeling his heat, tasting his sweat.

'See... see, I told you there were trolls living under that bridge. I told you.'

'Yeah, but we had fairy magic to protect us.' She smiled, full and beautiful, her disordered hair disrobed over her flushed face. 'Do you want to go back to the hotel?'

'In a minute.' He found her hand and squeezed it as tight as he could. 'Hold on,' he whispered, putting his face to her neck, 'hold on.'

'I'm here,' she whispered. 'It's OK, I'm here.'

When they stood up again his legs were still weak. They walked slowly away.

THE BIG PICTURE
BONNIE GREER

They had one day left in Paris. As usual, they decided to spend it together.

There were five of them: Patrice, Gloria, Odelle, Marie and Darlene. They had become the best of friends in kindergarten. Now they were forty, with seven marriages, three divorces and one widowhood among them. The ones who had been fat in their youth were now skinny, and the ones who were skinny were now fat. Their complexions ranged from sable to a translucent ivory. Two were tall, one was short and the other two fell somewhere in between. No matter what anyone thought, they considered themselves to be among the finest women on the planet.

And, like most close friends, they had one facial characteristic in common: a pair of large, luminous eyes, eyes with the clarity of a child, eyes that seemed to see everything, know everything. Especially about one another. They prided themselves on that: knowing the little joys, the secret sorrows, the delicate bits of naughtiness that female best friends always know. They were full of one another. Each was a living, breathing Tree of the Knowledge of Good and Evil, no angel with a flaming sword could block their way to one another's Eden. 'Open All Hours' was engraved on the silver bracelet each woman received from the others on her birthday. They all knew what that meant.

The bracelets marked their fortieth birthdays. This year, from late winter into autumn, they had enjoyed a succession of parties, culminating in a grand celebration thrown by their families and friends at an expensive downtown hotel.

It was toward the end of the party, when they had been sufficiently drunk, that they had entertained everyone with an a cappella rendition of 'We are Family' in perfect harmony.

Their birthday year had culminated in a trip to Paris. And here they were, in the City of Light, practically broke, but carefree, like the girls they were at heart.

They were sitting at an outdoor café and drinking champagne when Odelle of the alabaster complexion said: 'We should go see the *Mona Lisa*. That's supposed to be the greatest painting in the world, "The Big Picture", girlfriends. But my Aunt Susie saw it last year and she said she didn't get it. I've seen reproductions of it, and though I don't like agreeing with Aunt Susie, I have to say I don't get it, either.'

'How are you going to know anything from a reproduction? The world's got too many repros, and rewinds. We live in edit, I tell my students that all the time,' Patrice of the sable skin countered.

'But what is a "great painting"?' Marie asked.

When Marie asked a deep question, the women knew that they had drunk too much and it was time to go, so Gloria signalled for the bill.

'So what is it? Great art. What does it *do*?' Marie continued.

They all turned to Gloria, who had taken quite a few art courses at university, and who they had all once expected might have become an artist herself one day.

'Who knows what makes it great,' she replied. 'And do? What does art *do*? Does it *do* anything?'

'Anyway, THEY call it great,' Darlene added. They all nodded solemnly as if they were in church.

'But let's see it anyway.' Gloria was standing up now. 'We can't say we've been to Paris unless we've seen the *Mona Lisa*.'

They all had to agree with that, so they left the little café and made their way on foot to the Louvre, laughing and talking at the tops of their voices.

They reached the museum minutes before it was scheduled to close. They raced past the transparent pyramid near the entrance, through the doors, flashed their day-passes to the guards, hurried down the escalator, found the sign pointing to the appropriate gallery and, laughing and calling to one another like children, found the room where the *Mona Lisa* hung.

At first they did not see it. Like all legendary things, it was smaller than they thought it would be. The sounds of their voices and sensible footwear echoed through the great empty hall as they searched.

It was Darlene who found it. The others joined her.

They stood in silence around the small canvas. It was encased in protective glass, barely visible amidst the glare from the lights in the gallery. They did not move until it was time to go.

It was twilight when they emerged into the plaza outside. The transparent pyramid was awash in white light, the deep blue of the late autumnal evening framing it like a jewel in velvet.

Near it the great cacophony of the place de la Concorde hung in the air as the Parisians sped from Left to Right Bank through its open space in that great Grand Prix known as rush hour.

Just beyond was the wide boulevard of the Champs-Elysées, lights twinkling in the trees that lined it. And just behind it was the Eiffel Tower, ablaze, glittering like a gigantic Christmas tree.

But the women saw nothing.

They walked along without saying a word to one another.

They reached a bridge. It was dark by now. The light from the tourist boats, the *bateaux mouches*, swept the grand façades of the buildings on the quays. It was Patrice, the first-born, who broke the silence.

'Did you see it?' she said. 'It looked like it was breathing. I saw her chest move. It moved like my daughter's, like Shantell's neck does. That child hasn't spent one night at home in two years. I know she's a grown woman, I know I'm only her stepmother, but why did she have to just up and disappear like that?'

'Uh-uh,' Darlene countered. 'I didn't see any breathing. She wasn't breathing. Her breathing had stopped. Like his did. Just like his did. He said it would. I did what he asked me to do. I couldn't see him like that any more. I couldn't see my husband like that any more. I changed and washed him and then I did what he asked. I did. I'm not sorry.'

'It didn't do anything for me. Nothing,' Gloria muttered. 'It was cold. Just like her. That bitch. Took my promotion. I taught her everything I knew, tried to be a sister. She was really cold-blooded. I'll never trust another black woman as long as I live behind that.'

Odelle began to speak.

'Birds. Those black birds. Flying in the background like they did behind Nana's house. Nana. Nana really understood me. Knew me better than anybody else ever did. Ever will. Nana. They say God takes the good ones first.' Odelle began to tremble.

'It was her. Mona Lisa is who she meant,' Marie almost sang. 'Her. Rosamund, my psychic, told me somebody would smile at me, a very old woman and then I would know I was on the right path. I could stop therapy, I could…'

Marie stopped speaking. She, too, was feeling what the others were feeling – feeling, but not communicating.

It seemed now that a great curtain had dropped between each one of them, separating them one from the other.

They were each in an enclosure that the others could not enter. An enclosure whose entrance had been guarded by a mysterious face whose smile they now knew encompassed infinity.

A *bateau mouche* passed beneath the bridge. It was empty. Its light illuminated the five friends as it passed.

Soon, it went on its way, plunging the women into darkness.

ME AND THE REST OF THE WORLD
JOHN O'CONNELL

Apart from us, only the rugby teams came into school on Saturdays. You could see them from the roof of the music faculty if you could be bothered to look, rampaging across the pitch like randy wildebeest, their shouts catapulted high into the frosty November air.

Dan and I were up there messing about, waiting for Pete to arrive with the key. It was freezing. I blew into my cupped hands, pulled my jacket closed. Warm alternatives were flipping through my head, Rolodex-style, when Dan pulled me over to the edge.

'Look!' he said. 'It's him!'

Directly below us on the opposite side of the street Adrian Dyson, the 1st XV's bulked-up second row, was being dropped off in a glossy black BMW. It was a familiar scene. Nicer people might have construed it as poignant. Yet Dyson's father always managed to spoil it by leaning out of the window and bellowing, 'Go on, son! Give it your all!' at the poor bloke as he waddled up the tight aisle of concrete steps towards the changing rooms, Head bag slung over shoulder with what he clearly reckoned to be a sportsman's casual grace. We winced. 'Jesus,' said Dan. 'Anyone would think the match actually mattered.' He fumbled to light a cigarette then paused, lost for a moment in some filthy reverie. 'Wouldn't it be great if one day Adrian Dyson's dad lost control and patted his son's arse? You know, "Take care, son." A little slap. A wink. He'd need years of therapy to sort himself out.'

I laughed. 'You're appalling. I didn't realize you fancied him.'

'Who? Dyson?' Dan considered the allegation. He always considered my allegations. 'Mmm,' he said, and frowned. 'Maybe if he lost a bit of weight. And wore more leather.'

By the time we'd negotiated the rusty ladder down, Pete had arrived and let himself in. He was tuning up in the corner by a nest of mangled music stands. He nodded his welcome. 'Nice rollneck,' he said.

'Thanks,' I said. 'Nice sideburns.'

'Yeah, well...I thought it was about time. No half-measures, you know?' He ran a hand through his thick mop of hair. 'Have you finished those lyrics yet?'

'Yeah.'

'What sort of thing is it?' He looked across at Dan and winked, the bastard.

'It's a Lloyd Cole-y thing,' I said. 'It's called, er...' I couldn't bring myself to say it. 'It's called "Melancholy Jane".'

'Is it now?' Pete hunched over his guitar, leaning into it almost. He capped a thin fret by the neck with his left index finger before brushing the strings gently to release a soft harmonic chime. 'Oh well,' he said. 'I don't really care what it's called. As long as it's compatible with the Johnny Marr-y jangly thing I've been working on.'

'Johnny Marr-y?' I said.

'Yeah. Although to tell you the truth,' Pete continued, 'I think Mitch wants to try something a bit more Beatle-y.' Mitch was our drummer. He was an idiot.

'Beatle-y?' I said.

'Yeah,' he said. 'He's been perfecting his Ringo roll.'

'That can't have taken long,' I said.

'You'd be surprised.' Pete shook his head sadly, a slow swing heavy with the burden of others' musical incompetence.

Once Mitch had arrived and miked up his kit, we were ready to go. Dan sat cross-legged on the floor with his bass guitar balanced on his knees.

'Right,' said Pete. 'I need a straight four-four rhythm. I'll be going from D major to A minor seventh...Actually,' (he sounded bored already and it was only eleven o'clock), 'actually, let's just jam for a bit and you can follow me. It's not hard.' Then, to me: 'Ben, you might want to sort of scat your words over the top?'

'Yes,' I said. 'I might.'

'OK then. One, two, three, four...' As Mitch, Dan and Pete attempted to get what Pete unsmilingly called a 'groove' going, I started to sing, or at least pick a tune out of the ugly fuzz of power chords Pete unleashed, apparently under the impression that Johnny Marr, the former Smiths guitarist and Pete's hero, had carved a career out of inflicting this sort of racket on the record-buying, gig-going public.

'In time she learned to lose with grace,' I sang, 'with aspirin smile on pockmarked face...' I tried to lend my voice a hiccupy, mid-Atlantic twang. 'She betrayed a desire to acquire a more buoyant constitution...'

Puzzled glances were being exchanged. I carried on regardless. In my head, Lloyd, resplendent in a wine-red, snug-fitting rollneck, was tense with suppressed wonder. 'I said hey Jane that's oxymoronic, but I want this affair to be strictly platonic. It's been real nice but if you don't mind, I'll find my own way out.'

The playing stopped. There was a pause, then Mitch's gruff, stupid voice went: 'Oxymoronic?'

'Yeah,' I said. The thrill of performance had flushed my shyness away. 'Are you trying to tell me you don't know what oxymoronic means?'

Pete rushed to intercede. 'I think what Mitch is trying to say,' he said, signalling frantically to Mitch that he should stay where he was for the next ten seconds, 'is that perhaps your lyrics could do with being a bit simpler. I mean, they're often very affecting. My view is that the sticking point in this instance is the line about Jane's — and I'm assuming it is Jane's — "aspirin smile". What exactly is this? Do you mean her face is round like an aspirin tablet?'

'No,' I said. Jesus! Did Lloyd have this trouble with the Commotions? 'I mean that the expression of serenity Jane is wearing is forced. Only because she's recently taken an aspirin is she able to look as relaxed as she does.'

'Right,' said Dan. 'It's called hypallage. It's the inversion of the natural relation of two terms in a sentence, especially the transfer of epithets. Virgil does it in, er, something or other...'

'Yeah,' cut in Pete. 'Obviously I knew that. I was just questioning whether it worked.'

'I think Ben's lyrics are quite good,' drawled Dan through a haze of smoke. 'I mean, they're shit obviously, but that's the point, isn't it, Ben? Ben?'

At which point Mitch, displaying an unexpected flair for the dramatic flourish, threw his sticks down and stood up. A vein throbbed scarily on his forehead. Did this mean he was about to have a stroke? 'Right,' he said. 'I'm quitting. And if any of you have got any sense you'll do the same. Why you don't stop poncing around being in a band and piss off to university is beyond me. You're all so fucking – ' he scoured his brain for a suitable insult – 'middle-class.'

He put his coat on and left. It seemed another fruitless rehearsal had come to an end.

When I got home I called Jo. She sounded foggy, distracted. 'Are you OK?' I said.

'Yeah.'

'Is your mum in the room?'

'How did you guess?'

'I thought you were coming into town. To take photos of us.'

'I know, I was going to. But then I felt shit and decided against it. I think I've got flu or something. Then my little friend turned up.'

I felt my annoyance soften; Jo was so good with kids. 'That's OK. You could have brought her along.'

'I mean I got my period.'

'Oh, right. I'm sorry.' Embarrassment flushed hotly through my body. 'Right. Well, we're going to be there tomorrow too, if you feel any better.'

'OK, I'll probably see you then, then.' She winced. 'Listen, I'm going back to bed. Don't be offended.'

But that wouldn't do, you see. I needed to see her right then, immediately, without further delay. 'Can I come over?' I said, my desperate tone earning me a foothold somewhere between the enlightened and the prurient.

She didn't answer for a minute. I heard her muttering some request to her mother. Then she said, 'Yeah. Why don't you come over for dinner? I won't be eating much, but you can peel me grapes or something.'

'OK,' I said and hung up, happy.

It was five o'clock and almost completely dark. The fifteen-minute drive from Market Drayton into Whitmore, through neat hamlets with their single pubs and Spar shops, past frost-glazed fields, bare copseland and trophy houses set back from the road behind sloping banks of lawn, was safely familiar even at night. I was driving the white, Y-reg Fiesta my mum had bought for me and my sister to learn on. It was a miracle it had got through its MOT. If you went faster than sixty m.p.h., it juddered like a spaceship attempting re-entry.

I thought about Jo and how baffling it was that I should want to see her so much. She always had a camera round her neck: a big Olympus one with a scary-looking telescopic lens. Pete and Dan called her Astrid, after the German girl who befriended the Beatles in Hamburg – dazzled them with her leather-coated exi cool, styled their hair, took their pictures. I thought about the way her carefully shaped short brown hair lay across her forehead in a kind of French crop. I thought about the whiteness of her skin: ghost-white, flour-white, eighteenth-century-courtesan white. Dan had once said that Jo's face resembled a breast on which someone had drawn a face. It was a brilliant observation: exactly spot-on, and all the better for being borderline offensive. I'd always wanted to share it with her, but couldn't decide whether I could get away with it; I didn't know how she'd take it. And that was the rub: there was a rapport between us, certainly. But I was sometimes conscious of having to strain to sustain it, of nodding a little too emphatically and laughing a little too loudly. I could never predict how she would respond in any given situation, so to compensate I overstressed similarities between us when they did occur. Maybe I liked doing it. Maybe that was the appeal. I don't know.

At six months the band was still in its infancy, so it was important not to worry too much when things went badly. All the same, we hadn't been able to have a proper rehearsal yet. Either Mitch didn't turn up, or if he did he picked a fight with Dan about whether anal sex was natural. Or Pete told me my lyrics were crap. Or I told him he played the guitar like a chimpanzee wearing oven gloves. It was a triumph if a practice session lasted longer than half an hour.

We'd left school in July, but Mr Wallis, the head of music, didn't mind us using the faculty to rehearse in on weekend afternoons. A prefab shack mounted on breeze blocks, it wasn't anything special, but it was somewhere to go, and at least its storage heaters worked. The band was our year-off project. Pete had great plans for it; he had everything worked out, from the titles of our albums to the length of our first American tour. The fact that we had yet to play a gig and couldn't write songs to save our lives didn't seem to dampen his enthusiasm. We couldn't even agree on our influences. Dan liked lubricious funk with bass lines he could get his teeth into: Chic, Funkadelic, Sly Stone. Pete liked bands dominated by self-conscious guitar heroes: Led Zeppelin, The Who, Bowie's Spiders, The Smiths at a pinch. (He'd just been to see a new band called the Stone Roses in Manchester, who seemed to have a bona fide guitar god at the helm.) And I liked pop wordsmiths: Morrissey, Michael Stipe, Lloyd Cole…

Ah yes, Lloyd Cole. Lloyd, whose songs were inexplicably crammed with characters whose names began with the letter J: Judy, Jennifer, Jane, Jim, Jesus. How darkly romantic their lives seemed: always driving back in Citroën 2CVs from wild, Gatsbyish parties to basement flats in Charlotte Street, where they'd smoke Gauloises and drink cheap red wine. I wanted that life for myself. To that end, I always wore a rollneck to rehearsals. And in Jo, it looked as if I might have found a girlfriend who not only had a name beginning with J, but also a distinctly Cole-friendly hobby: photography. This cast her as an outsider, a neutral observer like the narrator of 'Speedboat' on *Rattlesnakes*.

I parked to the right of the drive so as not to cause an obstruction. Jo's mother opened the door. 'Ben,' she said, and the statement hung there for a second, unsure of its status. She was used to me by now. Sometimes I think she quite liked me. Certainly, she didn't seem to mind when I cut short our usual exchange of pleasantries in the interests of 'the invalid's' well-being.

Jo was propped up on a steep ridge of pillows, reading a book – *Franny and Zooey* by J. D. Salinger. (How the Lloyd within me leapt for joy!) She looked up as I entered. 'Hi,' she said. 'Don't bother to knock, will you? Did Mum offer you some coffee cake?' I looked down at the plate in my hand. 'Don't eat it, it's stale. She's been trying to fob it off on people for days. I ate some accidentally last night and it felt like someone was trying to film a Duran Duran video in my stomach.' I must have looked puzzled because she added unbidden: 'Wind.'

'How was the rehearsal?'

I sighed. 'Terrible. Mitch walked out.'

Jo wrinkled her brow. 'Didn't he do that last week?'

'Yeah.'

'Well, then. What are you called now anyway?'

'The World.'

'The whirled?' Her fingers did a piss-take pirouette across the duvet.

'Ha ha. No, the World. The globe. The Earth.'

'Isn't that a bit of a shit name?'

I had to admit it was. 'It wasn't my idea. It was Pete's. He said that then our first album could be called *News of the World*. It's like The Who used to call their albums things like *Who's Next*, *Who Are You* and *Who's Last*. Pete likes the idea of album titles which describe a group's career trajectory. We're only planning to make three albums, you see, so our second would be called *World in Motion* and the third...'

'...would be *World's End*, yes. I see. At least I think I see. It kind of depends which element you're trying to focus on, doesn't it?'

The dining-room table was lavishly laid. We had two glasses each, and side plates. I was expected to help myself to a crusty brown roll from a wicker basket. Jo's father was a dentist, so I supposed I was in good hands if any nutty bits from the bread lodged themselves in my teeth.

'So, Mr Healey,' I began, full of lordly bonhomie. 'Did you see any good mouths today?'

'Some, Ben. Some. Though it's amazing the state parents let their children's teeth get into.'

'Well, it's hardly surprising, is it?' countered Jo. 'I mean, it's so expensive to go to the dentist now, it's practically become a middle-class luxury. It's a wonder you don't see more people wandering about with inch-long fangs and molars where their incisors should be.'

No laughs.

'Yes, dear,' said her mother. 'I think we all know how you feel about it.'

Jo flashed me a perfect-toothed smile. 'Mum doesn't like me getting political. Do you, Mum?'

'I don't mind,' said Mrs Healey, who clearly did very much. 'I just think we all know what your worthy flags look like. Sometimes it's better just to run them down the mast and put them away. Otherwise it gets — I don't know — a bit boring, really. Don't you agree, Ben?'

'Yes.'

'No, he doesn't,' said Jo. 'He's just being spineless. That's a cheap trick to play on a guest.'

'What does your father do, Ben?' A canny intervention there from Jo's dad.

'He exports imitation Doulton figurines to the Far East,' I said. He did, too. Our house was full of the fuckers: crinoline-skirted ladies, mostly, with a few ballet dancers thrown in for good measure.

'That must be marvellous!' said Mr Healey, far too enthusiastically. 'I think we've got some figurines somewhere. We used to collect them. We certainly had a ballet dancer. What else?' He looked to Jo's mother for help. None was forthcoming. 'Ah, I know. We had one of those eighteenth-century ladies with the skirts. What do you call them?'

'Crinolene.'

'Crinolene, yes. Marvellous. We could have a look for them later, if you like?'

Back in her room afterwards, Jo was livid. 'You might have backed me up,' she said. 'You just sat there like some kind of lemon.' Now it was my turn to wrinkle my brow. 'And before you say anything, there's a rare type of lemon with a flat end which grows in the Caribbean. It's called the garumpa lemon, it's a delicacy, and it can, broadly speaking, sit.'

I was sixteen when I first met Pete, so that must be — what, 1987? Even then he was impressive. I realize I've made him sound like a bit of an arsehole, but really, he wasn't so bad. In fact, he was probably my best friend. It's funny what you remember and what you don't.

He'd attached himself to our GCSE music class, for no other reason, I think, than to disrupt it as much as possible. Because he needn't have turned up at all. He had Grade 12 piano or something. (Although, oddly, he couldn't play the guitar very well. While he knew a lot about it, he just didn't have an ear for pop music.) The mystery was why he hadn't been sent to some special music school to hothouse away his teens in the company of other prodigies.

Whatever, Mr Wallis soon grew to hate him. Crucial to GCSE was a laboured emphasis on base-broadening which obliged usually unflappable music teachers to educate their classes in the modes and procedures of something they knew nothing about: pop. This ignorance, coupled with every schoolkid's urge to pinpoint pedagogic Achilles' heels, was always going to make for some interesting lessons.

One day, Mr Wallis decided we were going to discuss the Beatles. Ripping the velvet dust-cover off the department's antique record player, he dropped the stylus on to Dan's specially brought-in single of 'Penny Lane'. 'It's marvellous, isn't it?' he enthused as the song got under way. 'That piccolo solo. Those evocative lyrics. I'm trying, and I can actually see the little nurse selling her poppies by the roundabout. I mean,' he went on, 'in some ways "Penny Lane" is almost as good as Mahler's Fifth or a Bach fugue.'

A torpid, resigned sigh went up. God, Mr Wallis was such a Joey. He probably didn't even know that at 7.55 on Wednesday mornings on TVAM, you could see a rundown of the week's new Top Five – with video clips!

And then this new kid suddenly said: 'Desh.'

'Ah, Williams!' Mr Wallis liked it when the quiet kids involved themselves; they conformed to his idea of what music students should be. Not like this GCSE rabble, with their synthesizers and noisy U2 'discs'. It didn't matter that this one seemed to have a speech impediment. 'I knew you'd have something to contribute.'

'Well sir,' began Pete, 'the reason "Penny Lane" is a bit like Bach is that they both employ the diatonic elaboration of static harmony, or DESH for short. Basically, you hold down a major chord while the bass descends the major scale, usually every half-bar, starting on the root note.'

'Right,' said Mr Wallis, who was shaking gently.

'And the prototype for this kind of structure is really Bach's *Air on a G String*. It's obvious really, isn't it, sir?'

I approached him afterwards – a shy, wary shuffle. 'Well done,' I said.

'Yeah,' he said.

His arrogance was all he had. He certainly didn't have any friends, not at that stage. In time I learned to ignore his manner. It was only a front after all, and besides, there was something unknowable about him which made him too interesting to dislike. What I did discover about Pete I was told much later, by someone else.

Before long we were seeing a fair bit of each other, though it was always Pete who came to my house rather than the other way round. He said his dad worked from home and didn't like the distraction of visitors. He didn't seem to want to talk about it. I thought that was fair enough.

Once we'd got our A-levels out of the way, Pete said: 'How about it, then? How about us forming a band. It'd be a real laugh. Dan's a good bassist, Mitch can just about keep rhythm.' Then he said: 'We must record our history right from the beginning, because you never know, do you? We should get Astrid to come in and take photos while we're rehearsing. What do you think? Will you ask her? She's more your friend than mine.' I said I would. I said I thought it was a great idea.

I saw Dan on the tube: that's how I found out. It was late afternoon – the cramped, airless couple of hours between the last expense-account lunches and the first clockings off – and I'd left work early, pleading a migraine, to collect a picture from a framer's on Charing Cross Road. I'd had a bad day. My temples throbbed and I could barely focus on the document I was supposed to be reading. Some reflexive urge forced my eyes upwards as the train stopped and the doors rumbled open. I noted the station sadly – Goodge Street, too close to Charing Cross to make dozing an option – and was about to return to 'Environmental liability insurance: what's the damage?' when the sight of a stooped figure clutching a handstrap at the far end of the carriage jolted my brain awake.

I had no idea Dan was in London. If, that is, it really was Dan: the resemblance managed to be at once undeniable and oddly incidental. His hair, which when I'd last seen him had been shoulder-length and blatantly home-dyed, was now a tuft of peppery curls, clipped short at the back and sides. And that black suit had clearly seen years of diligent service at weddings, funerals and interviews.

He saw me before I had a chance to call out, and the following evening we were sitting in a bar in north Clapham swapping life stories. You look different, I said. Your hair.

He laughed. He said it was funny, he'd only had it cut quite recently. He said he'd been in this synthesizer duo called Par Avion, playing Erasure and Pet Shop Boys covers to sensibly dressed thirty-something gay couples in a bar in Covent Garden.

I said that sounded great.

He said no it didn't, it sounded shit, and was. In fact, he'd quit. To get a proper job. Like me.

There was an awkward pause. I didn't have a proper job. I was temping at an insurance journal called Reactivity. *(It's a joke, but you have to know what reinsurance is to get it. And I'm not going to tell you.) If I acquitted myself satisfactorily, the editor had promised to consider taking me on as a trainee editorial assistant. I didn't tell Dan this. I don't know why. I suppose I didn't want to dishearten him. Instead I said, How's Jo? Have you seen her at all?*

The traffic splashed past. Dan cleared his throat and stared at the floor. You don't know, do you? he said.

My stomach dipped. Know what? I said.

I had to go on holiday for a week. It meant missing a week's rehearsals, which was bad news. A friend of a friend of my dad's had what he called a 'holiday cottage' near Abersoch in Wales, about ten minutes' drive from the sea on a good day. There was no TV. In fact, you had to really like Scrabble to have any fun at all. It was an especially bad time to be cut off in this way. Lloyd had disbanded his backing group, the Commotions, and made a solo album. The video for the first single off it was bound to be on *The Chart Show* this Saturday. I'd asked Pete to tape it, of course, but that didn't mean he would. He'd been behaving weirdly lately, really shiftily, and I hadn't seen as much of him as usual. When I asked him what he'd been up to in the evenings, whether he'd been out at all, he just said: 'Oh, I can't remember.' Or: 'I think *Where Eagles Dare* might have been on and I watched that.' Or, most revealingly: 'Why are you interested?'

Why was I interested?

At least there was the band. A focus for my shattered attention. The World. The name set me off: *World of the World*; *World Service*; *Around the World in 80 Minutes*. What other suitable album titles could there be with the word 'world' in? That expression my mum had always used when I was small and complained about feeling ill or put upon or unjustly treated: 'You and the rest of the world.' Yeah, that would do. *You and the Rest of the World*. Except that it was never any consolation, was it, when people said that to you? When you're young what you crave, more than anything else, is a sense that your problems are unique. So why does no one ever give it to you?

When I got back, weirdness had set in, big time.

We were about to run through an amended version of 'Melancholy Jane' when Jo turned up, weary and dishevelled-looking, stooping from the weight of the camera round her slim neck. It took her ten minutes to make eye contact with me. 'Astrid!' shouted Pete, and they kissed. Which was odd.

I'd written a new verse. It had taken me three hours and, really, it wasn't so bad. It certainly didn't deserve the muffled snorts that greeted its first airing.

'Jane said she was doing fine. We talked and drank some cheap red wine, while she tried to persuade me she'd died, from one complaint or another. The flat was cold and rather bare. She said, "It's the skeleton of a dead affair." I agreed its remains stank rank in the air. She smoked, I talked about my mother.'

'Wow,' said Dan. 'I like that. It has a sort of Proustian richness of evocation. You know, I think you're really maturing as a lyricist.'

'Hmn,' said Pete. Then, turning to Jo: 'Can you get me a hot chocolate from McDonald's when you go into town?'

'When'? That was a rather casual presumption, wasn't it?

'Are you going into town?' I asked her.

'Yeah,' she said. 'Will you come with me?'

It was dark by the time we got there. We sat by the clock tower in the market square, leaned back and stared up at the sodium-stained sky. Jo put her arm around me, which was pretty bloody exciting, I can tell you. She sighed. 'They don't like your lyrics much, do they?'

'You mean Pete doesn't. Dan couldn't care less. It's all Pete's fault. He's stupid and smug and stupidly, smugly pompously stupid...'

'No he's not.' Her tone was gently censorious. 'He happens to be your best friend. And you're his.'

Eh? 'How do you know?'

'He told me.'

'But that's impossible. He never tells anybody anything.'

'He does if you ask him.' She paused, and I could hear her heart pounding. I could hear, for once, that she was as scared as me.

'I spend hours writing those lyrics. And not once has Pete ever said to me that he likes them.'

'Well, have you ever told him that you like his guitar-playing? Tell me, what do you and Pete do when he comes round to your house?'

I thought for a moment. 'We listen to records,' I said. 'And then we talk about them.'

'Explain.'

'Well, we might listen to *Fruit Tree* by Nick Drake. And then Pete will say: "I don't like the string arrangement" or: "Isn't it amazing how Nick Drake evolved a whole new fingerpicking style?" And I'll maybe agree with him, or disagree with him, or make some comment about how Nick Drake uses a lot of Yeatsian imagery or something.'

'Do you ever talk about anything else? Did you know, for instance, that his mum died of cancer when he was ten?'

'No.' Whoops.

'Or that his dad might be about to lose his job?'

'No. OK, you've made your point. Whatever it is. I mean, you'd barely spoken to him before I went on holiday. I'm glad to see his tragic past has seduced you so completely.'

'Who said anything about seduction?' she said, her voice a crescendo of fake indignation.

'You're going out with him, aren't you?'

She nodded. My whole body went numb.

'Have you slept with him?'

She had the good grace to look awkward. 'What's it got to do with you?'

'You tell me. You're the one who thinks I don't know enough about him.'

I stared at her face. It was so weirdly white. Ghost-white, flour-white, eighteenth-century-courtesan white. Like a screen for projecting slides on to. So I said it. I knew it was hopeless, all of it, so I steeled myself, braced myself as if for a crash-landing, and said: 'Has Pete ever told you what he told me? That your face is like a breast on which someone has drawn a face?'

Silence. A pure sonic flatness, undented by anything: not the cars or the shoppers rushing past, or even our own jittery breathing. I blinked, taking a picture of Jo's face, stealing the moment for my own later perusal.

I wanted to stop time; to scramble determinism and fix the outcome. And the outcome is, well…that it could have gone either way. Because that's what photography does, that's why it unsettles. It returns you to the point before you knew the outcome. When I return to that image, I can convince myself that I'm looking at the beginning rather than the end, and vice versa.

So it doesn't matter that Jo slapped me and called me a scheming liar, any more than it matters that she went, 'No? Really?' and stormed off to confront Pete.

It doesn't matter that the World split up almost immediately afterwards, any more than it matters that we went on to enjoy global success and had a Brit Award presented to us by a gracious but (you could tell) inwardly grudging Lloyd Cole.

It doesn't matter that when I bumped into Dan and had that drink with him, he told me Pete and Jo were married, any more than it matters that, after Pete dumped her, Jo moved in with me, has lived here ever since and is currently pregnant with our child.

Or maybe it does. I don't know. You'd have to ask her.

THE DRESSING FLOORS
TIM NICKELS

Skin deep, deeper still:

Above the dressing floors the clotheless are nothing. Rumours. Phantoms-in-waiting. But not even *pantomime* wraiths – for ghost-sheets are in very short supply.

Above the dressing floors.

The dressing floors occupy the first three levels of the house by the reservoir. Rumours abound of a secret cellar and a super-secret tunnel below the lorry park in the basement. And *deeper still* the dark, dark waters that lead to the planet's liquid core: a domain of alien pressures and bathyscaped demons that wait for the first explorer from the light above.

But:

No frogsuits on the dressing floors. Monkey suits perhaps. Donkey jackets almost certainly. Maybe with a *touch* of frogging, the lick of the Crimea and lost dusty empires. Boots worn by Wellington and Blücher. Pixie boots from Whittington to Ultravox.

And Things to Keep Them In:

Vast wardrobes (such wardrobes!) and dressers on the dressing floors. The wardrobes that can clothe countries and harbour their allies. Coat hangers are strewn like a restless barbed wire – but those are for the new clothes: a mere century old. On hooks are the crinolines and bum-rolls of an earlier age, stained and charming. They throw skeleton shadows illuminated by dim – always dim but always on – electric candelabras. The electricity is inferior. It's not enough. It comes from too far away. The system has to work hard and sometimes sounds like the distant coughing of failing fridges.

In the attic above the dressing floors we remain undressed. It is chilly and bracing. The windows are open and wide. We have a clear view across the reservoir; the surrounding moorland that currently rusts with autumnal bracken. Our nakedness is unembarrassing. We have become accustomed to the comforting North European whiteness of fellow bodies. It is the thought of clothes that is frightening. That elusive sweetness of identity. We don't do a great deal. There are many settees and club armchairs. There's a coffee machine and a ping-pong table and a shower and loo with a lock on the door – for the naked are concerned about such things.

Miranda slips through the cat flap into *the attic*.

She returns from a scout of the dressing floors; under the feet of the tailors, fitters and seamstresses – their numbers disappear into infinity on the second level above the wardrobes. The tailors hate windows and electricity and make do with thick yellow candles, sickly with whale fat. The tailors are cross-legged on tables and on the floor facing away from each other; the catchers not of eyes but of stitches.

Miranda has seen a sight today that makes her purr with ear-twitchy pleasure. A young tailor with the head of an egg and purple socks has sewn his own trouser turn-up into the green felt of the table – because he daren't look down on the tailor who squats on the floor beneath him.

Thread slips in and out; eyes never touch.

Miranda purrs again in the attic as her memory transfers into instinct as is the way with animals. Animals live in the *now*. She will *now* gain pleasure whenever she's in the presence of needle and thread and heads like an egg.

And purple socks if she had the *eyes* for them.

Miranda slips now about the bare calves of the undressed as they read their Sunday supplements. She locates the comforting friendly foot of Alfredo. Alfredo is very old, perhaps the oldest of the undressed. A white beard foams down his chest – the happy home for many tiny spiders.

Alfredo smiles and lifts the cat on to his fleshless shoulder and takes her to the big window; he quietly avoids the ladies as they knit with number-fourteen needles and make-believe wool and discuss beetle drives and the new cooler weather.

There are people with clothes out on the moor.

They appear ponderous and thick. They have trouble standing up in their thick linen shells, their polyester carapaces. One even has boots on, lumberjack boots. The figure is a woman with blonde hair tied back with invisible faraway string. Alfredo has seen this woman before. He thinks she works on the reservoir, perhaps lives in one of its two hexagonal towers set at either end of the wall above the vast grey waters. Perhaps the others are her family down from the city.

Perhaps it's Sunday.

Alfredo glances over at Glenadine as she snoozes under several layers of supplements: there have been so many Sundays. Once one could tell quite easily. The bells from the church towers of the city might echo across the woods, ruins and tors of the wild countryside; filter through the incurious windows above the dressing floors. But the bells are a memory. Perhaps the steeples have been pulled down. Maybe the bells are *unclothed*.

Alfredo waves to the reservoir girl. She looks right up at the old man but seems unable to make him out. She seems aware of his presence but uncertain of his nature. Of his origin. The reservoir girl throws her head back and sniffs.

She turns away and looks into the reservoir. She can see her reflection – or thinks she does – and waves to that instead.

There's a flap on.

Miranda's familiar heaviness is absent from his knees and Alfredo is immediately awake in the dawn of tomorrow. The others in the attic snore quietly on; an occasional whimper from the rows of tall hospital bedsteads that line the inside of the eaves.

Alfredo shuffles his bare feet across the floor, cursing the god of careless nail hammerers. He makes his ears as wide as he can make them. They are large, transparent pieces of business like the dorsal cooling fins of Palaeozoic dinosaurs.

The air is full of shivers. It hums and the ears of the old man quiver imperceptibly.

The floors below are *dis-dressing*.

The tailors unpick the past week's labours and pile it into the articulated lorries. The building quivers again. Far below, just above the cellar line, lies the underground loading bay where the lorries back in every third Tuesday.

Or sometimes every second.

The truckers jump down from their cabs decorated with Walsall bunting and pictures of female Gladiators. They hitch open the rear trailer doors, empty and waiting for the latest knittings. Three tons of fishbone weave, an acre or two of corduroy (difficult stuff).

The apprentice tailors chuck in the week's makings that they wheel from the dressing floors in shopping trolleys. The tailors are pale under the arc lamps that the truckers insist on: these strivers of the whalelight. The tailors might eye the outsiders widely. The outsiders perhaps look around, down, up, muttering 'Jesus…' and adjust their fluorescent body warmers.

And when the job is done – when everything from the dressing floors is in the back of the big lorries – the tailorettes scurry back to their table tops, while the truckers laugh and roar up the ramps into the sunlight.

Miranda sees it all, curled up in a spare wheel on the docking bay; a tabby going to fat on cold milky Nescafé, the gift of apprentices.

Alfredo folds back his ears with his hands above the dressing floors. He lifts his nose and widens its nostrils. Like the reservoir girl.

Distantly, through the down-below mist of camphor and dry-cleaning bags, he smells today's diesel. The double glazing shudders very briefly. The passing of the great lorries is invisible as they take the circular underpass that leads out to the motorway.

Miranda flops on the crown of Alfredo's head like a humming ginger toupée. The attic letter box rattles sharply as the slush of newspapers falls through it. Presently, a melodic *clinckety-clank* as milk bottles touch the doorstep.

Alfredo waits the designated fifteen minutes (no watches – but he counts very carefully) and then opens their front door. The corridor ahead is lit with a dullish ambient glow; the walls are adorned with pictures of Neapolitan urchins more usually found in the bedrooms of cheaper airport hotels. Alfredo sniffs once more – but it is the reassuring smog of the dressing floors that touches his nose now: the camphor again; sewing machine oil, sweat and farts from a thousand tailors.

He pulls in the milk and closes the door.

Again, she is there. A week has passed. A week *perhaps* (Alfredo's counting is not trusted by all...).

Alfredo and Glenadine see the reservoir girl together. Glenadine puts down her bag of personalized vouchers ('...*IMAGINE, Ms G. Gurée, your name has already been selected for our competition's sensational second round...*' '...*IMAGINE, Ms G. Gurré, a brand-new hosiery and life assurance concept for you and your loved ones...*') and places her pretty old nose against the double glazing.

The girl walks from one of the grey reservoir towers with a tool box. She pauses far below and peers over the wall into the water. She unzips and shrugs off her yellow overalls. Underneath she wears more clothes – blue trousers and a jaunty red-and-orange shirt. She stands and looks at her feet; perhaps wonders whether to remove her lumberjack boots – *all the while* with her hand on her shoulder. Maybe she just worries at a bra strap; or perhaps she simply enjoys the texture of her sunny shirt. And *all the while* she stares across the greyness of the reservoir that sends water into the city.

She looks up at them with a restrained puzzlement. Glenadine waves.

The reservoir girl turns away: the tool box is in one hand, the overalls over her shoulder; she strides along the wall to the other tower.

And as she strides she looks ever, forever into the water; perhaps wonders if she can wear it. *If she could only quickly zip it on and dry her hands afterwards* –

That night:

Glenadine cries for clothes in her sleep. Her hands knit around themselves with the sheet in between. She is twisting the sheet into a blouse or pantaloons. Or perhaps even a handkerchief. (Few noses to wipe above the dressing floors; illnesses are unknown, injuries small – a tongue grazed licking an envelope, wrist-twists after gin rummy.)

'Thread, thread...' she whispers as the yellow half-moon glows in through the window. 'Come closer now. Come...'

Alfredo pulls the curtain, darkens the room.

Glenadine's eyes are open but Alfredo is unnoticed; as invisible to her as his own nakedness is invisible to himself.

'Come closer and I will *dress* you...' She sighs.

Alfredo crouches at the foot of the old woman's bed for some time. He rises: the crack of his joints make him jump in the still, breathing room.

He goes to the window, drags back the curtain and they are dressed again in moonlight.

The plumber comes on the morning of Glenadine's funeral. They watch her coffin as it slips out of the bowels of the building on the back of a pick-up truck and disappears down into the underpass.

The toilet is backed up. Some desperate soul has stuffed the U-bend with newspapers – water in the bowl is stained a deeper grey than the grey waters of the reservoir.

The plumber has been partially briefed on the situation above the dressing floors. His naked body is pale and pear-shaped. It is unused to being undressed. The plumber – Mr Stanley – carries his plumber's bag at genital level and the heavy tools prod him painfully as he stands on the edge of the loo seat and tries to peer into the ceiling cistern. He rummages around one-handed as the round faces of the attic dwellers beam up at him. He steps down and surveys the type-print waters of the toilet bowl. He closes the lid and sits on it.

Young Maisie brings milky coffee and Mr Stanley half rises to accept two Garibaldi biscuits from her seventy-year-old fingers.

'Well... it's a rum do, folks,' says Mr Stanley as he munches and hopes that his crossed legs don't break some attic etiquette. 'I'll be needing the electric pump and a towel. And a bucket or three, if you have any – '

'I'll get it, Mr Stanley.'

'Oh, I think we'll be needing more than *one* bucket, sir...'

'I'll get it, Mr Stanley,' repeats Alfredo. 'I'll get the electric pump. It'll be down in the van, I'll be bound...'

'And you'll be bounding down to get it, old chap? That's good of you, but I don't believe that you're allowed...'

'Oh, we *are*. Within the confines of the building, Mr Stanley – '

None of the attic dwellers seems to breathe any more. They stare at Alfredo while desperately... casually... casually... desperately... they attempt to glance in an opposite direction.

'It would save you time, Mr Stanley. Maisie girl could get the kettle going again and you could start rodding and then you'd be that much further ahead when I got back with the pump. It's *allowed*. Within the confines of the building. It's allowed. *Really.*'

The air is chill down in the basement. Alfredo finds the small plumber's van easily enough; and beyond it lies one of the big articulated lorries. The lorry is fully stuffed with knitting – he can see through the still-open rear doors. The loading men and the driver and a couple of uncomfortable-looking under-dressers stand in the Portakabin and watch a football match on television. Things are going badly and the men argue among themselves.

A new electrical coolness glides past Alfredo's shin.

'No, Miranda. I'm afraid your old Alfredo is going on a little trip by himself. A little trip to the outside. I need you to keep an eye on those naughty tailors, my sweet...'

He bends down and works the back of her neck with his hand. 'A little trip... A little trip...'

A goal has been scored. The Portakabin is in uproar. A glass breaks.

Alfredo rises and shuffles to the open rear doors of the lorry and plunges into the sea of wool; warms his naked feet and stifles a hundred sneezes.

The darkness moves:

Alfredo can't know how long he has lain here – his internal clockwork dims in the presence of shadows. His nostrils and eyes are clogged with wool fragments. The lorry is bumping along; the hum of the engine alternates with the hiss/bark of air brakes and gear changes.

Alfredo relaxes into his knitted ocean and dreams of the hours or days ahead, of his journey into a different planet. Or he might dream of the reservoir girl: as she stands on the battlements and looks ever deeper into the waters and wonders what her clothes are for.

★

The lorry stops with a final stagger of its braking system. The sound of the rear doors as they swing open reaches through the woolly fug: Alfredo has unknowingly worked his body deeper into the trailer's interior; *deeper still...*

And so light comes back into his world; the unloading of bales and scarves and the looser hanks of wool traitorously reveal his hiding place.

He sees them now.

He sees them...

His revealers:

Muffled with clothes, they hide under their weight, barely able to carry the new deliveries from the lorry. Some limp through the wearing of multi-layers of socks. Jumpers; cardies; waistcoats; greatcoats; shorts over plus-fours over track-suit bottoms over thick corduroy walking trousers... Bobble hats precarious above bo'sun's caps and balaclavas. Gender is impossible to tell – the bodies have been ballooned into the realms of androgyny.

Only the eyes:

Only the eyes – a flash of some pale male? female? colour: a frowned-upon revelation in this overdressed world.

Alfredo tumbles out on to tarmac.

He is outside.

He is outside in some sort of exterior counterpart to the basement lorry park. Low industrial buildings fill three angles; on the fourth, double gates and a perspex guard hut. The football match proceeds noisily within.

The unloaders – perhaps there are six of them – seem uncertain of this new arrival. Alfredo senses no aggression from them as he rises painfully and hopes a bloodied knee won't collapse under him. Rather, an odd sort of sadness communicates itself by the incline of a head, the limp mittened hands of some of them. He must seem such a tiny creature: a lower life form surprised during some vital shedding of skins. A forgotten thing: a prehistoric fish long thought lost, netted by accident and held up against the sun, the object of a poignant fascination.

Alfredo clears his throat but can think of no further sound to make. He totters forward on his cramped legs and they allow him through. They keep away (it seems) from his touch.

The gate is unlocked and he pushes through and closes it behind him. Most of the unloaders turn back to their work. One continues to watch him. *Perhaps it's curious*, thinks Alfredo as he rubs his knee. *Perhaps it wants to dress me*. And he remembers Glenadine and her thread of yellow moonlight.

And the colour of moonlight when morning comes.

The sun is hot and Alfredo feels his unused shoulders redden.

The streets of the city are awash with walking wardrobes. Pedestrians bustle each other off pavements with the weightiness of their clothing and fight at zebra crossings. One or two fall into the road; they lie helpless inside their bloated garments as the cars bump over them.

There is silence from the people of the city. In the attic – even when the most intense bridge game is in progress, *even* when the Sunday supplements are new – there is always a conversational hum from the undressed. Bickering – petty or otherwise – perhaps; but naked lives are *touched*, it seems. By comparison, the city dwellers try to keep as far away as possible from each other; and if by chance they fall into a fellow's path the silence seems to intensify – as if it can cocoon the occurrence more readily than any distant insurance claim for personal injury.

The slap of leather on pavement – or the strangled cough, the barely *breathed* breath. These are the sounds that Alfredo hears. The clothes seem to walk their inhabitants around. And perhaps some of the clothes are unoccupied.

Alfredo leans on a broken guess-your-weight machine and has a sudden urge to unravel these people, to cast off their knitted hearts.

Before he walks back into the countryside, Alfredo sits on a dustbin behind a restaurant where the orders are telephoned ahead by an answering machine.

He studies his hands. Perhaps his skin has been mistaken for one of the sheerer silks. He glances down at his old body: he could be dressed in a stained pillow leaking white goose feathers of body hair.

A bird lands unexpectedly at his feet and worries at a thrown-out piece of bacon rind. It is not a *goose* – this would have made a strange day stranger (*deeper still...*) – but it is of reasonable size: a pigeon perhaps. It's difficult to tell. Alfredo looks at the bird and the bird looks back – eyes bright in its featherless, free body.

The moors are beautiful in the dawn mist. A pinkish glow hangs in the sky as Alfredo glances back at the city. Perhaps it stirs itself awake. He might even hear a church bell – or the embarrassed rush of ten million water closets.

He sits between the two towers on the ramparts of the reservoir. His feet dangle over the water through the metal railing. He fully intends to return to the attic room above the dressing floors – but in a little while perhaps, when he's caught his breath. The seasons are changing. Although the day promises to be hot again, the night has turned his limbs blue and his progress back across the rough ground has been slower than he hoped. Yes. He will rest here for just a little while before he goes back to Miranda and tells her about his strange adventure.

There is a commotion in the waters of the reservoir. Nothing very large. Nothing terribly disturbing. For the first time he notices that the lumberjack boots and jeans and the colourful red-and-orange shirt lie in a heap by one of the towers.

He watches the girl as she surfaces and twists about to descend once more into the wet darkness: in the reservoir there is nothing between her soul and the water but her skin.

She might have surfaced again, but it's harder to see her now.

Alfredo glances up to where he thinks the big attic window might be.

HUDDERSFIELD VERSUS CREWE
ALAN BEARD

'Pools? God. Yes. Years since I did those. Frank never bothered. It's a man's thing, isn't it, the pools? The lottery's more women.'

I reassured her: lots of women on my round. Single women, too. She gave me a sharp look at this.

'I wouldn't know where to start with filling it in.'

I could help her. I wouldn't mind showing her.

'I'm just going out.' She was dressed up, plenty of eye make-up, a necklace catching streetlight. A long, long neck. 'Call next week, could you? I'm Kath, and you?'

'David. Dave.'

How things start. I nearly didn't call. I was drumming up business on a second round I'd just taken over. I wasn't having much luck among the narrow rows of terraces whose sloping streets always seemed to be in fog that autumn and winter. It was the last house I tried before I trudged back under the motorway home.

I've always kept up the pools round, all through the other jobs I've had, mainly factory work, but also shop assistant, maintenance man in a block of offices, supply postman. Itty-bitty jobs my wife Liz called them. But that's not quite right: the maintenance job lasted six years until the firm relocated to Scotland. The pools always brought in that little bit extra. It also got me out of the house.

The way I saw it, towards the end, that's what they wanted – me out the house. It seemed to me they were ganging up on me. My wife would say, 'You're just short of useless.' (*Just* being the money I brought in – she often earned more with her part-time nursing.) 'Why do you bother pretending to take an interest? You're so full of yourself,' she'd continue. 'Apologies for breathing,' I'd say.

My daughter Ruth (you could add a 'less') was no better. When I talked to her there was this sneer on her face the whole time. As if she couldn't quite believe what she was seeing. If she could she'd lie in front of MTV all day. An essay she wrote, on 'My Dad': 'He shaves in the sink and Mum is sick of him.' I pointed it out to Liz. She said, 'And?'

The cat was held in more esteem. I'd come home weighed down with shopping and park the stuff in fridge and cupboard, the kid's chocs, her yoghurts, my beers, and not say a word to either of them, busy anyway with TV watching, hoovering, on the phone. Of an evening we'd shuffle past each other between fridge and sofa. There didn't seem much to look forward to; I was sitting on the toilet reading pension leaflets and working out sums. My hair getting wirier, more like a wig each day. My latest job didn't help, fork-lift driving in a warehouse and a lot of it was waiting about between deliveries. I looked at the days in my life and could see no difference in them, unless we won the pools. I'm sure Liz thought that as a poolsman I should have been able to arrange that.

The night I first went into her house I smoked so much I silently vowed to smoke no more. 'Blimey. No doubt you can keep up then?' She wanted me to catch the doubleness of her words.

We sat on adjoining sofas in this small room. The former tenant's heavily patterned wallpaper – she hadn't bothered to decorate though she'd been there three years – made it seem even smaller. We pored over the coupon I put on the coffee table, our hands and knees close. Her hair smelt of tea; it was the colour nicotine leaves on the fingers. I explained the green panel, the blue panel, the booster entry. I could see how her eyes smiled – not quite her mouth – at that. She thought the crosses were like marks on a treasure map.

Every week she found some excuse for inviting me in. *Top of the Pops* on the television while she searched her bag for change. She always asked advice. 'Shall I go for Huddersfield versus Crewe, sounds like a draw to me.' I told her to stick to the same numbers, the same pattern. 'It's the best way.' She wouldn't. She'd come to the door and say she was on the phone and to come in and I'd watch her squat in a position she must have assumed hundreds of times she looked so comfortable. All the time I looked over the planes and corners and curves of her face for the beauty I saw there.

Sex with her was like dishes being served, one after the other, and all tasting new, ingredients you recognized but a new mix. She quite liked me to eat off her. I spent a long time gazing at her pale, rounded, marked skin, like a hoard of gold in the light from the angle-poise. It was a lazy, dabbling kind of sex, but occasionally she clung and dug into me hard, kneading, as if to make something new of my flesh. After I was tingling, felt the blood reach right down to my fingers and toes.

By now I was always late in from the round and told Liz I always would be – meeting a mate down the pub. She took this with a shrug – 'Enjoy yourself.'

Thoughts of Kath cut through the week, far-off lights calling through the fog as I stomped around the house. 'Wotcher strop-features,' said Ruth. 'Villa losing, are they?'

Liz finally noticed. I was spending too long in the bathroom looking into the mirror trying to figure out what it was Kath saw in me. 'You got a woman?' Her dark eyebrows arrowed. 'Yeh – you,' I said, but soon after I left, Kath had been saying I could, I should, and moved three-quarters of a mile away under the always roaring motorway to the other side.

We'd eat cheese on toast and do little. Didn't go out much. It was a relief to come home to such quiet. She liked me for the oil on me, the way I talked apparently. My steadiness. I was 'handsome in a way'. 'What way?' 'A way I like.' I liked her for the difference she presented. She was a Brummie but had spent time away and lost – almost – the accent. She was so pale after Liz's dark looks. 'My ghost,' I called her.

'You can save me from going under in this place,' she said, nodding towards the window. The fog was a mixture of weather and fumes from the battery factory, she said. She said she could hardly breathe out there and nothing would grow in the garden, a short one backing on to the motorway embankment. (She was later disappointed to find I didn't have the green fingers she wanted, but I made up for it in other ways.) She said the neighbours stole her catalogue parcels. She talked of moving out, somewhere 'nice' — Sutton, for example, but we couldn't afford that.

I didn't think it was so bad. True, when the motorway cut our district in two when I was a kid it was deemed the rougher part. Liz in particular didn't want Ruth mixing with the boys from here. But on my round I found little difference in the people — some were friendly, I got a kiss and a tenner from someone who won a couple of thou third dividend; others guarded their property as if you had a second job as a burglar. I had to admit it wasn't as pleasant with the high sagging factory walls, the shunting yards and the huge weathered billboard (a fading 'It Could Be You') welcoming you, but then the other side wasn't exactly Solihull either.

Kath was an actress. 'An actor,' she'd say, 'an actor. I am an actor. Or at least I was.' We watched the videos that proved it. In one she opened the door to police, in curlers, a shrugged-on dressing gown, and was pushed aside. An ageing moll. (I got her to play that role later, and I was a policeman who stayed to interrogate her.) A speaking part in the cable company ad. No, she couldn't tell the difference between a BT phone and this one. Except when the bills came in. Behind her was Central Library and the glugging fountain in Chamberlain Square. I saw that a few times, and noted again how she was cast as ordinary, hair blowing in the wind looked almost grey, and yet she seemed young to me. She actually got her phone installed and bills paid for a month as part of the deal. 'I made so many calls I ran out of people to call. My daughter got sick of me.'

Her daughter, Bernadette — Bernie — was going to be the one that did it. Actually be an actor. She was tall, brilliant, her face so expressive, camera-friendly. I asked her how she knew since she hardly saw her now. Bernie, at fifteen, had decided to live with her father after the divorce, and took his side always. 'All right, it's true at that time I was a bit messed up. I was seeing Frank, who I later moved in with, and doing drugs, a bit.' She regretted not fighting for custody through the courts. That would have sobered her up and Bernie would have seen her how she could be, straight, responsible. Like now. On top of things. Bernie would have stayed and by now

Kath would be visiting her in London, seeing her perform. Standing by her in photographs.

Kath told me it was she who did all the work with the baby and her bringing up. It was she who made Bernie what she was. How could she choose the father who left her to her own devices all those years? Neither was he the saint he made himself out to be. I sat and agreed with her word for word, because I felt too how children can be so heartless, unthinking.

One night in spring I came in from the job and she was listening to *Virgin Classic Album Tracks* – U2's 'She Moves in Mysterious Ways'. Doing a little dance. Sunlight was squeezing in from the tiny shred of sky visible above the embankment.

'Do you think I'm mysterious?'

'Yes, very.'

'I used to think I was an alien. Or been abducted by aliens. But maybe I just dreamed it and you know some dreams are so real they become real.'

Again I looked over the paleness of her face, the tiny red marks – neck creases – under her ear, her hair tied back gold in the late slanting sun. I wanted to get to the bottom of her.

'So you're an alien. I always wondered. Your slippery skin. Your bug eyes.'

'No, I mean it. I mean I'm not me.'

'Possessed maybe.'

The whole room was gold and she golden in it. I moved towards her.

She told me how handsome Frank was: 'All he had was nice black hair and a good couple of eyes. When all's said and done it's the eyes that get me on a man every time.' And how she missed her ex – a steady type like me, and although it brought a bad taste to my mouth, I understood it, it was a kind of accounting for herself. And because a similar thing was happening to me, thoughts of my wife, soon to be my ex, had begun where for long years when she was right beside me I'd done nothing but try and block her out.

Little things: finding Liz's photo-booth picture, the one that didn't make it into the passport fifteen years ago, in the inside pocket of a jacket I'd hardly worn and picked up on a forage back there. When Kath played music it was '70s stuff – T. Rex and Roxy Music. Her favourite single was Hawkwind's 'Silver Machine'. Liz had similar tastes, only Kath liked the treble high and Liz liked it low, more bass.

I thought it was to be expected really and it needn't be a problem, but one night during my first summer here I lay awake watching Kath undress. To cool us we had the window open behind drawn curtains. Her skin was still pale but glowed from the warmth of the day. I recalled a scene from an early holiday with Liz. Torremolinos in June. She took off her bikini in the hotel room. The evening light and her deep tan made it look as if she'd put on some bizarre skin-tight costume that left her private parts exposed. Through the night with Kath snuggling close but not wanting sex, I seemed to hear the sea breaking outside the window: maybe the noise of the motorway.

No one seemed to call on Kath, the phone never rang. The people on my round didn't know much about her, though they remembered Frank. I asked her where she was going the night I first called, all dressed up. She said some function, she couldn't remember, as if she went to them all the time.

One night though, when I got in, still thinking it strange to get my key ready on the corner of this street dominated by the motorway that rose above it, she was on the phone. She was crying, the receiver in her lap. Bernie was on the other end. I took the phone from her, despite her protests.

'Can't you be nice to your mother for once.'

'Who are you?' said the voice. 'Where's Frank?'

'Frank's gone. I'm here now.'

'But who the fuck *are* you?' And she put the phone down.

After that was our first argument. Because she hadn't told her daughter about me. How was that going to make me feel? I said she should write to her explaining I wasn't some fly-by-night. But she was still wet-faced from the call and I stopped and put my arms wide. 'You've got to believe in me. We've got to stick together.' She agreed and came close and kissed and promised everything would be all right. There was nothing wrong.

I was still doing my old round. Which is how I found out my wife was no longer there, nowhere in the district. A former neighbour said something about her going. Sure enough I called on our old house, even though Liz had cancelled the pools when I left, and a tall Asian in white robes and waistcoat opened the door. I asked him did he want to do the pools but he wanted to get rid of me and didn't give me a chance to look through, past him to my old world.

I didn't go back. I gave up my round there. I knew she'd have to contact me soon, for the divorce to progress. She did and she said she didn't require maintenance any more, they were all doing quite nicely now.

In her letter, which was almost friendly, she said I should keep in contact with Ruth, and that I should want to, and I did, although at one time I hadn't of course. Ruth came to our house a couple of times, nodded disdainfully at Kath and sat and watched television until it was time for me to take her back. So instead I met her on my own, once a month, and we'd go out, to the cinema mainly, the latest blockbuster — she liked special effects, *Independence Day*, *Total Recall*, and so did I — and a McDonald's after. More recently she wanted to go for a meal, she introduced me to Greek food, or a new balti at some place across the city. For many years, I told her, our diet had had to be as bland as possible because otherwise she wouldn't eat it. She said she was grown up now — she'd be sixteen soon.

She tells me of her new life, how Liz has changed — brighter, more relaxed apparently from the burden of me being lifted, and of Robert, her stepfather. I was glad to hear her say that though he was 'all right' and worked hard he was a bit of a creep. But then anyone over twenty-five was a bit of a creep to Ruth.

She pointed out that what I was doing, had done, was nothing new. Just the same as thousands of others, like her friends' parents, middle-aged prats running after younger women. But she's not, I said, only a few years. Same as your mother. (I turned it into a compliment for Kath when I got back, but she didn't want to hear anything Ruth might have to say.) Anyway, I added, your mother's no angel. I was referring to a brief (I think) affair she'd had years before which Ruth wouldn't have known about but she nodded as if she did.

We — Kath and me — went to see *The English Patient*. I practically had to force her out of the house. I thought she'd want to go. 'You're the actress,' I said. She didn't correct me. Before she went she read up on the film and during the screening she told me the critic's opinions.

After we dropped into a nearby bar, across from the Hippodrome. I thought she'd like to be near a theatre. When we'd settled in a corner by the window I asked her if she couldn't refrain from telling me what everyone else thought of the film during it, so I could make up my own mind.

'Oh,' she said, sniffing, and looked out at the crowds leaving the theatre. It was nice to be out among people. I'd thought about going back to the Villa again. I knew Kath wouldn't want to come, but she wouldn't mind me going.

'No, I don't mean I don't want to hear, but after the film.'

'No, you're perfectly right,' she said, still looking away. I gazed back towards the bar. I had been sat in a corner like this once out with Liz. She was at the bar and I watched as a few men glanced across at her, some not so slyly. How she stood on her toes in strappy shoes, waiting to be served, then dropped back on her heels. The backs of her knees bent in, one a deeper hollow. How she moved steadily across the room holding the two pints and not spilling a drop underneath her narrow, lopsided smile. A man was singing as we came out and for once it was a good, strong voice. A small mob who had been shouting and chucking things stopped to listen. His voice became larger, only drowned out by a passing bus, and he got on his knees for the finale. Me and Liz clapped and whistled for the man in the padded sleeveless anorak with his arms wide.

Me and Kath got the bus back to the motorway intersection and stopped on the corner by the billboard to light cigarettes. She had been quiet on the way home despite the rowdy passengers trying to get everyone to sing 'Three Lions'. She turned, she was smiling, she was trying hard. 'I'll get a job. Do something useful with myself, you see.' That's great, I said and apologized for what I said in the bar. For some reason we didn't carry on down the street, but stayed until we'd finished smoking. We watched lights arc into the sky as cars went up slip roads. Then we put our arms round each other and hugged for what we'd done in this life, and what also we had no control over.

She did get a job. At the local supermarket on the one till. But she didn't like the customers, got flustered with special offers and always feared armed robbery. She came home jittery. She took more and more time off and in the end I told her she should leave the job if it was getting her down so much, we could cope. (I thought she'd get the sack soon anyway.) But then we'd definitely have to stay here. She didn't care, she was grateful I'd said the words, and she rang up, went to get her wages and never went there again. I did – on my way home from work.

She hardly ever went anywhere again. One Sunday afternoon with fog again at the window she cried at *Oliver!* the musical, as much at Bill Sykes and Nancy's twisted relationship as over Oliver's plight. During the film I'd laughed at the mock-Cockney and now wished I hadn't. I'd say that was the beginning.

She started spending days in bed, or wandered downstairs in her dressing gown (I said was she auditioning for her old role but she didn't seem to know what I was talking about). I'd say, 'What you been up to?' 'Not a lot,' she'd say. She always had excuses – 'If I'd gone out I'd have *drownded*.' (Mimicking my accent.)

She got a cat, I don't know where from. It didn't like me; it scratched me. 'It's only a kitten,' she said. It wasn't. She put a dirt tray in the kitchen. You have to train it to go outside, I said. She wouldn't. Her fingers started smelling of cat food. Her breath was fags, but then so was mine.

At night with Kath in bed I zapped through cable channels (as Kath did in the day and evening: where's the zapper, she said once, things are no good without the zapper). I watched the weather in Norwegian, *Exotica Erotica*, Tommy Vance and MTV, which I imagined Ruth would be watching. You had to hand it to Liz, she had turned out much better than I would have imagined – I looked forward to seeing her now. I thought of Ruth's early life, not so much babyhood, because that was just a whirl of broken nights, mopping up, feeding, bathing. But of later, when she grew into who she was. How she couldn't get enough of learning. The phases she went through, I remember her doing the Ancient Civilizations: copying the alphabets of the Egyptians and Phoenicians (the trouble she had with that word) and writing messages in hieroglyphics. She made her bedroom into a museum, with a sign on the door and exhibits (bits of broken plates, paintings she'd done), and charged admission. Her

Bugs Bunny teeth, her shining face, the freckles beginning that she would hate later. The singing of hymns, trying to do handstands in the kitchen, her rending cries if she was hurt. When she was reading *The Lion, the Witch and the Wardrobe* she said I was like Mr Tumnus (something to do with my wiry hair). Telling me off about smoking even though I was doing it outside in the yard, in all weathers, wind and snow whirling about me.

Even though I'd lived here for a couple of years I couldn't get used to the place. Even though people would shout hello across the street, stop and chat about the Villa and whether Stan Collymore was any good, I didn't feel part of things here. I'd grown up just down the road but it could have been another city. Ironing one Saturday afternoon listening to the football on the radio, I was looking out into the back garden, the bare laburnum framed in the window above the low, square hedge. A leaf scraped along the path in a light wind, I could hear the cars and lorries moving always just beyond, out of sight. It seemed wrong. I couldn't get it to seem familiar to me.

She was ill, she had a pain in her chest. She called it her 'fear' pain. She was on the verge of being sick all the time. She wouldn't go to the doctor. I started to feel coming back from work like I did with Liz in our last years together and wondered whether all relationships ended up heading this way; this one had got there much quicker. I stayed out longer on the pools round. Started attending matches. Stan Collymore wasn't any good.

Two years almost to the night she came out of the house all dressed up like that first time. I was just arriving home. Even from my distance I could see she wasn't as expert at applying the make-up. She didn't seem to see me and walked off down the street. I followed her but she just walked down to the land underneath the motorway and wandered among the pillars holding up the rising road. I went back. She returned about an hour later, said nothing.

I wondered should I get help, call a doctor or something. Instead I called Bernie. The number I eventually found on the back of an envelope wasn't London, a Coventry one. There was no reply but I left a message. Could she just come and see her mother, could she just come and talk to her, it would mean so much.

*

'Hello, Dave,' I heard as I came in, dripping wet from the round.

I wouldn't have known it was her daughter, must have taken after the father, except for the pale skin which brought out roses in Bernie as opposed to her mother's milder, more mottled colouring: age.

Kath was watching the television, Michael Barrymore (early on she'd wanted us to apply to go on that show but I hadn't wanted to have the piss taken out of me), and keeping her eye on her daughter. I dripped, took my coat off, ran my hands through my wet hair, went to the kitchen and came back. I thought they must have had the big conversation, or Kath was so pleased to see her she could hardly speak, beyond the usual exclamations – well, look at you! Actually Bernie wasn't tall and didn't look glamorous to me. She wore trainers, dull green track-suit bottoms, splashed with rain. She chewed gum and looked around frowning at the room. When Kath went upstairs she leaned forward and asked what tale Kath was spinning now.

It turned out she wasn't a drama student, though she had applied once. She was working in a hotel. Assistant Manager, she reckoned. I thought of Ruth, who I was seeing at the weekend (Imrans, Balsall Heath), as Bernie went on to detail her mother's crimes. She was lazy, selfish, nuts. Hadn't I noticed?

'You could try being sympathetic,' I said.

'Tried that,' she said, 'so did dad, and look where it got him. Wrecked his life. Probably Frank's too – but who gives a toss about him?'

We heard the toilet flush, movement upstairs.

'Are you going to visit her again?' I hoped not, I was bristling, could have smacked her, but I was thinking of Kath.

'Nah,' she said. 'Don't see much point. And you? You going to stay the course?' She got up, stretched herself.

'Yes,' I said, feeling a last rain drop run down under my collar. 'I'm starting on the decorating next week.'

THE BALL
STEPHEN O'REILLY

The boy loved the sea and looked forward to those times each summer when the family climbed into the old Volkswagen Beetle and headed off for the long, clean stretches of sand a few miles further up the coast. Sometimes they took a dog if it managed to survive the year. The family had not much luck with animals. They tended to get knocked down on their quiet country road, which was strange enough in itself that nobody had a good explanation of why it should happen. The family didn't even live beside the road but down a long lane right-angled to it. The dogs never died right away either but rolled around in the dirt with their backs broken, biting at their dead haunches, howling in anger and puzzlement. His father would get a shovel from the shed and finish the dog off, burying the carcass in the adjacent field. It had become quite a graveyard. The boy loved all of the dogs and was sad when they died, but even at ten he realized that death was just an inevitable part of life and that, being ten, it would be a long, long time before he himself would have to worry about it. True, the previous year he had been worried that nuclear war would break out and kill everyone, bringing on bad dreams and desire to serve Mass, but that had been just 'a phase', as his mother said. To tell the truth, he felt embarrassed by the whole thing now that he was ten. Old women kept stopping him in the street and commenting on how he always looked so serious when serving Communion. During the summer months there were four Masses a day for the tourists and the boy tried to serve as many of these as he could. The phase ended rather quickly after a relation in England sent his mother her previous year's collection of *Reader's Digests*. He loved reading and had gone through them in a couple of weeks, reading about the SALT2 talks, MAD and how atomic war was increasingly unlikely. Then three weeks after the books had arrived, at Sunday evening Mass the year-long phase of prayer and terror came to an abrupt end. He was on the gong. A giant mushroom-shaped bell that sat on the floor behind the altar. It was his job to strike it with an ebony wooden mallet when the priest said the magic words. The boy was day-dreaming and missed his cue, over-compensating by giving the bell an almighty bang with the mallet when one of the lads beside him nudged him, deafening himself and the congregation and nearly blowing the speaker system from its mounts on the walls. When the deep bone-numbing tone of the bell had finally subsided and his eyes came back into focus he glanced up to see what the damage was.

It was bad.

He hadn't been the only one day-dreaming in the midst of the priest's low murmurings and smell of wax. The church was jammed that evening and the volume had been cranked up so that those standing in the entrances would hear. Now all eyes were trying to focus on the cause of the noise. Several old ladies were clutching their chests and breathing deeply. People were whispering to each other and nodding in his direction. Even the priest had stopped and had turned to look at the boy who had paralysed his congregation's nervous system.

The spell was broken.

The boy began to laugh. Shoulders heaving beneath the surplice as he tried to keep it in. Letting the air expel out through his nose until there was nothing left and dark spots in front of his eyes. All he could see now was the priest lifting a bony finger and pointing back towards the sacristy. Too much. He stood up and ran off the altar, face purple and robes flapping. He collapsed on the bench in the altar boys' changing room and roared with laughter at the image of all the old biddies clasping rosary beads to their chests as the shockwave hit them.

The journey to the beach was uneventful. His town had its own small beach but it was a dirty polluted affair that only the visitors used. His parents watched the houses go by and talked about who owned what. The boy lay on the back seat reading an American comic book, listening to the drone of their voices. In it a character called Deathlok was being hunted by cannibals who could smell him coming because he was in fact dead. His flesh was green, peeling away from his head, and he had been brought back to life by scientists as some sort of soldier. It was fascinating stuff even though he knew that he wouldn't be able to find out how the story ended. These comics trickled into the small town where he lived in a completely random order. In six months' time he might be able to find another issue but it wouldn't be about cannibals. Anyway, this Deathlok was armed to the teeth and looked as if he could look after himself. He felt the car go down a hill and the sudden change from tarmacadam to smooth, damp sand beneath the wheels, soaking up the vibration that had made him read all the speech bubbles twice. They had arrived. His father rolled down the window and the car filled with the smell of the beach and sound of portable radios as it weaved up the strand around the parked cars with their Northern plates and the pale bodies stretched out on towels around them.

The boy shucked off his trousers and headed down towards the water, carefully avoiding the jellyfish that littered the shoreline. His parents lay on the sand back at the car, eyes closed, white shanks pointing up at the sky, and he knew that he would have the afternoon to himself to swim and explore. They had made him take swimming lessons in the town pool after a doctor had told them that it would be good for his asthma. He hated it at first, mainly because it was something that he was being made to do, but now he felt comfortable in the water and considered himself to be a good swimmer.

The ball was the first thing he noticed. It was bright yellow with black octagonal-shaped patches and it was bobbing around in the surf a few feet offshore. Just sitting there. He stood for a few moments looking around him to see if he could see the owner, but nobody came to claim it. Some kids must have lost it playing football, he thought. He ran into the water and picked it up, turning it over in his hands to see if there was a name on it. Sure enough there it was in new, blue felt-tip.

Paul Mahoney
aged 13

He mulled it over. The afternoon was getting on. Chances were that Paul Mahoney had gone home with his family or maybe it had been lost further up the beach. He resolved to give back the ball to whoever asked for it. He was an only child and tended to be wary of other children, especially older ones. He had seen enough petty schoolyard cruelties to know that the return of the ball could be greeted with a poke on the nose or a Chinese burn just as easily as a thank-you. Anyway, the ball was his for a while now and he threw it lightly up into the air to get the weight of it, catching it again and letting it drop to his feet where it floated glistening in the sun. He stood there for several long moments staring down at the ball, letting it nudge gently against his ankles before stooping to pick it up.

He had an idea.

The boy passed some adults on his way out to sea. They were standing waist-deep in the water, bobbing gently up and down as the waves broke around them. Staring out to sea with nothing between them and America. Something about the image bothered him. Like they were waiting for something. They glanced at him in that uninterested fashion adults reserve for other people's children as he volleyed the ball with his fist out into the sea and waded out through the breakers after it. The ball spun around in the afternoon sun, light flashing off it, beckoning. Soon his feet no longer touched the bottom and he felt himself floating free, angling his body into the waves, and began to swim, lifting his head above the waves as they came in. The water stung the myriad grazes a boy picks up during the summer holidays but he left the pain behind as he caught up with the ball, hitting it harder this time and racing after it. This was great. He saw the headland that protected the beach and beyond that the open ocean. He wondered had anyone ever swum to America.

Whack.

He would look it up in his father's Guinness Book of Records. *It was five years old but it might be able to tell him. It couldn't be that far. Just over the horizon. That would be great. He could find out what happened to*

Deathlok and the cannibals instead of having to take pot luck in the newsagent's every Saturday.

Whack.

Maybe in the library. The woman there was nice and let him take books from the adult sections. It had started during his nuclear war phase when he told her that there were no survival books for under-twelves. She had laughed so hard her false teeth had been in danger of falling out and he could feel little bits of spit fall on his face. The kids' section was crap anyway. Sean and Maura books. He'd even read ghost stories about the sea from the grown-up shelves. Long-dead sailors coming back to their wives. A German submarine that kept killing its crew. Ships drifting empty with food on the tables. Yeah, you weren't going to get that in the poxy kids' section.

Whack.

And he believed it. Any kid would. How many times had he woken up in an empty house, his parents out, and lain there under the covers too scared to move, listening to the house creaking around him? The sly noises becoming ever louder and bolder until finally he could hear the creak of the bedroom door handle as something awful turned it. Then the sound of the Beetle's engine in the distance. His father shifting down gear at the same spot on the road every time in preparation for the turn up the lane. Lights shining on his bedroom window. He never moved until he heard the key hit the lock. Ten minutes later he was often asleep. Terror forgotten until the next time it happened.

Sooner or later. Yeah, it knew it had time on its side.

Whack.

Another wet smack sent the ball skimming over the tops of the waves. It landed deep in a trough.

He wasn't afraid of the sea, despite the stories. All that seemed very far away at four o'clock in the afternoon of a July day. He thought about the fishermen in the town. Most of them couldn't swim. He'd heard his parents talking about it. When he asked about it they told him that the fishermen thought that if the sea wanted you then that was it. Better not to prolong it.

The waves didn't break out here and the boy enjoyed the feel of them lifting him up.

He wondered if Paul Mahoney had thought of this game. Chasing the ball. Yes that's what it was. Was the tide going out? Yes. It didn't matter, he could still catch it. It was only a few feet away drifting steadily outwards. Look how it was shining. Paul had played this with his brother, hadn't he?

For some reason he couldn't think of his brother's name. His father had bought the ball for them in a little novelty shop by the beach. Making him responsible for it because he was the oldest. Making him write his name on it. Telling them that it was the last ball he was buying for them that summer so they'd just better look after it. Right? Then Michael (that was his name) had hit the ball out into the sea and they'd chased after it. Further and further out until the shore was a yellow streak in the distance and they couldn't see their parents and Michael was crying...

The boy felt a sharp sting on his arm, as a wave passed, and cried out in pain. The top of his arm burned and a brown jellyfish tendril was stuck to him. He brushed water on it to wash it off. A blister was already forming and he could see the jellyfish drifting lazily past him. He kicked out to get away from it. Treading water to get his bearings. The ball was near now and he grabbed hold of it only to feel it slither out of his grip. He tried again, catching hold of it with both hands this time, and rotated his body in the water to go back to the shore. He felt his testicles shrivel up and a sudden need to urinate. He vented into his togs and felt the heat dissipate around him. A comforting human touch. Then the water was cold again. He was in trouble. The shore was a yellow streak in the distance. He couldn't even pick out his parents' car from the others scattered across the yellow. What had happened?

He was nearly past the headland and out into open sea. He held tightly on to the ball and began to kick his legs, propelling himself inwards towards the shore. Panic welled up in him and he thought of crying out in the hope that someone might hear him.

Who?

There was no one near. He was on his own. No one could help him and he knew that he had only a few minutes left to help himself. His legs worked harder. There were hardly any sounds at all out here apart from the sea lapping against him, rising up and down. That awful slow, cold intelligence waiting for him to panic so it could wrap its cool arms around him and claim him as its own. It had tricked him into coming out this far and now it wanted him to go all the way.

Like Paul and Michael.

Part of him knew all this and also knew that the matter had not yet been decided. The work had been disturbed before completion and now the sea waited to see if it had been enough. The water churned behind him as he kicked. He didn't seem to be moving. If the tide took him out would it bring him back in again? How long would that take? He didn't know. He did know that he might die out here and the tide would bring him back in a few days after the mackerel had nibbled his ears and fingers off and carved a hole in his belly. He'd look like Deathlok and they'd stick him in a little box they kept for kids and plant him up there beside granny under a tree.

He wouldn't let that happen. He closed his eyes and concentrated on the rhythm of his kicks. He willed himself to keep his eyes shut while he counted to a hundred and then opened them. He had moved inward judging by the tip of the headland that was now slightly behind him. He was winning. His legs felt like lead but he'd got the boost he needed. The pain faded as he counted the kicks he made towards the shore. That was all that mattered. Kicks and holding on to the ball. In the end he lost count of the kicks and had to start again. It didn't matter, he was going to win. They'd been wrong. The fishermen. It could be beaten.

He passed one of the grown-ups on the way back in. He was still standing there bouncing up and down in the surf. Staring into nothingness. When the boy approached he seemed to shake himself out of his stupor. A man awoken from some unpleasant day-dream. He glared down at the boy. Don't go out there again, he shouted at him. It's dangerous. Where's your parents?

The boy gestured towards the beach, then gave the man a slow deliberate finger. He had swum past this man an age ago and he'd bet that if something had happened the man would never remember seeing him. The man turned and stared back out into the blue. Now he felt sand beneath his feet again. He waded past the men and women playing with their children in the surf. As he crossed the threshold between sea and land he felt the ball squirm under his arm. A woman was helping her child dig a hole in the sand with a plastic spade. Seawater was filling the hole as quickly as she dug. The child was staring at him, mouth open, eyes wide. Suddenly it burst into tears. He ran back towards where the car was parked, tightening his grip on the ball. His parents were still lying there, eyes closed. His mother's face was already pink and shiny. In the back of the car was an old half-filled Fanta bottle. Souvenir of another day out. He picked it up carefully, maintaining his grip on the ball, and went over to the sea wall where he smashed the top of the Fanta bottle against the concrete and used it to puncture the ball. When he was finished he buried the remains beneath the sand.

On the way home the boy sat up in the back and stared out the window. His parents glanced around to talk to him now and again. He could tell they were concerned about his quietness.

Was he all right?

Yes.

Was he hungry?

No.

He just wanted to go home. The whole day had the consistency of a day-dream. He felt that something bad had nearly happened but didn't understand how. It had been close.

A car passed them lights flashing, horn blowing. His father slowed and both cars reversed up to each other on the quiet road. It was a workmate of his father's. They were on their way to the Franciscan monastery for confession.

Had they heard?

No.

Two children had been drowned on the town's beach. The last time their parents saw them they had been playing football. Locals?

No. Tourists.

He didn't know their names.

The boy thought he might but said nothing.

They talked for a while more and then drove on.

The boy thought that he might begin to serve Mass again.

UMPH
HANNAH GRIFFITHS

I met Milly when Rob and I were still in the first fizz of falling in love. She's tiny with a black bob and eyes like shattered glass. Her lips make a little roof when she's thinking and when she's nervous she dabs at her nose. I met her on a Wednesday in a bar near me. It was a work-related matter but we couldn't hold on to the work conversation for long before we slipped over into other, more colourful stuff. She told me that the last time she'd been in this bar, she'd picked up a woman called Talula who had FUCK ME KILL ME tattooed on her sternum. I was surprised because she didn't *look* like a lesbian.

I told her about Rob, how I thought I was falling in love, how I liked that he was artistic – a guitarist in an unsigned indie band – *and* macho, how he drank and that I didn't mind, I wasn't interested in saving him or changing him. I was happy to occupy his sober hours and endure the ups and downs of his drinking because he was authentic and full of stories of life on a tour bus and riffs and strings. All that obsessional music stuff enchanted me. She looked sceptical as she wrung out her hibiscus tea-bag, said she'd never understood women's capacity for self-negation in the face of machismo. I probably made some comment about 'different folks' but felt a bit sorry for her. It had always seemed somehow ... less for a woman to be with a woman.

I told Rob about Milly that night. We'd arranged to meet round his place at midnight. I got there a bit early and let myself in. The place had filled up like a rubbish bin since I was last there and I thought it would be a nice surprise if I gave it the treatment. I picked up all the cans and take-away boxes, the tissue pieces and stray cigarette butts. With ten minutes left before twelve, I gave the carpet a quick once-over with his dust-buster and Pledged the television screen. I was feeling kind of sexy in my new scarlet underwear and my shine-smooth body. I went through to the bedroom and undressed down to the silky bits and pieces and climbed up on to the bed. I lay on top of the duvet, up on my elbows like a sex kitten, and waited for the key in the door.

At twelve-fifteen, I dropped on to my back. My muscles had gone a bit shaky from holding the pose. The flat was icy cold and my nipples had started to hurt inside the flimsy cups. I lifted my legs straight in the air, then lay on my tummy and looked at the spines of the books on his bedside table. I'd never read any Henry Miller or Philip Roth. I considered dipping in but was feeling quite tired. I really fancied a cup of tea but didn't want to get up and have Rob walk in on my filling the kettle in my underwear. No, it would be worth the wait. I got back into position.

Sometime during the next hour and a half I must have drifted off because I was woken by Rob at two o'clock collapsing sideways across me. He grazed my leg with his zip. He was unconscious with drink. I tried to push him off my legs but I had lost my strength in sleep.

'Rob, Rob – are you all right?'

'Umph.'

'Do you like my sexy underwear?'

'Umph.'

'Come on, sweetheart. I'll make you a nice cup of tea.'

I sat up and rolled him over my feet to the end of the bed. As I was getting off the bed, he grabbed my knickers and pulled me towards him. The flimsy elastic snapped and he held up the ripped scarlet shred like a burst balloon.

'Lovely,' he said and put the ball in his mouth. His eyes were shut and I watched him chewing and mumbling, still trussed up in his winter jacket. He was helpless and a bit useless and I wanted him to want me so much. I wrapped a towel around my waist and went to fill the kettle.

Later, sitting up together with our hot drinks, Rob still in his shirt and trousers but under the duvet, I couldn't resist testing the water a bit.

'Rob,' dragging on the 'o'.

'Yeah?' He sounded tired. He put his cup down and turned on his side to face the wall.

'You know tonight, like, when we had um arranged to sort of um hook up at twelve... what goes through your head exactly when you sort of know that you're going to be pretty late?'

'Don't fucking start, baby.'

'No, I'm not having a go... I just wondered whether you're... like... too drunk to remember or you keep meaning to call me but you just don't get round to it or whether you think, she loves me so much she won't mind. I just wonder what goes through your head.'

He turned slowly on to his back and, with a sigh, said, 'Look, Natalie, sweetheart, like I said when I met you, I'm not very good at the day-to-day shit and I will try my hardest but, with the drink, you're never really going to get much of a look-in on those nights.'

He gave me his special little love smile. 'But when I'm here, I'm the fucking best, aren't I?'

I had to admit, I had never met someone quite so interesting. Rob's the sort of guy who acts a bit dumb but, come to pub quiz time, he's your man. He has a huge frame of reference and a great vocabulary.

Now that I'd got him talking, I wanted to clear a few other things up too. 'But, do you think one day it will be like where you say, "Hey, baby, how was your day?" And where we'll make plans for the weekend and meet each other's friends and stuff?'

He shut his eyes.

'Hey, baby, how was your day?' His voice was flat and bored. I wanted to engage him.

'It was good. I met a lesbian called Milly.'

'Oh yeah?' He smiled, a bit dirty.

'Yeah. She's amazing. I think we'll be friends.'

'Well, you know what I think. I don't mind what lesbians get up to, as long as I can watch, heh heh heh.'

We had some very un-lesbian sex and I fell asleep wrapped around Rob's back.

The next time I saw her was round at hers. I'd invited myself to dinner. I wanted to break us out of a necessarily work relationship and establish that we could be friends. I thought about asking her round to mine but, well, I didn't want it to be awkward with Lara, my flatmate. It's not that Lara has any objections to lesbians, she's really open-minded about all of that stuff. It's just that I thought it would be nice to see Milly one-to-one this time. I thought the conversation might get watered down a bit with the three of us all joining in. Milly seemed more than happy to have me anyway. She loves cooking and said it would be a challenge to make something for me.

I didn't tell her about Rob finishing with me when I called her. I didn't want to give her the idea that I was at a loose end or wanted someone new to pour it all out to. I couldn't be bothered to explain how he dumped me in bed on our six-weeks anniversary because I was 'too demanding and too serious about everything'. I had really tried with Rob to keep my big mouth shut each time I felt insecure and needed his reassurance. But sometimes, when you're feeling really low, you need to hear that someone loves you. And Rob would never have said it of his own accord. I thought a bit of prompting would be a good way to solve the problem. I think now that maybe I prodded a bit too much.

Milly's flat is a work of art. When you first walk into the lounge bit, you can't quite work out what you're seeing because there are mirrored sections of wall which reflect back certain corners. It's quite disorientating. The rest of the walls are painted with terracotta chalk-based paint. The kitchen has pots hanging down like a French country house. There are exotic bottles of oil and different kinds of vinegars all along the sideboards. It's the sort of place you wish you'd grown up in.

She had it lit with candles and the smell of a deep, rich dinner made me want to curl up and sleep there for ever. I'd brought some beers. Milly took my leather jacket and hung it on the door.

'That's a lovely top.'

I was wearing my new grey velvet little cardigan thing. The V was deep enough to show a skim of white camisole. Milly was wearing black moleskin jeans and a grey T-shirt. Her hair was still damp and her amethyst drop earrings brought out a purple shine in her eyes. I thought about how many men must try to pick her up and be disappointed when they find out she doesn't do men. I mean, she really is the most exquisite-looking girl you've ever seen. And she smells good too, like blackcurrants.

'You smell nice, like blackcurrants.'

'I'm sure you say that to all the girls,' she said. I think she might have been laughing at me a bit. I couldn't work out whether I'd been inadvertently offensive. Surely you can say that a woman smells nice?

'You sit there and I'll sit here,' she said. There were two sofas facing each other and she'd directed me to sit opposite her. I clutched my beer and, as it had gone a bit quiet, I looked up at the ceiling. She had painted the constellations in white against a navy background.

'Do you like stars then?'

'Yeah, I love stars.'

'What, you're into all that astronomy stuff?'

'Not astronomy, I'm into astrology. In fact, though you'll hate this, I've done your chart.'

Now, I didn't know much about astrology but I knew that doing someone's chart took an awfully long time and that you needed to know quite specific details about time of birth and place of birth and all of that. I had tried to get one done for Rob when I first met him – well, more for me, to see whether the stars had anything to say about our being together. I tried to get the date and time of his birth out of him but he claimed that he was never born, he was the result of a big bang.

'Gosh. Don't you need to know my birthday?'

'I found it out.'

I couldn't stop myself smiling.

'Who the fuck did you ask?'

'I have my sources. Do you fancy another beer?'

She walked across to the fridge. I noticed the little holes in the heels of her wellington boot socks and how, when she opened the fridge, she didn't crouch down to get out my beer; she folded herself in half from the waist, like a gymnast.

'So, what does it say then, my chart?'

'Firstly, tell me how things are with Rob.'

She handed me the beer and went back to her couch, folding her legs up in the lotus position.

'Can I take off my shoes?'

'Sure.'

I undid my laces and slipped off the boots. I wanted to ball up on my sofa like she was. I realized that I had no idea whether she had a girlfriend. I guessed she lived alone but I wasn't sure. What if her girlfriend walked in and found me like this, shoes off, beer in my hand? She might think I was trying to seduce Milly or something.

'Well, Rob kind of dumped me. Isn't that awful?'

Though I had made hundreds of phone calls in the last few weeks to friends, emergency hysteria calls in the middle of the night when I was feeling really shitty and rejected, I just couldn't be bothered to talk about it with Milly. There was something superior about her when it came to men. I mean, she just didn't have any time for them and their ways. I love all that guy stuff, their funny obsessions, the repression, the way they can't talk about their feelings. I grew up on it and I like to think I understand them. But Milly, she just didn't see them in that way. She called them 'unevolved' and screwed her face up when she talked about their obsession with their own genitals. It was as if she could smell that stringy damp smell that stays in men's pants, even though she'd told me the first time we'd met that she'd never even touched one, a penis that is.

'Shit, that's terrible.'

She looked truly upset for me in my state of rejection.

'I can't imagine anyone finishing with you,' she said. 'You're beautiful and sexy and funny and smart and...well, like your chart says, you're going to have a great life. How come he ended it?'

The beer was giving me a little kick, and I touched my face, which was a bit flushed.

'He said I was demanding and too serious.'

'Same old shit then. And were you? Demanding? I can't imagine you being demanding. You're so...open and warm. And I could never imagine you being too serious.' Her head was tipped to the side as if she were considering my serious-capacity. And then she looked at me and her glassy eyes softened a little. 'I just see you as trying to do too much for other people and not letting anyone take care of you.'

It felt like someone had switched the central heating on inside my cardigan, Milly's gentle voice whispering my pain. She really is a very sweet girl with a golden heart. There's nothing strident or aggressive about her. I tried to imagine the sort of girl she went for – probably one of those butch diesel dykes who would crush little Milly in her muscled-up arms and carry her over her head to the bedroom. Where was the bedroom? I didn't notice any other doorways when I came in.

'Well,' Milly said, getting up from the sofa and heading for the oven, 'if you were my girlfriend, I would make you sleep for a week and feed you soup in bed.'

Aren't women lovely? Milly hardly knew me and she had already identified my vulnerable spots and understood just what I needed to hear. And she is a bloody good cook too. She had made meatballs in tomato sauce, just like in those Mafia films. She served it on her crooked wooden table with what she called 'leaves' but we would call salad. I had another beer and she sipped her second glass of wine. I noticed her pretty little hands making patterns in the air as she talked. The wine brought out two pink patches on her cheekbones.

I had seconds and another beer before we moved back into the lounge. This time, she sat on the end of my sofa. I think she was more comfortable with me now that we had talked more. And we had really talked. She wanted to know all about me and I loved filling her in – my parents, school, how I'd got my first job, what I felt about relationships, my favourite bands. I'd managed to ask her a little about herself. She is thirty-one, a couple of years older than me, and was born in Hampshire. She studied history and got a first from Cambridge.

She turned to face me on the sofa. We were facing each other with our feet up in front of us. It felt like when you're in the bath with your lover. Her little legs stretched out and my legs were in a Y.

'Have you got a girlfriend at the moment?' I asked, taking another glug of beer.

I had just imagined the key in the door and Gertrude or whoever finding us like that on the sofa.

'Yeah, I'm seeing someone.'

'Oh.'

I finished my beer. The room needed some music now.

'Shall we listen to some music?'

'Sure.'

Milly, once again demonstrating her suppleness, bent backwards over the arm of the sofa to reach her CD pile. Her T-shirt rode up a little. She had one of those belly-buttons that I'd always fantasized about having – shallow and tight-fitting in her drum-skin tummy. She managed to get the disc in and playing from that position and then sat up with a grin. Patti Smith's *Horses*.

'So, where is she tonight?' I asked.

'Who? Fia? She's at her aromatherapy class.'

One of those lesbians, all holistic and earnest. I couldn't imagine cool-chick Milly with someone earnest.

'Yeah, we're having a bit of a rough patch.' She picked at some fluff on her T-shirt. 'I think the x-factor is missing. I haven't wanted to have sex with her for ages.'

Now, I've always had a bit of a problem with the whole terminology of lesbian sex. I mean, sex to me is very definitely about penetration. It all seems quite nebulous with women. I mean, it's all orifice, isn't it? Like a jigsaw with no stick-outy bits. So when she said 'sex', I wondered whether she was referring to an actual penetrative act or the general area of bedroom activity. I considered clearing it up once and for all by asking her but I didn't want to sound ignorant. If I asked the question 'What exactly do you do in bed?' I'd sound like a Conservative politician. So I just nodded, trying to look knowing.

'Ah yes, the crucial x-factor. If that's missing, then I think people very quickly become just friends.'

'Yeah.'

Milly was staring at me, those lilac eyes. I started picking the label off my bottle of beer and concentrated on the task. I felt her foot pressing against my thigh. Her toes were wriggling inside those woolly socks.

'I don't know how to do this with you,' she said and my insides went all hot. 'I don't know whether you want me to.'

The beer was making liquid out of all my thoughts. I shut my eyes. I knew that if I spoke, I would be responsible for what happened next. I heard Milly manoeuvring in front of me and then felt her cold hair on my cheek.

'Look at me,' she said. 'What do you want?'

'Umph.'

I was silenced with her first kiss. Her lips were soft and her tongue pushed my mouth open. My body was held in a clench and all I could think was 'This is a woman, this is a woman, I'm kissing a woman.' And though the kisses were good and deep, I knew that soon we would start doing other things. What if I screamed when she touched me? I decided not to leave anything else to chance. I took control of the situation and flipped her on to her back so that I was on top of her. She gave a little kitten moan and smiled. I knew what I had to do next. I peeled up her T-shirt. She was wearing a black see-through bra. I didn't know where to begin but couldn't put off the inevitable any longer. I pulled down the cups of her bra and took one breast in each hand. She gave another little mew, so I knew I must be doing something right. Though a part of me was screaming 'Put on the brakes – you're feeling a girl's tits!' a greater part of me was caught up in the excitement of a new experience. With the pioneering spirit in mind, I bent over and sucked Milly's nipple (my right, her left). This went down very well, so I sucked a bit harder until my mouth was filled with breast like unbaked dough. It was great to be able to give so much pleasure to someone so easily, but now all I could think about was that she would expect me to start exploring down below. That seemed like a whole other universe.

Milly took my head in her hands and brought it up to her face. I took the opportunity to stock up on oxygen.

'I can't believe you have never been with a woman before,' she whispered, all breathy.

The situation seemed to be running ahead of me and, as she took my hand and led me out of the lounge, I allowed myself to be led by her fervour. We went downstairs and into her bedroom, which was dark except for the light from outside. The bed was high, with wrought-iron ends and white bedlinen, but there was no other furniture.

'Nat, I've thought about doing this with you since that first time I met you,' she said as she undid my cardigan. We were still standing up as I pulled her T-shirt over her head. She kissed me, flicking her tongue over my teeth and undid the button on my jeans.

'Lie down on the bed,' she whispered, and I did just what she told me. She pulled my jeans over my feet then wriggled up the bed until she was crouched over me. She pulled up my camisole and stared at my breasts.

'Oh God,' she whispered. 'They're beautiful.'

She started sucking my right nipple. I couldn't put it off any longer. I undid the button on her jeans. Her mouth was right by my ear and I could hear her breaths catching in her throat, faster and faster. I rammed my hand down the front of her jeans without bothering to slip them off, in case I wanted to bail out quickly. I felt the crunchy hair and kept going. It was difficult to get much of an angle inside the jeans waistband, so I stretched my fingers out then, with the middle one, broke in. Milly shrieked a little – with delight. I carried on pushing inside her. It was a strange feeling, like trying to reach for a lost earring down a plughole. It was all ... hole, all nothing. All I could think about was that diagram in third-form biology, shaped like ET's head with two ovary eyes and that long neck.

Her whole body was bucking like a big rabbit. She wriggled out of her trousers and shouted, 'Go down on me, go down on me, please!'

Now, I was having a good time and was aroused by Milly's sucking my breasts, but I couldn't imagine my face down there between her legs. I just didn't like the idea of it, all that wet on my face.

'I think it's a bit soon for that, Milly. Don't you like doing this?'

'I do but I want more.' She knelt up over me and pulled my knickers off. She put her thumb inside me, pulled it out, stuck it in her mouth and said, 'I want to taste you.'

I couldn't really say no after already refusing her first request.

'All right then,' I told her and she moved down between my thighs.

It was good, really nice.

Afterwards, Milly snuggled up under my neck, turning her face up to mine occasionally to give me little kisses. I was tired but jerky with all the new sensations. I needed to be in my own bed. Milly was settling into sleepy deep breathing and I didn't want to have to wake her later, so I decided to make a move right away.

'Milly – I'm going to head off now,' I said into her hair.

'Oh no.' Milly leaned up on her elbow. She made her mouth into a little kiss shape and spoke with a baby voice. 'Pleeeeeze don't go, Nat. I want to wake up with you tomorrow. Please stay with me.'

I felt hot and twitchy. I sat up and started to put on my clothes.

'Milly, it's not that I don't want that. I just have loads to do in the morning and I have to check my messages and stuff. I never sleep well in someone else's bed.' I stood up but she wrapped her arms around my legs.

'Well, I'm not going to let you go.' She pulled my trousers back down and kissed my bum. I pulled away but she clung on.

'Milly! Please!' I had to wrench her hands from my leg and almost push her on to the bed. 'Take it easy.'

Milly pulled her knees up and looked at me from under her fringe. I felt like a bear above her tiny bunny body.

'Why are you being so mean to me?' she said, still in that helium squeak. 'I only want to cuddle.'

I was tired and the air around my head started pressing on my ears. It was as if the walls were closing in and Milly was the walls. I didn't want to cuddle or even touch her. All I could think of was the last tube, which would be leaving soon, and how this conversation, if allowed to develop, could take us into the early hours. I needed to split.

'Please, Milly, let's talk about it tomorrow. OK?'

She reached for her last card, the physical appeal, and leaned back on the bed, propped up on her elbows like a sex kitten.

'Don't you...want me, Nat?' She dropped her head down so that she was looking at me through her fringe. I gulped to try to find some oxygen in the vacuum of her room and then I turned, grabbed the door handle, raced up the stairs to get my jacket then down and out the front door.

Outside the night was cold like a drink of water and I felt lighter, released. I had escaped, unscathed. Result.

NOT THAT FUNNY
GABRIEL BROWN

Have you met those kind of people that don't say *fried* breakfast, they say *fry* breakfast? If they exist, those kind of people, if I haven't just made them up. If they did exist they'd be fucking annoying. And some people say *proven* like it rhymes with *drove* with an *n*, albeit they're doing it to be annoying, my friend Tom is, he only does it because he knows it's annoying, and he's the only person I know who does it. And you wouldn't have thought that mushroom in foreign would be *mushroomo*, would you, that's just stupid. But it is, I know because I heard some people in Safeways saying it. It just goes to show something or other. And those people that call them *user cars*, not *used cars*, when that's clearly what they are. Anyone, but *anyone*, can see that. And this bloke in Luton Airport going *But there again* instead of *then again* when he obviously knew that's what it was. Why do they do that, those kind of people? They're like many other people out there, they're *trying* to annoy me, and they're succeeding.

But if *they* annoy me, how much more annoying am I? *Nightmare!* I murmured, the toast burned. But it wasn't a nightmare, just a bit of burnt toast. People are constantly lying their fucking heads off, especially me. And sometimes when I cough it's like a horse whinnying, but that's only because I exaggerate to make it sound like that. But I do have a bad cough, sometimes. And when I sneeze I make it deliberately noisy and squeaky. But I live on my own, so it's only me that's annoyed. Fucking annoyed.

And Safeways' storemanager, he's worked his way up to short

white sleeves, he's whistling, just about fair enough, he's whistling that tune *Duh-duh-doo-dee-duh-di-dah-doo-dah-doo-dah*, only he's gone on to add another stanza, *Da-ah-dah-dah-dah-duh-duh-du-uh*, barely pausing between the end of the first and the start of the second *as though they're the same tune*. That really pisses me off. It'd be OK, I wouldn't mind his musical liberties, if I didn't reckon he thought that was the *right* tune, like 'Yankee Doodle' or something, a *proper* tune, not one he'd made up. It was the way he did it, something to do with his certainty. It's true it takes a certain person to be a whistler; but an improviser, you'd expect them to be more cautious, tentative. Only storemanager, call him Brian, or Enoch, he had the certainty borne of plain wrongness. He'd got it wrong and he thought it was right. That fuck.

And this woman going to me *Could you just watch my basket, I've just got to get some eggs?* Like, I had to think about that, there was all manner of ramifications about which to think, but she just repeated it, like I hadn't understood, placing particular emphasis on *the eggs* that she claimed she had to get. But that was one of the first ramifications: why have you told me what you've got to go and get, as though that's going to affect my decision on whether or not I'll watch your basket, like certain products might be ruled out, say luxury goods, or non-consumables? And the other questions were like what do you mean, *watch your basket*, it's not *yours*, that's the whole point of checkouts, of money, of shops, of property, of theft, that's how it all works. No, her question was surely *Could you safeguard my place in the queue, as personified by this basket of produce that I have gathered, whilst I boost off to do more gathering?* Fair enough in the normal run of things, exactly the kind of thing that *I* do. And if she had asked that, my answer would have been no. Fuck you! I'm not defending a questionable queuing codicil on behalf of a woman who's neither pretty nor speaks posh.

How annoying is that? Me. I wouldn't do the simplest thing. I sort of looked at her, stunned, *Your basket?* and she was already moving off, confident that I'd do it. But I never. But I didn't *not* do it either. Filipina or something sort of half-joined the queue, sort of half-acknowledging the basket-representative, half-challenging it, whilst I moved down the checkout, into space vacated, half-inviting the

encroacher, but at the same time I looked back, and perhaps down at the basket, arguably half-bespeaking my proxy duties. And when eggwoman came back, which was sort of at the same time, in the half-argument which ensued...
— *I was in the queue.*
— *You? In queue?*
...she appealed to me and I like half-betrayed her, I didn't say anything, and I turned away, so she never thanked me, but just my presence, she seemed to invoke that in itself as supporting evidence. *I was in the queue. Look!* That's not *that* annoying, or that funny, just slightly. Like most things.

THE BEAUTIFUL SPACE
JASON GOULD

I lost both my parents and my grandparents at an age when I was barely conscious of which was which, of who in their quartet should have been protecting whom. It was almost as though God had decided to take the piss out of somebody, and I – hardly toilet-trained – had drawn the shortest straw.

As a result I became gradually bereaved as I grew older and older, as I saw in other people's lives what was missing from mine. There was no shock on the actual day of their deaths, no abrupt tears or tantrums; just the beginning of a space that it took me three decades properly to appreciate.

For tax purposes I am registered as a photographer, but prefer to see my output as more of an artistic calling than a profession, and the money I earn merely a means of pursuing my art. I grew up in and around Reading, and was a particularly weak child, having been hospitalized with pneumonia at the age of three. I still feel that my poor health was the reason why I remained friendless throughout my schooldays, and why it took me until twenty-four to lose my virginity. A lad called Rob Davis was the only one I ever truly made friends with at school. Like me, he didn't partake in team games or plays but messed about with electronics and model cars instead. It was Rob who first got me interested in photography. One afternoon in his parents' bedroom he showed me some holiday snaps that his father had taken; two or three featured his mother half-naked, and by the look in her eyes half-drunk as well. I was intrigued more by the sun breaking the horizon than the woman pressing her breasts together and grinning lasciviously in the foreground. And since that day you could say I've been obsessed by owning pictures of people.

During the final few weeks of what had once been a sound relationship with a woman I'd met through my work, I inherited a studio in Naples. The harsh truth is that though Salvatore considered himself a professional, he was no more than an enthusiastic amateur, an impressionable playboy who latched on to a fresh crowd each year. The image of European photography attracted him more than a desire to present reality in new and insightful ways; the parties and the sex and the lines of cocaine did their utmost to decimate his bank accounts and trouble his health. He was only thirty-five when he died from a heart attack in Berlin. I flew over for the funeral but because of bad weather arrived too late.

Even now I'm not sure why Salvatore bequeathed me his studio. I can only surmise it had something to do with a trip to Amsterdam we organized in the early 1980s. Kissing on the bed in his hotel room, the porno channel on low and the curtains flung wide to let in the neon, his tongue had tasted of the Cantonese food and the sake we'd smuggled through reception and up to his suite. I remember how the lights had filled the room from the sex shows outside, how they'd written XXX and EXTREM across my chest as I'd taken his cock to the back of my mouth and guided my own into his.

The studio looked out over the Bay of Naples, and had at some point in its history served as the storeroom for a bakery. The floor was ingrained with flour, and if I worked barefoot, as I often did, it would whiten my soles and cause them to slide across the boards as I moved.

Inside, apart from the free-standing lamps, some backdrop sheets and a lockable darkroom, there was little to break the atmosphere of emptiness. An adjacent chamber contained my bed, one or two works of fiction, my reference books, a stove and a cooler. Having the place virtually devoid of furniture was preferable to having it cluttered. It seemed purer that way; manufactured objects always remind me of forgeries and I find it impossible to inject authenticity into my work if my life is polluted by them.

Next to my sleeping area was a tiny bathroom that had hot water only on alternate days. During the summer, insects would climb from the drains and into the sink through the plumbing, dragging with them a strange-coloured ash.

In the eastern wall an arch-shaped window opened out on to a wrought-iron balcony. I could stand up there for hours watching Germans taking snapshots of Vesuvius, nine- and ten-year-old boys riding scooters with no helmets, and the occasional naked infant wrapped in a carpet and begging change from the tourists and fish scraps from the fishermen.

I was on the balcony eating olives out of a newspaper when I spotted my first ever mourner. In a part of the world as hot and fast as Naples I'd never expected to confront any sadness. Maybe I expected it to spill over from the literature and the art, which, though prevalent in the imagery of death, seemed to me more symbolic than real, its skulls and shrouds and preoccupation with dances more thematic than particular.

From my vantage point I could see her sitting on a cane chair, next to the ornamental gardens that separated the flats from the water. She was dressed in black, and appeared to be in her forties. Her hair was gathered up beneath a hat, and a veil, suspended from the brim down as far as her lower lip, distorted her view of the living. In her hands she held an overcoat, folded and arranged neatly on her lap. She stroked it unerringly, paying extra attention to the lapels and the collar and the pink interior lining. Passers-by lengthened their stride when they noticed her; a few women crossed themselves.

I went downstairs, walked outside and pulled up a chair. She edged away. I made a comment in the Italian I'd picked up from Salvatore over the years; a simple remark concerning the murders on Capri that had been splashed over the papers for weeks. She stood up to leave. As she rose I smelt something familiar; it reminded me of when, between foster homes, I'd spent two weeks in an orphanage and an older boy called Carl had forced me to eat a rotten peach he'd had stashed in a cupboard since the beginning of summer.

I asked her to stay. She glanced at me, her eyes bagged, and in that look I saw how her life had been hoodwinked by hope, how she'd been betrayed by everything, perhaps – worst of all – sleep, that universal of cures.

'He always wore this,' she said, as if I could only share her company if I was privy to her past.

'Really?' I said. 'Memories?'

She nodded. I should have felt uncomfortable but didn't. I'd been waiting for such an opportunity for some time.

'Tell me,' I said, 'do you have photographs of him?'

'Yes,' she replied cautiously. 'Why?'

'These pictures,' I went on, trying to sound blasé, 'are they posed for?'

'I don't understand,' she said. 'I think I will take a walk.'

'No, please.' I touched her arm to stop her. 'What I mean is, in these photographs is he smiling at the camera? Were they taken at a party, or on holiday? In a situation when he was overly aware of the camera and so deliberately posing?'

She thought for a moment, then nodded.

'I can help,' I said. 'I own the photographic studio up there.' I twisted round and pointed. 'I can give you photographs of your husband. New ones. Ones that are natural and uncontrived, free from the torment of memory. You won't look at these pictures and remember how you walked home from that party, discussing the wine or the cabaret or your friend's new mistress. You won't see these pictures and recall how on the fifth day of the holiday you'd argued over the pretty blonde in the bar, but then, later that night, made love on your hotel veranda.'

She mumbled something in the Neapolitan dialect that I couldn't translate, then repeated, 'I don't understand.'

'I'm saying I can give you photographs of your husband.'

'How?'

'Quite easily. Come to my studio tomorrow and I'll show you. You'll need to bring a selection of his clothes, and that – ' I indicated the coat she was now holding close to her chest ' – and the last photograph you have of him.'

I don't think she really knew what to make of this odd proposal. But she surprised me by turning up as agreed, and in return I performed the session free of charge, presenting all forty-eight treatments in a specially prepared album. When she flicked through them she didn't cry or quickly grab her mouth; instead, her brow smoothed, her shoulders lost their weight and sagged naturally, and despite my protest she gave me a wad of crumpled lire, and insisted I took it.

*

After that first session they flocked to my apartment. Word must have been fast and complimentary, for within the week they were queuing outside my door, streaming down the staircase and out on to the pavement, their arms overflowing with clothes.

Some wandered there straight from funerals, mud on their shoes and their fingers, hymns and prayers on their lips. Others came after years of keeping black and white photographs in cupboards for the dead, a candle burning either side of the frame.

They asked me to bring back their mothers and their fathers, their spouses and their lovers, their pets, their sweethearts, their murdered children. They carried bundles of skirts and jackets and trousers and jewellery up to my apartment, fell to their knees and begged me in barely understandable Italian to make the fabrics walk, the rosaries click…

In the early days I was unable to offer facial shots and had to position the mannequins with their features obscured, perhaps huddled in slumber or masked by a streak of orange as they gazed over the bay at sunset. In its way this only highlighted the realness of those sets, the nonchalance. But with time, and under the steady yet feisty tuition of a retired actor who still dabbled in the art of make-up, I came to master the craft of greasepaint and clay. If requested I would go to a potter's shop owned by a friend of his in Sorrento, and the whole thing would take anything up to a month to organize. The results, however, were astounding. I remember one man, no more than an adolescent really, whose father had died from a stroke while out boating with his brother. When I passed him his pictures he went deathly quiet and walked away without so much as a word. A fortnight later I learned from a waitress in a café that he'd tried to kill himself the following day in church. For weeks after, this news saddened me, not by the thought of what his despair had compelled him to do, but by his lack of success.

Generally, though, they went away smiling. And for a while I was happy, dressing dust.

Until I met Julee.

Perhaps slightly nervous of doing what I was in a predominantly Catholic country, I made sure to rest my camera on Sundays. In lieu of work I would rise late and eat breakfast in one of the street cafés famous for their bitumen-like coffee and dust-coated tables, then spend the remainder of the day in the gardens listening to headscarved old women tell stories about sex and death and bodily functions.

It was a Sunday when Julee approached me. Her body blocked out the sun and I glanced up from my week-old broadsheet expecting to be offered a pamphlet on Pompeii or a ride in a motorboat.

My instinct was to search my pockets for change, nudged by her ragged appearance. The clothes she had on were streaked with dirt and bleached of colour; her dress trailed on the concrete, its hem eroded. Her hair – thin and brown and held in place by a pair of metallic clips – was combed so her scalp showed through, bits of which had begun to flake. Her face had in it no bitterness or gloom; it had perhaps been stripped of every emotion, having exhausted them all – I was soon to learn – over the past few years.

'You're pale,' she told me in perfect English. Her accent would have been sultry had the circumstances been pleasant; the way she reverted to her native tongue when confused only added to the attraction.

'Sorry?'

'You are pale,' she repeated, 'much paler than I expected. When I was a child in Milan there was a doctor. He, like you, played resurrection. But he was different. He breathed life into the corpses of dogs and cats. When he pushed his fingers down their throats and tickled their hearts back to life his skin would glow: God shining, my grandmother said.'

'And I am pale?' I said with a bemused laugh.

'Paler than he was,' she replied. 'But that's good.'

I put my cup on the table and folded my paper. My first reaction was to dismiss her as an eccentric, but something – perhaps whatever weighed down every muscle in her face, especially those around her eyes – persuaded me not to.

'I'm a photographer,' I said, 'not a medicine man. I don't perform resurrections.'

'You help people see the dead, don't you?'

'I suppose so...'

'Then you resurrect.'

'What's your name?' I asked, picking up and finishing my drink.

'Julee.'

'And what do you want from me?'

She rummaged in the pocket of her dress and produced a picture. Holding it carefully between two quick-bitten fingertips, she turned the subject to my field of vision. I leaned forward to take it but she snatched it from my grasp, instructing me just to look.

The man in the photograph was young and athletic. He had long hair and was sitting on a barge, his feet up on a barrel and a copy of Kerouac's *On the Road* open on his lap. He'd looked up, smiled and lifted the cover of the book for the photographer.

'I can do a session for your husband – '

'He's not my husband,' she interrupted. 'We are lovers. It is better that way, like – ' she clicked her fingers and muttered in Italian ' – romantic, like a journey across the ocean.'

I didn't follow her, but said, 'You need to bring your lover's clothes, and more pictures of him. Do you know where my studio is?'

She nodded absently, as if everyone knew where my studio was.

'Come tomorrow night.'

'Thank you.'

'Your lover's name?' I asked.

'Pieter,' she said, and began to walk briskly away. She hadn't progressed more than a few yards, however, when she stopped and spun and returned to my table. 'I will pay you well,' she promised.

'There's no charge. Just a nominal fee for equipment and film – '

'I will pay you,' she said.

'There's really no need – '

'I will,' she insisted. 'I *must*.'

She turned again and this time made it past the old men playing cards in their vests at the corner of the street.

I dozed, and on waking couldn't work out whether Julee had been dreamed.

The next day Julee and her deceased partner lurked like guilt on the periphery of my thoughts. She'd somehow seemed different from my other clients, forthright and commanding whereas they were often hesitant, often embarrassed by their grief, by what they were asking me to do.

Whatever it was, it drew my focus away from the tableau in progress, that of a dead teenager, photographed through a door crack and sitting on a window-seat, strumming chords on a precious Les Paul. I tried to click off a few reels so the effort wouldn't be wasted, but the verve wasn't there. Not wanting to produce substandard work, I put the doll in the corner and covered it with a blanket, flicked off the lights and waited for Julee.

Just before eight I went downstairs and lit the torches on either side of the main entrance. Modern lighting also lined the thoroughfare but the torches were traditional, and – so the concierge explained to me every time I neglected to light them – the responsibility of whoever was in residence.

'Good evening,' she said as I reached up to blow the embers of the second. Her silhouette flickered on the alabaster beside me. She looked shorter and her arms were laden with bags.

'Hello,' I said, turning round. Though the light was poor and the street increasingly shadowed, I could see tiredness in her face, more concentrated than the day before.

I showed her into the hallway and we started up the stairs.

'Why at night?' she asked as we climbed.

'I prefer to shoot in the day, so I tend to greet new clients in the evening.'

'Why don't you shoot at night?' she asked.

'I don't know. I suppose ghosts look more convincing in daytime.'

'They're not ghosts,' she said.

'True. People think they are though.'

I stopped on the landing and waited for her to catch up. She wasn't as scruffy as she'd been at the café; her hair was combed to cover the parts where it had thinned, and she'd applied lipstick and eyeliner and a dash of perfume.

'Are you sure you want to do this?' I asked.

'Yes.'

'It's just, sometimes, people find it a little ... distressing.'

'It will be good for me, like a – ' she searched her vocabulary ' – tonic?'

'Yes,' I said, nodding, 'like a tonic ... '

I led her into the studio, switched on the lights and offered her a seat. She dropped the bag of clothes and perched on the lip of a stool.

'OK,' I said, 'while you're here I'll arrange a style for you to approve. I'll need those photographs to work from so I can slot together a mannequin that matches Pieter's height and weight and so on. Then I'll dress it. You can wait in the next room while I do that – ' I signalled to the antechamber ' – and if it's passable, if it resembles him, I'll do the shoot tomorrow, and you can collect the photos the day after.'

'No,' she said, shaking her head. 'Take the pictures tonight. I can't come back tomorrow.'

'You don't have to. Once you've OKed it you needn't do anything else.'

Again she shook her head, more vehemently now. 'I can only be here tonight. How can you photograph me if I'm not here?'

'I don't follow.'

'I want to be in the pictures too, with Pieter.'

'I can't do that.'

'You must,' she said.

'But...why?'

'Because I want his skin to rub against mine. I want to feel his breath in my nostrils and hear his heart in my ears.'

'But – '

'Please...' she said.

'All right,' I agreed, shrugging. 'We'll do it all tonight.'

'Good,' she said, and began unbuttoning her blouse.

By the time I woke the next day the sun was half-eaten by the horizon, and far bloodier than the one I'd seen rise that morning as I'd waved goodbye to Julee. I got up, washed and dressed, and boiled a pan of water. With two cups of coffee inside me, I went to the darkroom and began work on the hundreds of photographs she'd persuaded me to take the night before.

In the dark I watched both him and her become whole; her naked, he fully clothed to retain a semblance of the person she cherished.

I'd used up every reel of film I had, but still she'd complained that it wouldn't be enough, still she'd wanted more. I developed in batches of fifty, and although a lot were identical I kept them for her anyway.

Perhaps the most awkward aspect of the session had been Julee's absolute lack of direction. I'd wished, as I'd moved around the makeshift bed watching her feign passion for the lens, that a spark of life could have twitched in his fingers, that they could've flexed and cracked and gone to work on her hips, her shoulders and her breasts. If by a quirk or stitch of anatomy it had been possible for them to have made love, it would've been far easier to photograph, and much more rewarding. But because of Pieter's clumsy limbs all they could do was hug loosely, put their dry, passionless mouths together and hope it looked better than it felt.

It was all tokenistic. The notion was everything, the act itself meaningless.

I completed the set by dawn. Julee dressed silently and quickly, checking her watch every thirty seconds. She thanked me, scribbled her address on a scrap of paper, kissed Pieter on the cheek and rushed downstairs.

Realizing she wanted her pictures delivered, I opened the door to the balcony and stepped out into the brightness. I shouted down and told her I would take them round as soon as I could. She waved in agreement before hurrying away, almost twisting her ankle in her haste. I stood there until she'd rounded the corner out of sight. When she had, I went back inside and dismantled her lover, then lay on my bed and waited for sleep.

Dejected women were reeling their washing in over my head as I set off for Julee's, shoebox under my arm. It was seven at night and already the scratched and narrow doorways of the pensions were more than foreboding. I walked part of the way parallel with the beach, but was eventually forced to branch off and ascend the slope into which the greater part of Naples is carved.

Julee lived in a dangerous part of the city. About five years ago it was popular among Camorra-run prostitutes; transsexuals mainly, caught up in the wave of cross-gender fanaticism that was surging over Europe. In an uncharacteristic crackdown, the motive for which is still hazy, the Polizia had swept through the district collecting anything that loitered. Since then the rumours concerning unprovoked Camorra killings had tripled, in both volume and inventiveness. Bearing this in mind, and also the fact that I'd been fortunate to have escaped a visit from them for so long

– considering how much attention I'd generated – I moved as fast as I could, and didn't turn when I heard scuffling in one of the alleyways behind me.

The address she'd given me was one of the cheap apartment blocks used to house large families with little or no income. Playing on the front steps amid the debris of a dismantled Kawasaki were two toddlers, their hands covered in grease.

I stood across the road and tried to guess which window was hers. As I peered up, someone tipped the contents of a pot off one of the balconies. On another, a man in a Rolling Stones T-shirt was eating a roll of salami, his face fat and tired, his family quarrelling in the background.

The building's main door opened and I ducked into the alcove of a shop. I'm uncertain why I hid. I felt awkward, the same as when I'd woken up beside Salvatore with an uncharacteristic tang of salt in my mouth.

Julee stepped over the threshold and trotted down the cobblestone street, away from where I was secreted. I let her gain a good fifty yards before following. Although my premise for tailing her was to give her the photographs, I was also intrigued to find out what – or who – enticed her so hastily.

She maintained a healthy pace, boasting a worthy knowledge of the town I still found it so easy to lose myself in. She was confident in her stride; but then, I presumed, she'd lived in Naples most of her life. And in her current state of mind, I don't believe she was shocked or worried by the city's brutality. Had she been plucked from the street, robbed and fucked and dumped at dawn, I don't think she would've been surprised, or all that bothered.

After a fifteen-minute journey she stopped in a locale I'd never visited. It was a square, around which lads on scooters – two and three to a machine – raced. At a table outside a wine bar a gigolo was trying to charm a bored-looking girl of about seventeen; two of the waiters were watching him through the window. She glanced up as Julee strode past, and as I followed, seconds later, I heard him mention something about France and orchids.

At the rear of the square was a church, set behind a row of disconnected fountains. It was old and, like the San Gennaro cathedral, Gothic in origin. Above the door, through which Julee had vanished, was one of those incredibly sanguinary crucifixions. There was none of the metaphor that I'd witnessed elsewhere in Italian art: the sugary blood, thick on his hands and feet and forehead; the limp, bare genitalia; the calm face forever trying to die...

Was it here then, to this almost medieval place, that she ran for comfort? How could she one night make love to a plastic doll and the next kneel before Christ and pray?

Clearly she was in greater distress than I'd thought. This wasn't just a few photographs that I carried with me tonight, snapshots to be wept over on Sunday evening and forgotten by the following dawn. These would be what her life revolved around: they would hear anecdotes from her dreams as she stretched in the morning, reports of her day when she got in from work; they would counsel her decisions and allay her fears; they would help her through the days and the weeks and the months. They would be everything to her. But perhaps most of all, she and they would watch friends' relationships flounder and fracture, and swear on their souls that they would never fall foul of a similar fate, never split.

I knew it was speculation but I knew it was true. And I knew it would never be enough. Not for her.

I waited for Julee to emerge from the church, and when she did – after about ten minutes – she dashed across the square more quickly than when she'd arrived. I was too far off to see if her visit had been beneficial, if it had lifted some of that weight from her features.

She was so anxious to return home, she jogged most of the way. I followed her again, merging with anything large enough to conceal my identity should she glance over her shoulder.

About half-way through the journey was a hole in the road, the result of some Byzantine excavations dug by the University of Rome. As we passed it I loosened my grip on the box and let it slide quietly and peacefully into the earth.

Back on Julee's street I waited a couple of minutes before going into the building and taking the stairs up to the flat number she'd given me. Standing in the corridor, I realized I had no real reason to visit her; I'd thrown away the one thing that linked her life with mine. Nevertheless, I still knocked on the hand-painted number 19, and still accepted when she stepped aside to welcome me in.

'Did you bring them?' she asked before we'd reached the main room, turning as she walked, her palm outstretched.

'No. There's a problem with development. It'll take a day or two to fix.'

Her face, which in the gloom of the hallway seemed to have lightened – perhaps at my presence – reacquired its former load. I didn't look at her, but around the lounge we'd entered.

The furniture, most notably the television, the radio and the red and amber lava lamp bubbling slowly by the window, had about it something of the 1970s. On my right a door opened out on to the unlit accoutrements of a kitchen, and on my left was another, coloured purple and closed. Pinned above a record player was a poster of two women wearing nothing but transparent underwear to advertise an album by Roxy Music, and leaned against the wall beneath them was a boxed set by Yes. Hanging from a hook was a baseball cap, bearing the Coca-Cola trademark; stuck to its brim was a badge showing two fingers held up in a peace sign, a stars and stripes flag grafted over their skin.

'So when can I have them?' she said.

I crumpled my mouth as if perplexed by the offending chemistry. 'Tomorrow, with luck. The day after at the latest.'

'We had a deal,' she said. 'You don't get paid until I've got them.'

'I told you from the start, I don't want paying.'

'I thought you would. Didn't you find what we did a little...unsavoury?'

'Perhaps...'

I crossed to the window and looked down at a young couple strolling by. His hand was resting against the small of her back, stroking the waistband of her miniskirt.

'You're...in a bad way, Julee,' I said. 'I've seen lots of people who, while being like you, manage...somehow...to handle their loss. You can get...What I mean is, there are people – experienced people – who might be able to help – '

'Did I ask you to judge me?' she asked.

'No – '

'Then don't. If I'd wanted psychiatric help I would've gone to a hospital. If I'd wanted shit about grief, I'd have gone to a priest. All I want – ' she coughed huskiness from her throat ' – all I want is something to remember him by.'

'A memento?'

'Yes.'

'Nothing more?'

'No.'

'What about last night?' I said. 'You wanted more last night; a lot more than a memento.'

After considering this a second, she said, 'Maybe. But is it any wonder? All he does is lie there; lie and watch the sun and moon go round and round...'

I turned from the window and faced her. 'You mean he's alive?'

'Just.'

'But I thought he was dead...'

'No,' she said. 'If I were to leave he would probably die.'

'Why didn't you say – '

A soft thump came from behind the purple door. Ignoring me, Julee rushed over, turned the handle and went inside.

Though the temperature that day had topped ninety the bedroom was artificially heated. Through the entrance I could see three electric fires, one either side of the bed and one at the foot, each trailing its wires across the floor into sockets that were hanging off the wall. A basket, also at the foot of the bed, was filled with empty medicine bottles and soiled cotton wool balls; thrown on top of the rubbish were two or three paperbacks, their pages crinkled as if they'd been dropped in water then dried in the sun. Once the door had been open ten or twenty seconds a hint of human waste came to me and I switched to breathing through my mouth.

She retrieved the pillow from the floor, lifted his head with one hand and with the other patted the cushion into place. She reached under his sheets and checked something, then, satisfied, tucked them and the blankets back in. As she went to the sink to fill a glass I caught a glimpse of his face. It had the dirty whiteness of slush and was heavily bearded. She leaned over him to help him take water. After he'd drunk she put the glass on a bedside table, combed his hair out of his eyes and left, gently clicking the door closed behind her.

'He usually lifts a hand to greet me,' she said, 'or follows me with his eyes. But not tonight. It's because I've been out. He's been the same since I spent so much time at your studio.'

'You lied,' I said.
'No, I didn't.'
'You said he was dead.'
'You assumed him to be.'
'Because you wanted photos…'
'You don't understand…' she said, shaking her head.
'Understand what?'

She didn't answer immediately but sat on the couch, lit a cigarette and started flicking aimlessly through a copy of *Oggi*. After a few intense drags, she said, 'Pieter is English. He added the "i" to his name in the 1960s to annoy his parents; it was the type of thing you did. There used to be this guy in Hyde Park who'd do portraits of you for nothing. He did one of us. It was very accurate. We didn't ask him to paint it but he offered, insisted even. We sat there on the grass over four hours while he worked, taking breaks when it rained. I still have it. When I look at it now I see how much I've come to resemble my mother. But Pieter…'

'What's wrong with him?' I asked so she wouldn't have to finish.
'Does it matter? Does it make any difference whether it's cancer or AIDS or heart disease?'
'Is he in pain?'
'Yes.'
'Has he long…?'
'Yes.'
'Is there nothing – '
'No.'
'Surely there must be – '

I was interrupted by a muffled syllable from the bedroom. Again, Julee stepped towards Pieter's door.

'I'd better go,' I said.
'My photos?'
'I'll make some copies as soon as I get back. You can have them and the negatives tomorrow.'
'Thanks,' she said. 'I'd like to book another session.'
'Ah… not at the moment. I'm going to take a break. I might give it up altogether actually…'
'Why?'
I shrugged and said, 'It feels wrong, imitating people who are – ' I

glanced at Pieter's door ' – he looks so, I don't know, so different from how I'd expected…'

'Do you not make enough money out of it?'

'You know very well I don't do it for that.'

She moved towards me, and up close I was again reminded of how pretty she'd once been. 'If you don't do it for the money,' she said, staring at me intently, 'why do you do it?'

'No reason.'

'There has to be.'

I shrugged again, as if it was all so casual. 'I do it to help people in need, to help them get over their losses.'

'Your Christian duty…' she said, raising her eyebrows cynically.

'If you like.'

'I think there's more,' she pressed.

'And I think it's none of your business,' I said, moving towards the exit.

'Quite right,' she replied from behind me. 'Just like my grief should be none of yours…'

I stopped before reaching the door, aware of her eyes on my back. I'd never met anyone like Julee. She was so naked; simply by glancing at her in the street you could tell how all the emotions that most of us are lucky enough to elude for the best part of our lives had for her become a kind of normality. And if I'm honest I suppose I was a bit jealous that I'd never known such extremism myself, and in all probability wouldn't.

I turned back to her. 'If you must know,' I said, 'my parents died when I was young.'

'I'm sorry.'

'No need. I wasn't old enough to notice.'

'How old were you?' she asked.

'Three,' I said matter-of-factly, 'and two months.'

'And you never got over it?'

'There wasn't anything to get over,' I explained. 'I only know about it from hearsay, from newspaper clippings and suchlike.'

'What happened?'

'Nothing spectacular. They just died. That's all.'

'Can I ask when?'

'February 1967.'

'I don't want to pry,' she said, her face apologetic, 'but may I ask how?'

'I...'

'Forget I asked – ' She lifted her hands in contrition.

'No, it's OK,' I assured her, 'it's been a few years since I told anyone. It just feels a little weird.'

'I'm the same with Pieter,' she admitted. 'I tell people he's left me for another woman.'

'Really?' I said, then, hoping her attention had drifted back to her lover, quickly added, 'My parents and grandparents were driving into Reading one night when they had an accident.'

'Oh – '

'It was two in the morning,' I continued before she could ask questions, 'and five miles after the Newbury turn-off an articulated lorry jack-knifed in front of them. The police report said the driver had been driving without a break for three days. My father's car got trapped beneath the lorry's trailer – between the front and rear wheels – and was dragged a quarter of a mile before both vehicles veered from the road, down an embankment and into a field. By the time the emergency services arrived there were no survivors. The lorry had been destined for a chain of gift shops and tourism outlets in central London; the pictures in the papers the next day showed the field littered with birthday and Christmas cards, mugs painted with horoscopes lying in the frost, empty photograph frames floating in a ditch...'

Julee looked confused and I assumed it to be a combination of sorrow and disgust. 'Pieter had a friend who crashed on the way home from a party,' she said as though competing, 'but he'd been drinking.'

'They hadn't been to a party,' I replied, 'they'd received a call earlier on reporting that someone they knew had only a 60–40 chance of making it through the night, so they were on their way to Reading General Hospital.'

'And did they?'

'Did they what?'

'Make it through the night.'

'Yes,' I said. 'Oh yes.'

She reached up and touched my face, so soft, so unlike how I'd imagined her to feel. After a lengthy silence she asked, 'Why don't you bring them back?'

'I could. I've a garage in England filled with their clothes. But...'

'But what?'

'But...I won't.'

'Why?'

'Because I don't miss them.'

'Please – '

She was interrupted again by Pieter. I recognized the word as her name, breathed rather than spoken.

'Please don't go,' she said. 'We can talk...'

She opened the bedroom door and went inside, this time shutting it straight away.

I lingered a second then let myself out, went downstairs and into the street. I didn't want to talk any more and would post her the photographs so we wouldn't have the chance. It was only a matter of time before she realized that meeting me had done her more harm than good, that to have compared our lives any further would have been tantamount to gloating.

Across the road the boy and girl I'd seen from her flat were kissing in a doorway. She had her back to me, and I could see he'd lifted her skirt and slipped his hands beneath the silk of her knickers. Before starting home I looked up at Julee's window to see if she'd noticed the couple. Thankfully there was no silhouette, just the room turning slowly from amber to red, then back to amber, then back to red.

To Rosalia

FISHY TALES
FRED NORMANDALE

As a boy I grew up among some wonderful characters. I thought this was a normal background, that everyone lived in a world such as mine. I couldn't have been more wrong, it was unique.

My father was a fisherman working on a coble, fishing from Scarborough, a small fishing town in the middle of the Yorkshire coast. I loved the harbour, spending every possible minute on the piers or on board the many boats which plied their trade either catching fish or taking trippers around the bay on small motor or rowing craft.

From an early age I knew all the fishermen and was known to everyone. To some it must have seemed a rough environment for a small boy, but from my vantage point I was surrounded by big men with even bigger hearts. The sense of humour, which I hope I've inherited, could be found in the most serious situations.

Old Walter was talking to Harry. They'd stopped for a chat and a cigarette at the top of the slipway from which they operated their boats, taking tourists for trips around the bay. Walter had a rowing boat which was licensed to carry seven passengers. It was called *Unexpected*, which I thought was an appropriate name. Harry operated a motor boat equally appropriately called *Happy Days*.

As I passed by, bag of sweets in hand, Harry shouted in my direction, 'Hey, young Nommy, can you sing?'

I was confused. 'I can sing a bit but not very well,' I replied hesitantly.

'Well, if you can sing, go an' get in my boat.'

I was even more confused, then looked down to where his boat was berthed at the bottom of the slipway. It was full of lots of other kids. There must have been fifteen or sixteen of them and I knew them all.

'We'll jus' get a few more an' we'll be off,' he said as the situation dawned on my confused face. 'But ya' not coming if ya' can't sing.'

'I can sing,' I hurriedly assured him and rushed down the slipway to join the unruly mob in the *Happy Days*. The bag of sweets was snatched from my hand and quickly distributed as I piled into the throng.

The boat, which was licensed to carry eight passengers, eventually had twenty or more youngsters on board. We were singing 'I Love to Go a-Wandering' at the tops of our voices, drowning out the noise of the engine. At the stern, holding the steering tiller, stood Harry with a grin from ear to ear as he pointed the boat down the harbour towards the entrance.

'Louder,' he was shouting. 'Louder, I can't hear you.'

The harbour was ringing with the sound and many people stopped their work to watch the *Happy Days* on her first cruise of the year.

When the passenger trade was quiet, Harry fished with a few pots for crab and lobster to supplement his income.

One day he was hauling his pots, close to the pier wall, when a body appeared, floating alongside his boat.

He dragged the dead man into the boat, then propped him at the stern. He placed an arm over the steering tiller and a sou'wester on the head, then continued to haul his pots.

Fishermen passing by, leaving or returning to the harbour, thought he'd acquired some assistance for the day. He relaid his pots, then headed back to port.

After steering his boat slowly through the harbour mouth he walked for'ard, leaving the dead body slumped at the tiller.

Turning to the corpse, he was heard to shout, 'If you can't steer any straighter than that, don't bother coming tomorrow.'

Before the advent of radar and modern navigation systems, fishermen were able to return to the position in which they had left their gear by time and compass bearing.

For example, steering north by east for twenty-five minutes or east south-east for twenty minutes.

Alf didn't have a timepiece. If he had owned one, it wouldn't have helped much, as he couldn't tell the time.

He was a chain-smoker, each new cigarette being lit from the previous one.

As the coble men returned from sea to the harbour after laying out their lines, one skipper would say, 'We went north-east by east, half an hour.'

Another would say, 'East by north twenty minutes.'

Alf would say, 'Due east three and a half cigs.'

Sadly, he died quite young of lung cancer.

The cliffs along the Yorkshire coast are spectacular. Many thousands of visitors are attracted to the rugged beauty, rocky shores and caves. Gannets, puffins and guillemots breed in abundance on the sheer cliffs.

George and Robert fished from a coble, working close inshore, under the cliffs, fishing for crab and lobster.

One day, while hauling their pots, they heard a shout from the shore. On investigating, they found a man trapped by the incoming tide. He was stranded thirty feet up the cliff face with no way up or down.

They manoeuvred their boat as close to the cliff as possible, then instructed the man to jump into the sea so they could pick him up from the water. Being a non-swimmer and afraid of the rocks below, the fellow refused this offer.

It was impossible for a helicopter to fly close to the cliff face and the lifeboat would be unable to get any closer than they could in their small boat. How were they to get him down?

George picked up a coil of light rope. Weighting one end with a small shackle, he then threw it to the stranded man.

'Tie the rope around your waist,' he shouted up to the unsuspecting man, who quickly followed the orders.

George tied the other end to a strong point on the coble, then yelled to his brother, 'Head out to sea at full speed.'

His brother promptly followed these directions and the poor unfortunate victim was plucked, screaming, with arms and legs flying from the cliff face into the sea. He was then hauled, spluttering, unceremoniously into the boat.

It is not recorded how he expressed his thanks for his rescue.

Soon after I left school I was shipped up by Bob on board the *Success*. My other shipmate was Terry.

Trawling, one fresh breezy day, in the company of several other vessels, we hauled our trawl to discover there was a very heavy object in it. With the aid of the winch and the lifting mast in the centre of the vessel, we were able to swing our unwanted catch inboard.

Just how unwanted it was became very apparent on releasing the catch on to the deck. Surrounded by fish, seaweed and shells was a large, circular, threatening mine.

Bob, the skipper, radioed to the other vessels in the area informing them of our predicament, only to see them disappear over the horizon at a rate of knots previously unrecorded by fishing vessels. We were on our own.

It's fairly easy, even in poor weather, to lift heavy objects on to the deck of a trawler. The design and layout are perfect for lifting anything inboard. Getting the same object outboard again is very difficult. Gravity cannot be reversed. Nevertheless, somehow we had to eject this unwanted catch back into the sea and we had to dump it where it could not be caught again.

It was decided to drop it close inshore on rocky ground where it was impossible to trawl. Bob set the course and as we steamed slowly to the west he instructed Terry to go below to rustle up some bacon sandwiches and a pot of tea.

Hanging over the boat's side were the large steel trawl boards which keep the net open on the sea-bed. As the boat was rolling quite heavily, these boards were frequently banging on the boat's side.

After steaming for about fifteen minutes, Bob looked down the cabin hatch to see why his sandwich had not arrived. He saw Terry, frying pan in hand, holding it over the stove. Each time the trawl boards clanged on the boat's side our cook jumped, as did the bacon in the pan. Hardly surprising with a thousand pounds of high explosives just above his head.

Eventually we arrived at the designated dumping ground, then debated the best way of jettisoning our unwanted cargo. It was decided to fasten a rope around it, then, with a wire hawser through the pulley wheel on the top of the lifting pole leading to the winch, we would be able to lift the thing off the deck. It would still be in the centre of the vessel, but so far, so good.

Terry was appointed winch man. When the rope was in place he passed three turns of the wire round the winch capstan then heaved. The mine was lifted from the pitching deck and immediately began to swing to and fro with the rolling of the boat. It is impossible for two men to prevent a thousand-pound object from obeying the law of gravity and it was at this point that panic set in.

I suggested that rather than stop it swinging, if we were to encourage it by pushing, it would eventually swing out over the boat's side. Above the noise of knocking knees and rumbling bowels, Bob shouted to Terry, 'Next time it swings to starboard, throw off the wire. The momentum will take it clear of the boat's side.'

Something must have been lost in the communication of this message, for instead of totally releasing the wire at the end of the swing, Terry lowered it down about six feet. Here was our unexploded bomb, having reached the peak of its projection now hurtling back at our boat's side.

It's true, all your life does flash before your eyes. I was just wishing I'd been more considerate to my fellow men when – CRUMP! – the mine hit the boat's side with a mighty crack, then crumpled into several pieces which fell harmlessly into the sea. No bang, no agony, ten fingers, two arms, two legs, everything normal. It was a dud. Could we have been this lucky?

There was plenty of time to doubt the parentage of our trusty cook while steaming back to the fishing grounds.

Eventually I too became a skipper. My boat was the *Courage*. She was more than twenty years old but in good condition. Billy and Bluey were my crew.

'Haul oh! Hauling time, come on, my lovely lads, let's have you out.' We had been dragging the trawl for over three hours and it was time to haul it up. I was shouting down the cabin hatchway to wake the two crew sleeping below.

Billy, an experienced hand, tumbled from his bunk, sat on the seat locker, then proceeded to roll a cigarette. There was no movement from the other bunk. 'Come on, Bluey, it's hauling time,' Billy called to the inert teenager opposite. The call went unheeded.

He finished his smoke then proceeded to make two mugs of coffee from the ever simmering kettle. 'Come on, Bluey, show a leg, it's hauling time.' Nothing stirred. He sipped his coffee, growing more exasperated. This happened all the time. 'Come on, you idle sod, get out of ya' pit,' he bawled. Nothing happened.

His eyes lit on the wooden shutters at each end of Bluey's bunk and inspiration struck him. 'I know how to get the little bugger out.'

He picked up an old newspaper from the table, separated the sheets, then crumpled them into a ball. Picking up his cigarette lighter, he set light to the bottom of the ball, waiting until it was blazing. He threw the burning ball into his shipmate's bunk, shutting the shutters, then holding them closed.

There was a delay of about three seconds then a thumping, kicking and clamouring unlike anything he had ever heard. Billy released the shutters and Bluey shot from the bunk through a cloud of smoke, like a genie from a bottle. He was coughing, spluttering and swearing.

Ever after, if Bluey wouldn't get out of his bed it only took the rustle of a newspaper from Billy to raise an immediate response.

We were having a gruelling trip. From sailing, the three of us had toiled more than forty-eight hours and, with the exception of coffee breaks and a few sandwiches, it had been non-stop. We were on fish. Trawl up, trawl down, gut, wash, box and ice fish, coffee, trawl up, then repeat the process. It was relentless but we were on fish and on pay. We had found an area abundant with cod.

We were trawling close to a huge shoal of herring on which the cod was feeding. A prohibition order on fishing for herring had been introduced that very week and the fleet of factory trawlers fishing the herring with small mesh nets had all left the area.

Despite this, here again was the Fisheries Patrol Vessel in close proximity. The crew were preparing to send their inflatable dinghy with a boarding party to measure our nets and to check our catch, the third time since we had sailed. It was becoming annoying.

We were tired, busy, and we were being hassled. We were not fishing for herring. Our mesh size was too large to catch them. There was not a single herring on board our vessel, yet here was the Navy about to inspect once more.

Billy, speaking through the side of his mouth so that he would not be observed by the officer of the watch, whispered, 'Stand by the scupper door, Bluey, an' when I give you the nod, open it.' (The scupper door is a small sliding door in the side of the boat which enables excess water, offal and debris from the trawl to be jettisoned overboard. We had a large quantity of it on the deck.)

Billy put the hosepipe among this heap and it soon began to slop from side to side with the rolling of the boat.

The inflatable with its unsuspecting crew pulled along our port side just as our vessel rolled to port. 'Now!' he hissed through clenched teeth.

The results exceeded his wildest dreams. Looking over to port for the first time, he saw the inflatable with its deflated crew. It was brim-full with seaweed, starfish, sea urchins, fish guts and lots and lots of water.

'Oh dear!' he said with mock surprise. 'We never saw you there, we never expected to see you back again. Sorry.'

We fished undisturbed for the remainder of the trip.

On the following trip, during the night, Billy and Bluey were standing on the deck gutting fish when a searchlight stabbed out of the dark, lighting up the entire vessel, resembling a stage spotlight in a theatre.

The unlit Fisheries Patrol vessel had crept up alongside the *Courage* unnoticed. I should have detected it on the radar but had failed to. As if rehearsed, my two oilskin-clad crewmen dropped the fish which they were handling, linked arms and began a chorus line of high kicking in the glare singing, 'There's no business like show business.'

It can't have been the response the Navy was expecting, for the light promptly went out again and the vessel steamed off into the night.

The *Courage* had been sold and Billy had now become skipper of his own boat. I'd recently taken delivery of the *Independence*, a new boat almost sixty feet in length, requiring a crew of five to operate it.

Our children, Paula and Danny, were growing up. Danny was six and a half and wanted to go to sea on a fishing trip with his dad. Having had an early introduction to the sea myself, I could see nothing wrong with this, but I would wait for the finest of weather forecasts before taking him.

His mother remained tight-lipped and noncommittal but his grandmother was outraged. 'That bairn is far too young to go to sea yet.'

I remained unmoved and one fine Saturday in August I informed Danny that he was sailing at midnight. He didn't sleep that night and was quickly dressed when I called him at eleven-thirty.

We walked hand in hand down the cobblestone street to the harbour. In my other hand I had a clean pillowcase containing two or three books and a change of clothes. In his, a rolled-up sleeping bag stuffed with sweets and crayons. There was not a breath of wind and the stars shone brightly.

We sailed out from the harbour, rounded the lighthouse, then headed out north-east on a sea which was so smooth that it appeared to be glass. I suggested that he should turn in and get some sleep until we arrived at the fishing grounds, some three or four hours distant. He would have none of it and was going to stay in the wheel-house to keep me company. Ten minutes later he was asleep under the chart table. It was eight o'clock in the morning when he stirred.

We had reached the fishing grounds, streamed the trawl, towed it along the sea-bed for four hours and were about to haul it up.

He looked out of the wheel-house window and then at me, perplexed. Instead of the bright summer day and miles of sea in all directions which he'd expected, he saw only fog. It was a thick peasouper and we had been enveloped in it since daylight.

The trawl was hauled up and the bag of fish lifted inboard. Danny was amazed as the wriggling mass dropped on to the deck, half a ton of fish, tails kicking and flapping.

The trawl was quickly lowered to the sea-bed again, a process which was repeated several times until late evening. Danny spent the entire day going back and forth from the deck to the wheel-house, getting in everyone's way and, when not eating, asking unanswerable questions or wanting to play games, as six-year-olds do.

By this time he was exhausted and didn't complain when I took him below, pulled off his wellington boots, then tucked him into the back of my bunk. 'That's the last we'll see of him until tomorrow,' I thought, somewhat relieved.

We continued fishing, the fog got thicker and the atmosphere more and more heavy. It was oppressive; something was going to happen. It did, just before midnight. The heavens opened and rain of monsoon proportions fell from the sky. Huge forks of lightning pierced the night, lighting it up as though daylight. Thunder rolled overhead. It was indeed a storm to remember.

I would be lying if I said we were not all a little apprehensive. Lightning was stabbing the sea all around us and we were the only target in the area above sea level.

A little voice behind me said, 'What's happening, Dad?'

My first thought was to say, 'Go back below, Danny, it's very scary up here,' but an inner voice said, 'He'll be more frightened down in the cabin on his own,' and I heard myself saying, 'Come up here and watch this, it's really exciting. Every time the lightning flashes, it lights up the whole sky.'

He spent the next two hours, eyes like saucers, exclaiming things like 'Wow!' or 'That was a good one, Dad.' I enthused as best I could.

The storm abated and as we had caught a reasonable amount of fish during the twenty-four hours and we were not far from home, I decided to take the catch back for Monday's market and to take Danny home.

Arriving in port early next morning, we left the crew to unload the catch, walking back up the hill together, once more hand in hand. Unfortunately, we had to pass my mother's house on the way up. I held my breath and tried to tiptoe past. It was no use. She saw us passing and was out in an instant.

'You should have more sense than to take that poor bairn to sea in a storm like that,' she ranted. The verbal battering stopped as Mother paused for breath, then, feeling a tug at her skirt, she looked down to see two saucer-like eyes looking up at her and I heard the unforgettable words, 'But Grandma, it was brilliant, every time the lightning flashed it lit up the whole night sky.'

By the time Danny was ten years old he was spending most of his school holidays at sea on board the *Independence* and he had gained his sea legs.

One early evening we were trawling on a favourite piece of ground when an unusual mark appeared on the echo sounder screen. I was sure we were going to catch a big haul of cod.

After plotting our exact position for future reference, I called the crew from the cabin and after a quick pot of coffee we began to haul the trawl. First the 120 fathoms of thick wire cable to the otter boards. These were quickly disconnected. We then hauled in the thirty fathoms of chain and wire bridles to the mouth of the trawl.

All fish have a swim bladder inside them which acts as a depth regulator. When fish are pulled to the surface quickly, the air in this bladder expands and the fish then become buoyant. If there is any quantity of fish in the net, it floats to the surface.

All eyes looked to starboard as the net was heaved alongside. There was a mass of foam, the water boiled and the entire trawl burst to the surface. Bonanza! Realizing just how much fish there was in the net, my immediate thought was, 'Don't burst, please don't burst.' It didn't. The air inside the fish was quickly expelled with the crush and the net rapidly sank again. We now had tons of dead weight hanging down over the starboard side.

The cod end has a rope strop around it so that, on encountering large hauls, it is possible to lift the catch on board in small amounts of approximately one ton each lift.

We lifted the first bag inboard then emptied it, then repeated this manoeuvre twice more, marginally lightening the strain on the net. The decks were filling up and the crew were throwing cod for'ard and aft, making room for more to be lifted on board.

I felt someone tap on my back and little voice said, 'That's a good catch, Dad.'

'I don't think we've got half of it on board yet, Danny,' I hurriedly replied. Another four bags were lifted in and we again stopped to redistribute the deck-load of fish. There were still fish in the net to be brought on board.

'It's a good haul, isn't it, Dad?'

'Yes, Danny, it sure is.'

There was cod stacked as far for'ard and aft as we could get them. It was now possible to haul the remaining fish on board. The boat was full from stem to stern with cod.

It had grown dark by this time. We had been hauling fish on board for three hours. Now it all had to be gutted, washed, boxed and iced. First we streamed the trawl overboard again, more to gain some deck space than to catch more fish. A quick pot of coffee and then the laborious gutting began.

Danny, who by this time was getting a little tired, was led to the wheel-house, then sat in the watchkeeper's chair. The automatic pilot would steer the boat but someone had to keep pressing the cancel button, stopping the autopilot alarm bell ringing. This bell rings at five-minute intervals to ensure the watchkeeper remains awake.

I was now free to help with the work on deck. I could still keep a lookout for other vessels and would pop into the wheel-house every twenty minutes or so to check our position.

By two a.m. we were making inroads into the huge catch and had cleared some deck space. Danny was now very tired and asking to be relieved of his position. With the tremendous workload still ahead this was not possible, but he perked up a little when given a can of Coke and a packet of biscuits.

We stopped only briefly for coffee and the deck space grew as more and more fish were cleaned then dropped below to be iced and boxed.

By five a.m. poor Danny was a little tearful and although now wrapped in his sleeping bag, he was still sat in the wheel-house chair. How could I cheer him up and keep him interested?

'You can have a little sleep if you want.' His eyes lit up. 'As long as you keep pressing the button,' I added. His face fell again. 'You are on pay, you know.' The smile came back.

'Am I, Dad, really?' That clinched it. Although he was shattered, he managed to keep going until we dropped the last few fish below.

He crawled into his bunk about eight a.m. and didn't get out again until eight a.m. on the following day.

We landed a bumper catch that morning and it was a very different Danny who ran home to show his mum the wage packet with his name on it and ten crisp one-pound notes inside.

Time has moved on again. I'm shore-based now. Most of the old hands have pulled in their cod ends and gone to the great fishing grounds in the sky. Bluey is one of the top skippers in the port. Danny has been skipper of his own boat for some time.

Regulations and bureaucracy have taken much of the freedom from this unique way of life. A new generation of characters are now to be found around the port. The humour and mischief still abound and on quiet mornings, if you listen very carefully, you can faintly hear a boat-load of kids singing 'I Love to Go a-Wandering'.

THE GIFT
LOUISE DOUGHTY

There are many pictures. Pictures live easily in her head – but words need lips and oxygen. Being voiceless at thirteen is no great shame but by her age it becomes a little childish. By twenty-three one should have spilt the beans. The pictures? Well, there is the stab, the blue surprising eyes, the bite, the choke, the tube and the discussion way way up above her head. The small white coat, the scarf she fiddled with. The look. The card. The Black Hand gang, the way she did it. Pain.

Words are another thing. They creep out retrospectively, like mist. They keck from her in moments. She spills a drunken confidence or, more, it spills itself. In a dim room there are a friend and a gas fire late at night. They twist the stems of glasses in their fingers. She leans forward and the friend tells of the night a murmuring uncle slipped in through the door. (Her body is quite still. Her eyes are milky.) In return she tells her, well, the first for me, it was November...It becomes a social detail, a current event. They laugh. They think it would sell newspapers perhaps. They think if we can speak, well, that is something. If one can say it, like good morning, it must be similarly dull.

Hiding behind gestures, they are simple. They think of telling as a healing process but it is a pleasurable phenomenon: a slow evening and a tune and medium wine and while we are at it, a catharsis, after the second yawn.

The friend leaves. It is dark and she feels whorish. Her inner self should be a little more select.

She was select with the man they sent her to when they became confused. He stood as she went in and shook her hand. She thought him short, behind his desk, but then she was tall for her age. Outside the cold air tap-tapped at the window and the room was bright with knowledge. Do sit down. The tape recorder was concealed. She sat and he began. She watched him as he spoke and thought how fat his fingers were. How desperately interested he seemed. At that time she was bitter and thought he was a liar like the rest. His questions made her smile; the weather, school, homework and home, then, out of the blue – were you trying to kill yourself?

No.

Are you going to do it again?

I don't know.

Thinking her simple answers might be disappointing, she began to fiddle with her scarf, as if she was on edge. As soon as she had noticed it she stopped. When there was a lull, a pause, she started it again. Later she felt guilty about teasing him. He told her mother she was bright – an attempt at flattery and quite successful too. He wore an indiscreet white coat, embarrassing the parents, probably, but inducing none the less a certain pride. It was confirmation. There *is* something wrong. It's not just her. Perhaps she isn't quite mad after all.

They never travelled anywhere, the short psychiatrist and her. After three months of weather talk she was handed back, certified adolescent. It was an anticlimax to all concerned.

One thing he never asked her: why?

She asked it, in the hospital as the orderly gripped her arm and the sister waved the rubber tube. Why? By then she knew she was not going to die. Retribution she could understand but not to this extent. They seemed so bored with the task. They turned her on her side so deftly. They opened her mouth. She did not help them. The tube slid down her throat and she gagged and choked and could not breathe. She thought, a symbol. First that thing at that end and now this tube at this. Perhaps the two will meet inside and I will be skewered. (Or perhaps she didn't. Perhaps she was too young. Maybe it was a subconscious image.) Then there was the pain, the gluten clinging round her neck, the stickiness in her hair. There was the blood pouring from her nose, the stomach lining plummeting from her mouth: the retching on and on, and vomit pinked by the violence of the deed. There was her insides heaving upwards hard enough to wrench her head up from her shoulders, nerves and all. Tiny tiny stars exploded in her brain and her throat gagged so hard she thought it might give way. Her whole body jerked in rhythm — ah, another image. (I am being fancy here, bear with me.) She became that pain.

It was almost worth it for the feeling of release as it slid out of her. It was over, for the second it would take for them to realize she was there. Then there was the lifting up and the chastisement and the knowledge that the punishment had only just begun. You have sinned, my girl, and we are going to make sure you know it.

Guilt. Now there's an interesting thing. She didn't feel guilty as he laid his coat on the pine needles and leaves. It was lined and soft, although she wished the weather was warmer. She was curious, but so ignorant despite her smile that she didn't even know what she was curious about. There is something pleasant about that sort of slavery. One can fool oneself. The responsibility for the distance between her knees was his. There were the usual preliminaries. She was kissed. A hard hand performed the necessary exploration, loosened her. Then there was the weight of him between her thighs. She felt a rush of fear. His face tensed and suddenly there came a pain so surprising, so unlocated, that she opened her mouth and let out a shriek. Her face shot upwards, teeth clashing against his nose. He pulled back and out.

She was embarrassed, wanted to apologize. He said nothing; got up, did up. She began to do the same, with a confused feeling that whatever it had been, it had not been a success. It was only then that she noticed the stream of livid red down her white thigh, almost to her knee-high socks. She cried, God...

When are you due?

Next week.

You've come on early.

He gave her his hanky to put in between. She felt faint, but grateful. When they got back she flushed it down the lavatory and they went to their history lesson; the assassination of Franz Ferdinand and the Serbo-Croatian crisis. When he asked who knew the exact date she raised her hand and was disappointed when he chose her friend to answer. When his wife gave birth she signed the card along with all the others. *Wishing you much joy and a little sleep.*

For a while the secret was a thing to hug, a baby of her own. She was a pioneer. She was proud – until the novelty wore off. Then she looked around and saw the silence. She thought there would be words in deeds, perhaps, but she was wrong. There was the rubber tube and small white coat and choking and reproachful looks. A black life. Deafness all around.

On cold nights round a gas fire, she has something now. She serves it like a delicacy. She speaks in mouthfuls. As the evening slips towards the confidence a secret wrapped in tissue paper is unfolded. Words trip lucidly from adult lips and fill the space between them, on the carpet where they sprawl, unfallen. Here is the gift that I bestow. Here is a sign that you have touched me and I am fond. Be fond in return or pity me at least. I need your kindness for an hour or two. You may take it with you when you leave. In return I will restrict my generosity. I will say nothing of the rest. I will not tell you that in every single union there is pain, in every kiss a choking. Nothing so close to melodrama (dears). Such shouting would be selfish. You would be chained and so would I, too much for anyone. I'll buy a pet, I think, and feed it fruit and grow old with my tongue cut out.

She can count those who know on the fingers of one hand. She has this fantasy that when she needs her toes she will be free. She does not fight it now, although she has. We all must be obsessed. Her burden is herself. She can't complain. Some are obsessed with cars or mortgage rates.

I have much to be grateful for.

LOOKING FOR JAKE
CHINA MIÉVILLE

I don't know how I lost you. I remember there was that long time of searching for you, frantic and sick-making... I was almost ecstatic with anxiety. And then I found you, so that was all right. Only I lost you again. And I can't make out how it happened.

I'm sitting out here on the flat roof you must remember, looking out over this dangerous city. There is, you remember, a dull view from my roof. There are no parks to break up the urban monotony, no towers worth a damn. Just an endless, featureless cross-hatching of brick and concrete, a drab chaos of interlacing backstreets stretching out interminably behind my house. I was disappointed when I first moved here, I didn't see what I had in that view. Not until Bonfire Night.

I just caught a buffet of cold air and the sound of wet cloth in the wind. I saw nothing, of course, but I know that an early riser flew right past me. I can see dusk welling up behind the gas towers.

That night, November the fifth, I climbed up and watched the cheap fireworks roar up all around me. They burst at the level of my eyes and I traced their routes in reverse to mark all the tiny gardens and balconies from which they flew. There was no way I could keep track, there were just too many. So I sat up there in the midst of all that red and gold splendour and gawped in awe. That washed-out grey city I had ignored for days spewed out all that power, that sheer beautiful energy.

I was seduced then. I never forgot that display, I was never again fooled by the quiescence of the backstreets I saw from my bedroom window. They were dangerous. They remain dangerous.

But of course it's a different kind of dangerous now. Everything's changed. I floundered, I found you, I lost you again, and I'm stuck above these pavements with no one to help me.

I can hear hissing and gentle gibbering on the wind. They're roosting close by, and with the creeping dark they're stirring, and waking.

You never came round enough. There was I with my new flat above the betting shops and cheap hardware stores and grocers of Kilburn High Road. It was cheap and lively. I was a pig in shit. I was happy as Larry. I ate at the local Indian and went to work and self-consciously patronized the poky little independent bookshop, despite its pathetic stock. And we spoke on the phone and you even came by, a few times. Which was always excellent.

I know I never came to you. You lived in fucking Barnet. I'm only human.

What were you up to, anyway? How could I be so close to someone, love someone so much and know so little about their life? You wafted into north-west London with your plastic bags, vague about where you'd been, vague about where you were going, who you were seeing, what you were up to. I still don't know how you had the money to indulge your tastes for books and music. I still don't understand what happened with you and that woman Theo you had that fucked-up affair with.

I always liked how little our love-lives impacted on our relationship. We would spend the day playing arcade games and shooting the shit about x or y film, or comic, or album, or book, and only as an afterthought as you gathered yourself to go, we'd mention the heartache we were suffering, or the blissed-out perfection of our new lovers.

But I had you on tap. We might not speak for weeks but one phone call was all it would ever need.

That won't work now. I don't dare touch my phone any more. For a long time there was no dialling tone, only irregular bursts of static, as if my phone were scanning for signals. Or as if it were jamming them.

The last time I picked up the receiver something whispered to me down the wires, asked me a question in a reverential tone, in a language I did not understand, all sibilants and dentals. I put the phone down carefully and have not lifted it since.

So I learned to see the view from my roof in the garish glow of fireworks, to hold it in the awe it deserved. That view is gone now. It's changed. It has the same topography, it's point for point the same as it ever was, but it's been hollowed out and filled with something new. Those dark thoroughfares are no less beautiful, but everything has changed.

The angle of my window, the height of my roof, hid the tarmac and paving stones from me. I saw the tops of houses and walls and rubble and skips, but I couldn't see ground level; I never saw a single human being walk those streets. And that lifeless panorama I saw *brimmed* with potential energy. The roads might be thronging, there might be a street party or a traffic accident or a riot just out of my sight. It was a very full emptiness I had learned to see, on Bonfire Night, a very charged desolation.

That charge has changed polarity. The desolation remains. Now I can see no one because no one is there. The roads are not thronging, and there are no street parties out there at all, nor could there ever be again.

Sometimes, of course, those streets must snap into sharp focus as a figure strides down them, determined and nervous, as I myself stride down Kilburn High Road when I leave the house. And usually the figure will be lucky, and reach the deserted supermarket without incident, and find food and leave and get home again, as I have been lucky.

Sometimes, though, they will fall through a fault line in the pavement and disappear with a despairing wail, and the street will be empty. Sometimes they will smell something enticing from a cosy-looking house, trip eager into the open front door and be gone. Sometimes they will pass through glimmering filaments that dangle from the dirty trees, and they will be reeled in.

I imagine some of these things. I don't know how people are

disappeared, in these strange days, but hundreds of thousands, millions of souls have gone. London's main streets, like the high road I can see from the front of my house, contain only a few anxious figures – a drunk, maybe, a lost-looking policeman listening to the gibberish from his radio, someone sitting nude in a doorway – everyone avoiding everyone else's eyes.

The backstreets are almost deserted.

What's it like where you are, Jake? Are you still out there in Barnet? Is it full? Has there been a rush to the suburbs?

I doubt it's as dangerous as Kilburn.

Nowhere's as dangerous as Kilburn.

I've found myself living in the Badlands.

This is where it's all at, this is the centre. Only a few stupid shits like me live here now, and we are disappearing one by one. I have not seen the corduroy man for days, and the glowering youth who camped down in the bakery is no longer there.

We shouldn't stay here. We have, after all, been warned.

Kill. Burn.

Why do I stay? I could make my way in reasonable safety southwards, towards the centre. I've done it before, I know what to do. Travel at midday, clutch my *A–Z* like a talisman. I swear it protects me. It's become my grimoire. It would take an hour or so to walk to Marble Arch, and it's a main road all the way. Those are reasonable odds.

I've done it before, walked down Maida Vale, over the canal, full these days of obscure detritus. Past the tower on the Edgware Road with the exoskeleton of red girders that jut into the sky twenty feet above the flat roof. I have heard something padding and snorting in the confines of that high prison, caught a glimpse of glistening muscle and slick fur shaking the metal in agitation.

I think the things that flap drop food into the cage from above.

But get past that and I'm home free, on to Oxford Street, where most of London now lives. I was last there a month ago, and they'd done a decent job of it. Several shops are operating, accepting the absurd hand-scrawled notes that pass for currency, selling what items they can salvage, or make, or find delivered to them inexplicably in the morning.

They can't escape it, of course, what's happening to the city. Signs of it abound.

With so many people gone, the city is generating its own rubbish. In the cracks of buildings and the dark spaces under abandoned cars little knots of matter are self-organizing into grease-stained chip wrappers, broken toys, cigarette packets, before snapping the tiny umbilicus that anchors them to the ground and drifting out across the streets. Even on Oxford Street every morning sees a fresh crop of litter, each filthy newborn piece marked with a minuscule puckered navel.

Even on Oxford Street, every day without fail in front of the newsagents, the bundles appear: the *Telegraph* and *Lambeth News*. The only papers to survive the quiet cataclysm. They are generated daily, written, published and delivered by person or persons or forces unseen.

I already crept downstairs today, Jake, to pick up my copy of the *Telegraph* from across the road. The headline is 'Autochthonic Masses Howling and Wet-Mouthed'. The subhead: 'Pearl, Faeces, Broken Machines'.

But even with these reminders, Oxford Street is a reassuring place. Here, people get up and go to work, dress in clothes we would recognize from nine months ago, have coffee in the morning and resolutely ignore the impossibility of what they are doing. So why don't I stay there?

I think it's the invitation from the Gaumont State which keeps me here, Jake.

I can't leave Kilburn behind. There are secrets here I haven't found. Kilburn is the centre of the new city, and the Gaumont State is the centre of Kilburn.

The Gaumont was inspired, preposterously, by New York's Empire State Building. On a miniature scale, perhaps, but its lines and curves are dignified and impassive and easily ignore the low brick and dirt camouflage of their surroundings. It was still a cinema when I was a child and I remember the symmetrical sweep of the twin staircases within, the opulence of chandelier and carpet and marble tracings.

Multiplexes, with their glorified video screens and tatty decor, are unimpressed by cinema. The Gaumont is of an age when film was still a miracle. It was a cathedral.

It closed and grew shabby. And then it opened again, to the electronic chords of slot machines in the vestibule. Outside, two huge pink neon standards explained the Gaumont's new purpose in vertical script, reading downwards: BINGO.

You were my first thought, as soon as I knew something had happened. I don't remember waking when the train pulled in to London. My first memory is stepping off the carriage into the evening cool and feeling afraid.

It was no ESP, no sixth sense, that told me something was wrong. It was my eyes.

The platform was full, as you would expect, but the crowd moved like none I had ever seen. There were no tides, no currents moving to and from the indicator board, the ticket counter, the shops. No fractal patterns emerged from this mass. The flap of a butterfly's wing in one corner of the station would create no typhoons, no storms, not a sough of wind anywhere else. The deep order of chaos had broken down.

It looked as I imagine purgatory must. A huge room full of vacant souls milling atomized and pointless, each in personal despair.

I saw a guard, as alone as all the others.

What's happened? I asked him. He was confused, shaking his head. He would not look at me. Something's happened, he said. Something...there was a collapse...nothing works properly... there's been a...a breakdown...

He was being very inexact. That wasn't his fault. It was a very inexact apocalypse.

Between the time I had closed my eyes on the train and the time I had opened them again, some organizing principle had failed.

I've always imagined the occurrence in very literal terms. I have always envisaged a vast impossible building, a spiritual power station with an unstable core shitting out the world's energy and connectivity...I've always envisaged the cogs and wheels of that unthinkable machinery overheating...some critical mass being reached...the mechanisms faltering and seizing up as the core explodes soundlessly and spews its poisonous fuel across the city and beyond.

In Bhopal, Union Carbide vomited up a torturing, killing bile all over the land. In Chernobyl the fallout was a more insidious cellular terrorism.

And now... Kilburn erupts with vague, surreal entropy.

I know, Jake, I know, you can't help smiling, can you? From the awesome and terrible to the ridiculous. The walls here are not stacked high with corpses. There is rarely any blood when the inhabitants of London disappear. But the city's winding down, Jake, and Kilburn is the epicentre of the burnout.

I left the guard alone in his confusion.

Got to find Jake, I thought.

You're probably smiling self-deprecatingly when you read that, but I swear to you it's true. You'd been in the city when it happened, you had *seen* it. Think of it, Jake. I was asleep, in transit, neither here nor there. I didn't know this city, I'd never been here before. But you'd watched it being born.

There was no one else in the city for me. You could be my guide, or we could at least be lost together.

The sky was utterly dead. It looked cut out of matt black paper and pasted above the silhouettes of the towers. All the pigeons were gone. We didn't know it then, but the unseen flapping things had burst into existence full-grown and ravenous. In the first few hours they swept the skies quite clean of prey.

The streetlamps were still working, as they are now, but in any case there was nothing profound about the darkness. I wandered nervously, found a telephone box. It didn't seem to want my money but it let me make the call anyway.

Your mother answered.

Hello, she said. She sounded listless and nonplussed.

I paused for far too long. I was groping for new etiquette in this new time. I had no sense of social rules and I stammered as I wondered whether to say something about the change.

Is Jake there please? I finally said, banal and absurd.

He's gone, she said. He's not here. He went out this morning to shop, and he hasn't come back.

Your brother came on the line then and spoke brusquely. He went to some bookshop, he said, and I knew where you were then. I thanked him and rang off.

It was the bookshop we found on the right as you leave Willesden Green station, where the slope of the high road begins to steepen. It is cheap and capricious. We were seduced by the immaculate edition of *Voyage to Arcturus* in the window, and entertained by the juxtaposition of Kierkegaard and Paul Daniels.

If I could have chosen where to be when London wound down, it would be in that zone, where the city first notices the sky, at the summit of a hill, surrounded by low streets that let sound escape into the clouds. Kilburn, ground zero, just over the thin bulwark of backstreets. Perhaps you had a presentiment that morning, Jake, and when the breakdown came you were ready, waiting in that perfect vantage point.

It's dark out here on the roof. It's been dark for some time. But I can see enough to write, from deflected streetlamps and maybe from the moon, too. The air is buffeted more and more by the passage of those hungry, unseen things, but I'm not afraid.

I can hear them fighting and nesting and courting in the Gaumont's tower, jutting over my neighbours' houses and shops. A little while ago there was a dry sputter and crack, and a constant low buzz now underpins the night sounds.

I am attuned to that sound. The murmur of neon.

The Gaumont State is blaring its message to me across the short, deserted distance of pavement.

I am being called to over the organic nonsense of the flyers and the more constant whispers of young rubbish in the wind.

I've heard it all before, I've read it before...I'm taking my own sweet fucking time over this letter... then I'll see what's being asked of me.

I took the tube to Willesden.

I wince to think of it, now, I jerk my mind away. I wasn't to know. It was safer then, anyway, in those early days.

I've crept into the underground stations in the months since, to check the whispered rumours for myself. I've seen the trains go by with the howling faces in all the windows, too fast to see clearly, something like dogs, I've seen trains burning with cold light, long slow trains empty except for one dead-looking woman staring directly into my eyes, *en route* Jesus Christ knows where.

It was nothing like that back then, not nearly so dramatic. It was too cold and too quiet, I remember. And I am not sure the train had a driver.

But it let me go. I came to Willesden and as I stepped out on to that uncovered station I could, for the first time, feel something different about the world. There was a very slow epiphany building up under the skin of the night, oozing out of the city's pores, breaking over me ponderously.

I climbed the stairs out of that underworld.

When Orpheus looked back, Jake, it wasn't stupid. The myths are slanderous. It wasn't the sudden fear that she wasn't there which turned his head. It was the threatening light from above. What if it was not the same, out there? It's so human, to turn and catch the eye of your companion on a return journey, to share a moment's terror that everything you know will have changed.

There was no one I could look back to and everything I knew had changed. Pushing open the doors on to the street was the bravest thing I have ever done.

I stood on the high railway bridge. I was hit by wind. Across the street before me, emerging from below the bridge, below my feet, the elegant curved gorge containing the tracks stretched away. Steep banks of scrub contained it, squat bushes and weeds that tugged petulantly at the scree.

There was very little sound. I could see only a few stars. I felt as if the whole sky scudded above me.

The shop was dark but the door opened. It was a relief to walk into still air.

We're fucking shut, somebody said. He sounded despairing.

I wound between the piles of strong-smelling books towards the till. I could see shapes and shades in this half-hearted darkness. An old bald man was slumped on a stool behind the desk.

I don't want to buy anything, I said. I'm looking for someone. I described you.

Look around, mate, he said. Fucking empty. What do you want from me? I ain't seen your friend or no one.

Very fast, I felt hysteria. I swallowed back a desire to run to all the corners of the shop and throw piles of books around, shouting your name, to see where you were hiding. As I fought to speak, the old man took some kind of contemptuous pity on me and sighed.

One like the one you said, he's been drifting in and out of here all day. Last here about two hours ago. If he comes in again he can fuck off, I'm closed.

How do you tell the incredible? It seems odd, what strikes us as unbelievable.

I had learned, very fast, that the rules of the city had imploded, that sense had broken down, that London was a broken and bloodied thing. I accepted that with numbness, only a very little astonished.

But I was nearly sick with disbelief and relief to walk out of that shop and see you waiting.

You stood under the eaves of a newsagent's, half in shadow, an unmistakable silhouette.

If I stop for a moment it is all so prosaic, so obvious, that you would wait for me there. When I saw you, though, it was like a miracle.

Did you shudder with relief to see me?

Could you believe your eyes?

It's difficult to remember that, right now, when I am up here on the roof surrounded by the hungry flapping things that I cannot see, without you.

We met in the darkness that dripped off the front of the building's façade. I hugged you tight.

Man... I said.

Hey, you said.

We stood like fools, silent for a while.

Do you understand what's happened? I said.

You shook your head, shrugged and waved your arms vaguely to encompass everything around us.

I don't want to go home, you said. I felt it go. I was in the shop and I was looking at this weird little book and I felt something huge just... slip away.

I was asleep in a train. I woke up and found it like this.

What happens now?

I thought you could tell me that. Didn't you all get issued... rulebooks or something? I thought I was punished for being asleep, that's why I didn't understand anything.

No, man. You know, loads of people have just...disappeared, I swear. When I was in the shop I looked up just before, and there were four other people in there. And then I looked up just after and there was only me and this other guy, and the shopkeeper.

Smiles, I said. The cheerful one.

Yeah.

We stood silent again.

This is the way the world ends, you said.

Not with a bang, I continued, but with a...

We thought.

...with a long-drawn-out breath? you suggested.

I told you that I was walking home, to Kilburn, just over the way. Come with me, I said. Stay at mine.

You were hesitant.

Stupid, stupid, stupid, I'm sure it was my fault. It was just the old argument, about you not coming to see me, not staying longer, translated into the world's new language. Before the fall you would have made despairing noises about having to be somewhere, hint darkly at commitments you could not explain, and disappear. But in this new time those excuses became absurd. And the energy you put into your evasions was channelled elsewhere, into the city, which was hungry like a newborn thing, which sucked up your anxiety, assimilated your inchoate desires and fulfilled them.

At least walk with me over to Kilburn, I said. We can work out what we're going to do when we're there.

Yeah, sure man, I just want to...

I couldn't make out what it was you wanted to do.

You were distracted, you kept looking over my shoulder at something, and I was looking around quickly, to see what was intriguing you. There was a sense of interruptions, though the night was as silent as ever, and I kept glancing back at you, and I tugged at you to make you come with me and you said Sure sure man, just one second, I want to see something, and you began to cross the road with your eyes fixed on something out of my sight and I was getting angry and then I lost my grip on you because I could hear a sound from over the brow of the railway bridge, from the east.

I could hear the sound of hooves.

My arm was still outstretched but I was no longer touching you, and I turned my head towards the sound, I stared at the hill's apex. Time stretched out. The darkness just above the pavement was split by a wicked splinter which grew and grew as something long and thin and sharp appeared over the hill. It sliced the night at an acute angle. A clenched, gloved fist rose below it, clutching it tight. It was a sword, a splendid ceremonial sabre. The sword pulled a man after it, a man in a strange helmet, a long silver spike adorning his head and a white plume streaming out in his wake.

He rode in an insane gallop but I felt no urgency as he burst into view, and I had all the time I needed to see him, to study his clothes, his weapon, his face, to recognize him.

He was one of the horsemen who stands outside the palace... are they called the household cavalry? With the hair draped from their helmet spike in an immaculate cone, their mirrored boots, their bored horses. They are legendary for their immobility. It is a tourist game to stare at them and mock them and stroke their mounts' noses, without a flicker of human emotion defiling their duty.

As this man's head broke the brow of the hill I saw that his face was creased and cracked into an astonishing warrior's expression, the snarl of an attacking dog, idiot bravery such as must have been painted across the faces of the Light Brigade.

His red jacket was unbuttoned and it flickered around him like a flame. He half-stood in his stirrups, crouched low, grasping the reins in his left hand, his right held high with that beautiful blade spitting light into my face. His horse rose into view, its veins huge under its white skin, its eyes rolling in an insane equine leer, drool spurting from behind its bared teeth, its hooves hammering down the deserted tarmac of the Willesden railway bridge.

The soldier was silent, though his mouth was open as if he shouted his valedictory roar. He rode on, holding his sword high, bearing down on some imaginary enemy, pushing his horse on towards Dollis Hill, down past the Japanese restaurant and the record shop and the bike dealer and the vacuum cleaner repair man.

The soldier swept past me, stunning and stupid and misplaced. He rode between us, Jake, so close that beads of sweat hit me.

I can picture him on duty as the cataclysm fell, sensing the change in the order of things and knowing that the queen he was sworn to protect was gone or irrelevant, that his pomp meant nothing in the decaying city, that he had been trained into absurdity and uselessness, and deciding that he would be a soldier, just once. I see him clicking his heels and cantering through the confused streets of central London, picking up speed as the anger at his redundancy grows, giving the horse its head, letting it run, feeling it shy at the strange new residents of the skies, until it was galloping hard and he draws his weapon to prove that he can fight, and careers off into the flatlands of north-west London, to disappear or die.

I watched his passing, dumbstruck and in awe.

And when I turned back, of course, Jake, when I turned back, you had gone.

The frantic searches, the shouts and the misery you can imagine for yourself. I have little enough dignity as it is. It went on for a long time, though I had known as I raised my head to your lack that I would not find you.

Eventually I found my way to Kilburn, and as I walked past the Gaumont State I looked up and saw that neon message, garish and banal and terrifying. The message that is there still, the request that tonight, finally, after so many months, I think I will acquiesce to.

I don't know where you went to, how you were disappeared. I don't know how I lost you. But after all my searching for a hiding place, that message on the face of the Gaumont cannot be coincidence. Although it might, of course, be misleading. It might be a game. It might be a trap.

But I'm sick of waiting, you know? I'm sick of wondering. So let me tell you what I'm going to do. I'm going to finish this letter, soon now, and I'm going to put it in an envelope with your name on it. I'll put a stamp on it (it can't hurt) and I'll venture out into the street – yes, even in the heart of the night – and I'll put it in the post box.

From there, I don't know what'll happen. I don't know the rules of this place at all. It might be eaten by some presence inside the box, it might be spat back out at me, or reproduced a hundred times and pasted on the windows of all the warehouses in London. I'm hoping that it will find its way to you. Maybe it'll appear in your pocket, or at the door of your place, wherever you are now. If you are anywhere, that is.

It's a forlorn hope. I admit that. Of course I admit that.

But I had you, and I lost you again. I'm marking your passing. And I am marking mine.

Because you see, Jake, then I'm going to walk the short distance up Kilburn High Road to the Gaumont State, and I'm going to read its plea, its command, and this time I think I will obey.

The Gaumont State is a beacon, a lighthouse, a warning we missed. It jags impassive into the clouds as the city founders on rocks. Its filthy cream walls are daubed with a hundred markings, human, animal, meteorological, and... other. In its squat square tower lies the huge nest of rags or bones or hair where the flying things bicker and brood. The Gaumont State exerts its own gravity over the changed city. I suspect all compasses point to it now. I suspect that in the magnificent entrance, framed by those wide stairs, something is waiting. The Gaumont State is the generator of the dirty entropy that has taken London by storm. I suspect there are many fascinating things inside.

I'm going to let it reel me in.

Those two huge pink signs that heralded the Gaumont's rebirth as a temple of cheap games... they have changed. They are selective. They ignore certain letters, and have done ever since that night. Both now scorn the initial B. The sign on the left illuminates only the second and third letters, that on the right only the fourth and fifth. The signs flicker on and off in antiphase, taking turns to blaze their gaudy challenge.

IN...
GO...
IN.
GO IN.
GO IN.

Go in.

All right. OK. I'll go in. I'll tidy up my house and post my letter and stand in front of that edifice, squinting at the now-opaque glass which keeps its secrets, and I will go in.

I don't really believe you're in there, Jake, if you're reading this. I don't really believe that any longer. I know that can't be so. But I can't leave it alone. I can leave no stone unturned.

I'm so fucking lonely.

I'll climb those exquisite stairs, if I get that far. I'll cross the grand corridors, wind through tunnels into the great vast hall that I believe will be glowing very bright. If I get that far.

Could be that I'll find you. I'll find something, something will find me.

I won't be coming home, I'm sure.

I'll go in. The city doesn't need me around while it winds down. I was going to catalogue its secrets, but that was for my benefit, not the city's, and this is just as good.

I'll go in.

See you soon, I hope, Jake. I hope.

All my love,

DADDY'S GIRL
EMMA DONOGHUE

I just now came up from seeing Daddy.

I never walked in here without knocking before. His study is real cold; the back of his big chair is smooth like an icicle.

The newspaper folded on the desk says 18 January 1901. I still can't get used to it, this century I mean. It sounds most improbable.

Doctor Gallagher said he would have to show me if I couldn't take his word for it. But I've never seen Daddy without his necktie, even. I guess I always thought he was a modest kind of man. So when it came to it, I just couldn't bear to lift the sheet. It seemed disrespectful.

Even with the sheet up to his chin Daddy looked kinda peeved, like when Momma was alive and dinner went on too long and I could tell he wanted to stroll down to the saloon on Seventh and smoke a great black cigar.

He looked just like that last Saturday, the last time I saw him. It strikes me now, he must have known. He must have felt it coming. Nobody ever could pull the wool over Daddy's eyes. He called me in — he was sitting right here in this chair — and he told me to go stay with my friends in Brooklyn for a week. No reason given, no questions to be asked. 'Get on, girl, I won't be disturbed.' I thought it must have had something to do with politics.

I reckon we ought to bury him right away. Before the reporters burst in and get a look at him.

Why couldn't Doctor Gallagher have kept his big mouth shut and let a man rest in peace? I don't see that the public's got a right to know. There was a fellow from the *New York Times* on the stairs five minutes ago, hollering through the keyhole.

'Miss Hall, Miss Hall. Could you tell? How long have you known? Are you a millionaire now, Miss Hall?'

All today I have kept a good hold on myself, because I am known to my friends as the sort of girl you can rely on, but now it is all starting to shake loose. My mind runs round in little circles.

My name is Miss Imelda Hall, known as Minnie. I am twenty-two years of age. I help my Daddy, Mr Murray Hall, run an employment agency at 145 Sixth Avenue. Used to, I mean to say.

All in all, I am glad I didn't lift the sheet. There are some things you shouldn't look at, because what are you supposed to do afterwards? Like that baby I saw once in a trashcan behind the market.

Oh my good Jesus.

I can hardly throw up if I haven't eaten a bite since supper yesterday, can I?

If Daddy was here now he'd give Bridget a smack around the head for letting the fire go out.

He left his hat on his desk. Inside it's black with grease.

Why, what a fool I was, we all were. Daddy's friends used to complain that all the years they were going bald as taters, he never lost a hair off his head. And another thing, his face is always smooth, as if he's come up directly from the barber's, even when I know for a fact he's only just got out of bed.

I should have wonderered about that, shouldn't I? But a girl's not inclined to set to wondering, when it's her own Daddy and he doesn't care for being stared at. And he never seemed like anything but your regular poker-playing whiskey-drinking good fellow. Not exactly handsome, but a real charmer with the ladies.

It turns my stomach.

How could Momma? How could she?

I am sitting here in Daddy's study at Daddy's desk in Daddy's big leather chair, and any minute now he is going to walk in here and catch me.

I know what he would rather I did. 'Put a match to the whole damn lot,' he'd say. 'No use rooting around in a dead man's papers.'

But the thing is, Daddy, I'm a little curious. And this is not your private study any more. You're not really going to come across the landing and find me poking about, are you? I can do what I please now.

The thing is, quite above and beyond the thing itself, this changes everything. For instance, if Daddy's not my Daddy, who is? I just can't see a fine upstanding woman like Momma carrying on with another... with a man. Did he tell her, 'Go right ahead, Cecilia, don't mind me'? I just cannot see Daddy putting up with that.

I'm counting on him to have left me something, some kind of clue. Surely it would be here if it was anywhere, wedged in one of these bursting drawers or pigeonholes, slipped in between these old campaign handbills and Democratic Party Meeting notices and postal cards to 'good old Murray Hall'.

Something you never got around to mentioning, something you always wanted to say. You and Momma did plan to tell me, didn't you? I expect you just didn't quite know how. Surely you didn't reckon to let me go my whole life through not knowing who in the hell I am?

This must be it. I knew it would be here. So simple, a folded paper with 'Minnie' on the outside. I can hardly bear to open it.

'Gone to hustings, home late, don't wait dinner.'

Damn him. His notes were never more than ten words long.

This desk is full of the junk of a whole lifetime. My stomach is growling now. But what I'm looking for must be in here somewhere.

He always said I had Mamma's eyes and his nose. The Senator used to say, 'Isn't she the dead spit of her Daddy?'

I must have been adopted.

Now I am making a right mess and papers are falling on the rug but I don't care. It has got to be written down. Where I was born, how they got me. Surely there must be a letter or a certificate or a photograph even. Something with my name on.

Could be my name is not my name, of course. It could be staring me blue in the face and I'd never recognize it. Could be I had another name before they adopted me and turned me into Miss Imelda (Minnie) Hall. Maybe I am not an Imelda but a Priscilla or an Agnes. And of course I am not a Hall either. God knows what I am. Come to think of it, I've got no proof I'm twenty-two years old. Could be it's all lies.

I am not rightly anyone or anything now. Just like a bit of paper floating down the gutter.

It makes me shake to think of it. Not about my name so much as about Daddy. When I think of him now I could just rip him to pieces.

The other day I came down all ready for a party and Daddy said something very cutting about the neck of my bodice. I told him it was all the fashion but he said I might as well serve up my bosoms on a plate for the fellows. He made me go right upstairs and change my whole ensemble and I was late for the party. And to think that all this time, all these years – well, there's no other way to put it, but Daddy had bosoms himself.

What kind of monster plays a trick that lasts a lifetime?

What kind of woman decides to be a man?

These cards are so old they've gone yellow. 'Best of wishes from all the boys to good old Murray Hall.' 'With the compliments of State Senator Barney Martin to his old friend Murray Hall.' 'Merry Christmas, dear Murray, from all your pals on the Committee.'

I never could stay awake when Daddy talked politics. Who promised his vote in which ward, and which man could be trusted, and which other fellow would slit your throat as soon as look at you. How Daddy'd started out as a nobody with a nickel in his pocket and now he was a professional bondsman, but best of all, he was rich in friends, and what else could a man rely on in this world?

There was that one time Daddy got wild at Skelly's on Tenth Avenue and whipped a policeman in the street and ended up in the station house. But his buddies squared it in the right quarters, and he was home for breakfast. Momma had been worried near out of her mind. But the Tammany Hall men can fix anything. Sometimes it takes a bribe or a riot or maybe even a body in the river, I've heard, but the job gets done. You keep on the right side of the Tammany Hall men, Daddy used to say, you wear a permanent smile.

I wonder what they would say to him now.

When I went over to draw the curtains I could hear those jackal reporters down below, shouting up at me. 'Miss Hall, Miss Hall.' But I will not talk to them. They put words in a person's mouth.

Here it is in my hand: 'The Last Will and Testament'. It doesn't take long to read.

Well I guess I needn't worry about anyone marrying me for my money. Oh Daddy. Was any of it true?

It's not that I'm not grateful for the two hundred dollars, but where's all the rest gone? What kind of deals did those friends of yours do? And I see I'm supposed to 'cause to be erected a suitable headstone over the grave of Cecilia, the deceased wife of the testator'. That is a sweet thought, Daddy, but what would a 'suitable headstone' for Momma say? 'I Married a Woman, Lord Forgive Me'?

Momma will just have to move on over and make room; I sure can't afford two headstones if I'm to feed myself this winter. She was a sweet-looking woman, was Momma, even if she was twice Daddy's size. Now there is a queer thought: I don't expect you can tell the difference between a man and a woman, after a few years in the grave, when you get down to the plain bones.

He'll have to mind his manners now. Daddy was never seen around the Lower West Side without some class of female on his arm. Younger than me, sometimes; even the maids who came to our office looking for a job. He just couldn't keep his hands off the opposite... I mean, girls. It saddened Momma so, she stopped speaking to Daddy years before she died.

But I've got to try to be merciful, I suppose. There's nobody else left to forgive him.

I guess he had simply got to be a man's man, and a ladies' man, and every kind of man, so no one would suspect he was no such thing. I bet he was sick when he tasted his first cigar, but he kept right on. And he got so he could drink his weight in beer and stand up under it too. As if he'd found a book on being a man and was set on following it page by page.

It strikes me now that I do not even know where Daddy came from. He sometimes used to talk about making the crossing, but he never said from where. Daddy never did care to be interrupted with questions when he was telling a story. His tales made the crossing sound such a hoot: all the farmers down in steerage green as grass, and the fiddler carrying on regardless. Maybe it was Ireland he started out from? Or Scotland? Daddy never said much about his life from before he crossed the ocean. Whatever I asked him, he claimed he couldn't remember.

He doesn't have a name now either, no more than me. I wonder what he was born. Mary Hall? Jane Hall? Or no kind of Hall at all?

I almost set to laughing when I think of calling Daddy by a girl's name, and him in no position to stop me.

Oh Lord, I could cry to think of him as a Nancy or Eliza.

I don't even know how old he was when he made the crossing. I see him at the rail of the ship, heading into New York harbour, but his face is blank. What is he wearing? What name does he go by? Where is he coming from? I wish I could be there, leaning on the rail, looking out to sea. Just for a moment. Just to ask why. Is it so bad to be a woman?

I guess I could have been a better daughter. Daddy used to say I'd inherited his temper and Momma's sulks together, but now it turns out my faults are all my own. I used to get uppity with Daddy when he would forget his key and haul on the bell when he crashed in at two in the morning, especially after Momma died.

No wonder he drank. Doctor Gallagher says it was a cancer in the left breast. He says Daddy had been sick for five years before he said a word, and by the time the doctor got to see it, the cancer had worked right through to Daddy's heart. It sounds like woodworm, I can't help thinking, or like when the mice get into the cheese. What a ninny I was; I thought all those books on medicine Daddy collected were some sort of hobby. I saw him take a spoonful from a bottle once but he said it was cod-liver oil. Five years of being eaten away, for fear of being found out.

The papers are all in one big heap now, and I'm so cold I had best go down to the kitchen. There's nothing left to read. Only one last drawer that comes unstuck with a shudder, and there's nothing in it but a bit of card at the back.

An old brown photograph: a girl with too many ringlets. One of his hussies, from the early days. That goes on the top of the pile, face down; I'll toss the lot in the range after supper.

Unless.

It couldn't be.

Daddy?

I turn the picture up, and all of a sudden it changes; I see past the ringlets, into the face.

It looks like Daddy dressed up as a girl, for a game. Eyebrows drawn together; a faint smile.

I have got his nose.

Well, he looked better in trousers. But I will tuck the picture into my pocket.

I did not know before today that you can hate and despise a person and still love him on the other side of all that.

He is still my Daddy. Even if he is dead. And a woman.

Doctor Gallagher says 'she', now, when he remembers, and so do the reporters. But I won't, not ever. Daddy wouldn't like it.

A note

Murray Hall (perhaps born Mary Anderson, or Mary or Elizabeth Hall) was said to have come from Ireland, Scotland or New York's Lower West Side. Murray Hall's first wife died, or disappeared; the second marriage ended in estrangement after about seven or perhaps twenty years. At the time of death Murray Hall was forty-two or sixty or possibly seventy.

When her father was discovered on death to be a woman, Hall's daughter Imelda (Minnie) refused to talk to reporters. Nothing is known of her origins or her subsequent life.

A HIGHER AGENCY
TOBY LITT

I am a writer; I write screenplays. You know, like for films before they are made.

I first became serious about this during the eternal summer of stoned fucking that followed my last term at Uni.

For five years I tried to interest agents and producers in my work – and, in all that time, there was no serious interest. I would send off customized letters, well researched and personable; back, six months later, along with my now totally tatty script, would come a formula rejection.

About a year ago I finished what I felt was my best screenplay yet. Unfortunately, I am not at liberty to discuss it in any detail. I can say – I think – that it is set in west London, that it is very violent, very strange, and that the ending still makes me cry.

When I finished the script I sent it off to the agent whose formula letters had always come back fastest. His name was Mr Harold Oliver, and he was a partner in the Sykes-Oliver Literary Agency. All I knew of Mr Oliver was his address, his promptness in reply and the thick black ink of his fluid signature. But I felt, somehow, that we had a relationship: he respected me, and I him.

At this time I was living in a top-floor bedsit half-way along a litter-strewn street just off the Shepherd's Bush end of the Uxbridge Road. In the last days before I finished the script, I noticed a sign up in the window of a nearby Italian restaurant:

★

DISH-WASHER WANTED
APPLY WITHIN

I needed work, any work – the social were on my case big-time. My script had taken all of nine non-job-seeking months to write.

Straight after sending the script off from the post office, I went along to the Italian restaurant.

From the outside there was nothing special about it: a back-lit red and white sign above a large glass window with an aluminium-framed door in the middle.

As I couldn't afford to eat there, I walked in and went straight up to the till.

'I'm here about the dish-washing job,' I said. 'If it's still going.'

The Co-Manager – whose real name I'm not at liberty to give – was, as it happened, working the till.

He was a dark-complexioned man, burly and broken-nosed, with no trace of an Italian accent.

'Do you have any experience?' he asked.

'Well, I've washed dishes before,' I said, jokily.

'How many?' he asked.

'I never counted them.'

'Roughly. How many at one time?'

I remembered a large dinner party at Uni, then multiplied by three.

'Thirty-six.'

'Do you have stamina? I need to know. I can't introduce you to the Manager if you haven't. Thirty-six isn't that many.'

'Well, it's all I've done. Take it or leave it.'

The Co-Manager leaned over the till. 'Show me your hands,' he said.

I lifted them, palms upwards.

He made me turn them over then inspected my fingernails very closely, one by one.

'Come with me,' he said.

He ducked out from behind the till and walked between tables to the back of the restaurant. Parting a beaded curtain with his boxer's hands, he led me into the noise and heat of the kitchen.

We approached a man in a dark suit who stood with his back to us.

'What do you think?' asked the Co-Manager.

The man glanced at me over his shoulder.

If possible this man was even broader and more blunted-off than the Co-Manager.

'What do you think?' he asked back. He too had no Italian accent.

'It's been five days,' said the Co-Manager.

The broad man looked me up and down.

'Go with your instinct,' he said.

The Co-Manager put a hand on my shoulder and pulled me away.

'That is the Manager,' he said – and, even if I were at liberty to tell you more, which I am not, I never heard the Manager referred to by any other name.

The Co-Manager rumbled into my ear: 'Respect the Manager.'

'Does that mean I've got the job?' I asked.

'Come back tonight at seven.'

The Co-Manager walked me to the fire door and pointed the way back on to the Uxbridge Road, past overflowing and sour-smelling dustbins.

'Come in the back way when you come back,' he said.

Just before I left he shook my hand – and I took this as a good sign.

Back in the communal hall of my bedsit building I saw that one of my ever-changing neighbours had left me a note – pinned up on the greasy corkboard by the phone.

'Call Oliver soon.'

Another hand had added, in a different-coloured pen:

'And your mother too.'

While I went to get Mr Oliver's number from my top-floor room, I left the payphone off the hook – hoping that this would warn everyone off from using it (and also, of course, prevent any incoming calls).

The payphone was still free when I got back downstairs.

I dialled, excited — no agent had ever phoned me before.

'Mr Oliver,' I said — and gave my name (which, as you'll already have guessed, I am not at liberty to give you).

'This script is just fantastic,' he said. I loved his low cigaretty voice straight off. 'I've already talked about it to some people,' he said. It made me think of Orson Welles and my dead Dad and God. 'Interest is already firming up, I have to say — but we'll need to go to a second draft as soon as possible,' he said. These were the words I had been waiting five years — and all my life — to hear. 'It would be an honour and a privilege to be your agent — and to make you very rich and very famous,' he said.

I had an erection, and I said: 'Yes, Mr Oliver. Please.'

'Call me Harold,' he said, and put the phone down.

As I had no one else to tell I phoned my mother.

'Mr Oliver is famous throughout the industry,' I said. 'Everyone has heard of him.'

She said, 'Oh, really?' and 'That's nice' and 'Will you be coming home for Easter?'

I needed to do something to celebrate.

Back in my room I counted my money and decided that now — probably — I could afford a bottle of decent vodka.

I had honestly forgotten about the dish-washing job until I was walking past the Italian restaurant on my way back from the off-licence. In my joy, I had strolled past the first time without even seeing it.

Being a decent sort, or so I like to think, I didn't want to just disappear and never see them again — not when they'd been so kind in taking me on in the first place — so I decided I'd go in and tell them that, thank you, but I no longer needed the job.

This time it was the Manager who, squat as an impacted British bulldog, was standing behind the till.

'Didn't the Co-Manager tell you to come in the back way when you came back?' These were the first words he addressed to me.

'Yes, he did,' I replied. 'But — '

'You're early,' said the Manager. 'That means you're keen to start, does it?'

'Not really, you see – '

The Manager reached over the counter and grabbed the off-licence bag from my hands.

'Staff are forbidden from drinking on the premises,' he said. 'Unless expressly invited to by the Management.'

'No, this isn't for – '

'We can't have you dropping plates because you're pissed. Now, get in the back.'

'But I'm not working here,' I finally managed to say. 'I don't need the job.'

'You don't *need* the job?' the Manager said, turning overtly nasty for the first time. 'You don't *need* the job? Well, what if the job needs you?'

'You see, I've had a very lucky break. I'm going to – '

'I don't care *what* you've had, you agreed to do a job of work for us – in the back, now!'

I was about to walk out but the thought of all the money I had spent on the vodka held me back. I decided that the Co-Manager might be a little more approachable.

After only a slight pause to see if the Manager would relent, I went down the aisle towards the rear of the restaurant.

As I walked into the kitchen, the Chef was just barricading the fire door. The Co-Manager had his ear closely to the phone. He looked at me as the beaded curtain fell back in place behind me.

'He said *that*?' he said. 'To *you*, the Manager?'

He shook his head ruefully. I'd seen actors do this in movies – this was the sadness before violence.

I skipped over to the sink, pulled on an apron and gloves, and started washing dishes.

Six hours later I was finished.

In all that time I had hardly dared look over my shoulder.

I had listened, though – I had listened to the Chef shouting at the Waiters and the Waiters shouting at the Chef.

The Co-Manager had been there – occasionally on the phone, more often than not talking about me.

I had listened and cowered.

The Waiters had kept bringing me greasy crusty charcoaly dishes – dishes with cigarettes stubbed out in them – dishes with blood-soaked tissues on them – dishes with phlegm slopping across them.

Finally, when no more dishes came, I took off my apron and gloves and tried the back door.

'No, my friend,' came the Manager's voice. 'Come out *this* way. We're all having a nightcap.'

I turned to see his face, poking broadly through the beaded curtain.

Out in the restaurant the Chef and the Waiters were sitting up and down on either side of a long table, smoking and drinking.

Bottles of House Red stood in pairs on the red gingham. My vodka bottle was present too – intact and at the head of the table.

As I walked in there was a round of applause, led by the Manager. He picked a full glass up off the table.

'To the best bloody Dish-Washer we've ever had.'

'Hear-hear,' said everyone else, then applauded.

The Co-Manager came over and stuffed a wodge of crumpled notes into my hand.

'Great job,' he kept saying. 'Really great job.'

'Sit down,' said the Manager.

I took hold of my vodka and got ready to make my excuses.

'Please,' said the Manager, pulling back a chair – with just the hint of the hint of a threat.

I sat. The Co-Manager sat on my left-hand side, the Manager on my right. We sat.

The Manager poured me out a glass of House Red.

'Cheers,' he said.

'Cheers,' I replied, unable not to.

'Cheers,' everyone said.

We all took large loud glugs.

For a moment afterwards we just sat there, tired and smiling. Then the Co-Manager said, 'Speech.'

'Oh yes,' said the Manager. 'A wonderful idea.'

'Really,' I protested.

'Speech!' cried one of the waiters. 'Speech!' chorused the rest.

'Go on,' stage-whispered the Co-Manager, nudging my elbow.

I stood up, unsteady on my feet through fear and exhaustion. My hand grabbed the vodka bottle for support. I looked down the two lines of brightly lit, heavily fleshed faces.

'Well,' I began, having no idea whatsoever what my speech was meant to be about. 'First of all I'd like to thank the Manager and Co-Manager...' There were lots of hear-hears: I seemed to be on the right track. '...for all their help and encouragement — and for giving me this great opportunity in the first place. And I'd also like to thank the entire Waiting Staff, each and every one of them, for their...' A word was fluttering round my head like an injured bird. I grabbed it. '...forbearance.' There was laughter and heavy-handed applause from the two Managers. 'I must also mention the Chef, whose innovative and expressive use of some of the most obscure areas of the English vernacular has kept me most entertained.' More applause. ('Most entertained!' gasped the Manager, as if I'd told the joke of the century.) God, I was almost enjoying this. 'And finally I'd like to say how much I've enjoyed working in this fine — '

'Enjoyed?' said the Manager, all hilarity gone.

'Past tense,' said the Co-Manager.

They both stood up. It was like being between two sides of beef in a refrigerator.

'Is leaving?' said the Manager.

'Thinks is leaving?'

'Yes,' said the Manager. 'But isn't.'

'How could he?'

'It's a vocation.'

'A gift from God.'

Again I looked down the table at the Waiters, at the Chef. They looked back — but not at me, at Judas.

'To leave would be a travesty.'

'Almost blasphemous,' said the Co-Manager.

'As near as makes no difference,' said the Manager.

'Look,' I said, 'I'm really sorry, but you'll have to find someone else.'

'There is no one else,' said the Manager, almost distraught. '*You* are the Dish-Washer.'

'I'm a writer,' I said, weakly.

'What you do in your spare time is no concern of mine,' he said.

'A *full-time* writer.'

'Well, then,' he said, 'what have you been doing for the past six hours?'

'That's — '

'What have you been doing?' There was the hint again — and the sadness.

'Washing dishes.'

'Yes,' the Manager said. 'And what will you be doing for six hours tomorrow?'

I didn't dare hesitate.

'Washing dishes.'

Hilarity instantly returned. There was another round of toasts. My back was mercilessly clapped. Another grubby note somehow found its way into my pocket.

It was half-past two before I hit the cool quiet air of the Uxbridge Road.

There was no time to work anything out on the short walk round the corner and home.

It was clear that, for some reason, the Managers had decided to make me stay on. Perhaps only until they found someone else, though it didn't seem that way.

I could always not go in the following evening — but somehow I felt sure that the Managers would make me suffer for this: the restaurant was on my route to the tube station, the off-licence, the launderette, everywhere. I could always avoid it by walking round the block, but I would bump into them in the end — and it would be a very, very hard bump. And the end might really be the end.

I could go and stay with my mother, but that was always a last resort.

Still undecided, I went to bed.

The next morning I woke up late — achy-armed and slightly hungover.

I tried to get started on the second draft, but my brain just couldn't click into focus. Desperate, I went out for an inspirational walk.

As I hurried past the Italian restaurant, I saw that they had taken down the Dish-Washer Wanted sign.

The vacancy had been filled.

★

Seven o'clock found me back in the kitchen.

I had been terrified going in, but the Managers greeted me like the proverbial prodigal, the Waiters called me by my first name and the Chef promised to think of a good nickname for me.

Eventually he came up with Emu – because, he said, I was good at keeping my head down.

The hours sloshed past – dish after dish after dish.

The orders thinned out. The orders stopped.

Standing in the propped-open-by-a-broom fire door, the Chef had a cigarette.

In came the Co-Manager to pay me, filthy cash.

Out I was again in the cold air – free and not free.

This routine carried on for a week.

On the way home I would think of escaping; in the morning I would be unable to work; come evening I would be back in the kitchen.

And then Mr Oliver rang.

'Hey,' he said, when I made it down to the payphone, 'how's that second draft coming along?'

'It's a bit difficult,' I said.

'Creative work is never easy. But the rewards...'

'No, you see – I've got this job I can't seem to give up.'

'What? You love it so much?'

'No, it's dish-washing. I hate it.'

'Why can't you just give it up?'

For a moment I thought I'd be able to control myself, then I started sobbing – right there in the communal hall.

Mr Oliver was very understanding. He asked me where the Italian restaurant was. He said he was sure the whole thing was a silly mistake. He mentioned someone very important he needed to consult.

When I asked him what I should do that evening, he said: 'Go in just as normal. But I promise you, it'll be the last time.'

God, did I hope it was.

My hands were raw from rubber and my elbows covered in cuts. The Chef's emu jokes had become more and more elaborate.

Now, he reckoned, emus only stuck their heads in the ground because they loved taking it up the arse.

The Waiters were starting to booby-trap dishes with olive oil and broken glass and glue and faeces.

The Co-Manager was pinching my bottom and the Manager was ignoring me completely.

At about midnight, just when we were usually starting to turn customers away, my agent walked in.

I knew the moment he was there because he shouted my name in the loudest voice I'd ever heard.

I walked towards the beaded curtain, but the Co-Manager stepped into my path.

'Let us deal with this,' he said, and grabbed and squeezed my balls – hard, very hard indeed.

Winded and dizzy, I fell to the floor.

From this position I found I could see under the bottom of the beaded curtain and into the restaurant.

My agent, Mr Oliver, was standing beside a very tall, very thin man – a man I'd never seen before but who I assumed to be Mr Sykes. (Unless it was the other way round – which I later found out it wasn't.) Mr Oliver was also tall and thin, but not so tall and thin as Mr Sykes. Both of them had skin that, in the dim light of the restaurant, looked luminously blue.

The Manager stood before them, barring their way into the kitchen.

I decided to stay down – it seemed the safest place.

Mr Oliver shouted my name again.

Obviously, I didn't appear.

Mr Oliver and Mr Sykes conferred for a moment, then Mr Oliver said to the Manager: 'I'm sure we can come to some arrangement acceptable to both parties.'

'The boy is mine,' said the Manager. 'I am not giving him up.'

'We have a prior claim,' said Mr Oliver.

'Do you?' said the Manager. 'Well, we have a stronger claim.'

From his inside pocket Mr Oliver produced a gun. 'Stronger than this?' he asked.

'Oh,' said the Manager. 'Much.'

As he said this I looked round and saw the Chef reaching for something far back in a steel cupboard: a double-barrelled shotgun. Once he'd grabbed it, he tiptoed over to the Co-Manager and handed it to him.

I looked back out into the restaurant. The Waiters and customers were clinging to the walls.

Mr Oliver hadn't moved.

But Mr Sykes was now also pointing a gun at the Manager, who had raised his hands over his head.

The Co-Manager quietly clicked the two firing hammers back into position.

For the first time Mr Sykes spoke up: 'The boy is ours – give him back to us or face the consequences.' His voice was a strangely penetrating hiss.

'I'll tell you what I'm going to give you,' said the Manager, and dived to one side.

Immediately on cue the Co-Manager stepped through the beaded curtain and fired off his rounds. But Mr Oliver and Mr Sykes had been prepared for this. They were already going for cover behind tables on either side of the aisle.

The Co-Manager, sensing his exposure, turned to dive back into the kitchen – but too slowly.

The first shot pumped through his shoulder. The second lodged in his gut. The third ripped open his throat.

Bits of the Co-Manager spatted down on to me where I still lay on the kitchen floor.

Hidden by the till from Mr Oliver and Mr Sykes, I could see the Manager pulling his pistol out of an ankle holster.

'Mr Oliver!' I shouted. 'Be careful! He's armed!'

Then I felt the Chef sit down on top of me. For a moment he allowed me to examine my reflection in the broad blade of his favourite vegetable knife. 'Shut up,' he whispered.

The Co-Manager's blood was soaking up into my trousers, from my hips to my knees.

Out in the restaurant the Manager started firing. He was trying to cover himself as he made a dash for the kitchen.

The tactic failed miserably. Without him noticing, Mr Sykes had crept under one of the longer tables.

When Mr Sykes shot the Manager, he was practically aiming up his nose. And, if this was – in fact – where he was aiming, then Mr Sykes was a pretty good shot, for the nose, along with the chin and forehead, was the first part of the Manager to hit the ceiling.

As the Manager snapped forwards in total pain, Mr Oliver shot him a couple of times in the stomach. But somehow the Manager kept firing – completely at random, waving here and there.

The window at the front of the restaurant shattered.

Mr Oliver dodged from side to side, trying to outguess a blinded dying man.

A fifth bullet, a sixth – they all went wide.

Then, cleverly, Mr Oliver dropped to the floor. All the remaining bullets would go over his head.

But he hadn't reckoned on Mr Sykes, who – in an attempt to save Mr Oliver from further danger – had all this time been planting bullets up into the Manager's chest and guts. Now, though, he tried a shot to the ankle.

The Manager crumpled – and his last living bullet got Mr Oliver through the left eye.

There was a period of calm during which two of the customers dashed out the front door.

I was completely soaked in the Co-Manager's blood.

The Chef whispered in my ear: 'Stand up.'

I did so.

He pushed me through the beaded curtain and into the restaurant, the knife close to my throat.

'You can have the boy,' he said. 'Just let me have the restaurant.'

There was a silence. I looked for Mr Sykes, but he'd hidden again.

'That's all I want,' said the Chef. 'The restaurant.'

'Yes,' said Mr Sykes. 'We can do that.'

Mr Oliver groaned and died.

'Let him come forward,' said Mr Sykes, from somewhere on the left.

'I'm trusting you on this,' said the Chef.

He pushed me forwards.

Mr Sykes' voice said: 'Walk towards the door.'

I did, leaving bloody footprints behind me.

When I reached Mr Oliver, I stepped to one side so as not to tread on him or his blood.

Crack – and behind me the Chef went down.
The bullet must have missed me by nothing.
Crack – Crack – Crack.
The Chef slumped back through the beaded curtain and fell on top of the Co-Manager.
'Come on, boy,' said Mr Sykes, standing up from behind a table on the right and placing his thin hand on my shoulder. 'We've got to leave, quickly.'
'But the police – '
'You have work to do. We have to get away. To a safe place.'
'Where?' I asked.
He didn't reply until we were in the car, moving.
'You know,' he said. 'Your mother is very proud of you.'
I looked at him closely.
'Very, *very* proud,' he said, deadpan.

BREATHING UNDER WATER
CHRISTOPHER KENWORTHY

For the first three hundred kilometres south of Perth I tried not to think about Cassie, and concentrated on driving. The roads in Western Australia are the longest and straightest in the world, edged with car-wide verges of orange gravel. The scenery beyond them is the same for hours: scrub and eucalyptus. Some of the trees have skin coloured like bone, others a ginger granite. Where the limbs of branches fold out of trunks, the bark sags over itself, wrinkled like the swell of a small tummy.

I stopped the car, telling myself I needed to stretch my legs, but in truth I wanted to run my hand down the smoothness of a milk-coloured tree. It felt as cool as stone, but soft, a fuzzy nap making it yield slightly. It was too hot to linger in the direct sunlight, so I retreated to the car, driving with both windows down.

In all the years I'd passed through this area, my Dad had never stopped to let us explore. We used to go to Hopetoun every summer, three cars full of brothers, uncles, aunties and cousins. Cassie would travel in Uncle Harry's green Holden. The distances between the cars would vary as we drove, but none was ever out of sight. The journey was always carried out at a frantic pace, seeing if we could beat the five-and-a-half-hour record, though it usually ended up nearer to seven. As the children all grew into their twenties, the group visits stopped. Cassie and some of my other cousins travelled down with their friends occasionally, but I hadn't been back until now.

Fifty kilometres out of Newdegate, the road passed through the bowl of a dried salt lake; it was like driving through the rim of a volcano, the ridge-horizon cupping an expanse that looked like fresh snow. Three days before, on the other side of the planet, I'd walked through a circular park in Prague, trampling real snow. It was this vague similarity that interested me, and I pulled the car over again.

The grasses by the road were crisped with crystals. The lake-bed looked like set sugar and it crunched underfoot, sparkling. I walked out on to it, as nervous as though walking on thin ice, though I knew the salt was packed feet deep. When I touched it I was surprised at how smooth it felt; expecting grains, I found it was more like touching flour. I couldn't resist tasting the residue on my fingers, and the flavour of salt reminded me of my cousin.

Six months previously Cassie had driven me to Perth Airport, for the start of my trip to Europe. We didn't talk much in the car, the volume of rushed air from the open windows a good excuse not to speak. She waited with me to watch aeroplanes taking off until my check-in time. When I had to leave, there was no smile, but her face held a sadness that made mine feel worse, and she put her arms around me. Her hair was down that day, long enough to brush against my arms as we hugged. She moved her face into my neck, and mine pressed against hers. My lips must have touched her skin, because when I pulled away I could taste faint salt.

A numbness encompassed me on the plane, and I tried to put it down to the awe of my journey. I'd never been away from home for more than a few weeks, and thought I must be focusing my impending homesickness on Cassie.

I managed to believe that for half a year. On the return flight, however, I kept wondering whether Cassie would pick me up at the airport, and that prevented me from sleeping. So I flew back from Prague wide awake, but the build-up was pointless because my parents came to collect me. I didn't hear from Cassie for two days. When she called, she didn't even ask about my trip, or how I was, but said, 'Can we meet up somewhere?'

'Should I come and see you and Ron?' I wondered if she'd broken up with him, because six months was a long time.

'No, let's meet up.' The way she phrased that suggested it wasn't the usual sort of get-together.

We met at a café in Subiaco, but didn't even get as far as the tables. Cassie was waiting in her car as I drew up and walked over to me before I could get out. There was no big hello; the look on her face was matter-of-fact, almost resigned.

'I wrote this for you,' she said, handing a letter to me through the window. 'You'd better read it.'

Then she got in her car and I watched her drive away. The envelope was so well sealed she must have used a lot of spit on the glue, but I fished out her letter. I tried to read it line by line, but my eyes jumped to words such as 'touch', 'heart' and 'love'. By the time I finished it, my breathing was painfully rapid and shallow. I have no memory of driving away, but I must have done, because some time later — half an hour, an hour? — I found myself in a remote suburb. It took me five minutes with the map book to work out a route home.

It was a surprise to find that I slept well that night, but it may have been because of my decision to leave. Rather than go away with her, as she'd suggested, I wanted to go alone. My parents watched in bewilderment as I packed the car, because I'd only been back a few days. I made jokes, saying that until I got a new flat they should be relieved to get me out from under their feet. Once Dad was resigned to my decision, he started checking oil and water in the car, advising me of the best route to Hopetoun.

Just before I left, Cassie rang. It was difficult to talk, I explained, because Mum and Dad were within earshot.

'Stephen?' she said, as though that might elicit a response, then, 'Did you read my letter?'

'I read it.' The sounds of our breathing mingled in the phone. Looking through the doorway, I tried to work out whether or not I could be heard. 'And I could love you too,' I said. 'But not like this, Cassie. Not while you're with Ron.'

I expected her to address that directly, but instead she said, 'Don't go.' I didn't know whether she thought I was going to put the phone down, or if she knew that I was leaving the city.

'I have to go.'

She didn't speak again, but waited for me to put the phone down. I left straight after, my brief goodbye making Mum and Dad look more upset than when I'd gone to Europe.

Driving kept me occupied, and I managed to get as far as the salt lake before I thought of Cassie again. As I stood up, swallowing the salty taste away, I resolved to drive faster, hoping the momentum would prevent me from thinking about her again.

Having spent six months travelling through Europe, I'd become used to twilight; darkness comes gradually after hours of dusk. It's like being under water, because there are no colours other than misty blues. In Australia, the sun holds overhead for most of the day, then steals away, turning daylight to dark in minutes. Being used to twilight, I miscalculated the speed of the coming night. The first indication that darkness might be on the way came when I stopped at the Ravensthorpe Roadhouse. The tubular grain silos were like a row of huge missiles, but they looked pinkish, rather than the pure aluminium-white I remembered them to be. As I drove away I saw that the orange verge was glowing, and there was a red glare of sunset in my rear-vision mirror.

The sun met with the horizon, cloudless sky banding with weed-green light, darkness following within a few kilometres. The journey went slowly during the last stretch, because I was afraid of hitting animals. To give me the best chance of avoiding kangaroos and foxes, I drove in the centre of the road, always ready to switch my foot from the accelerator to the brake pedal.

When I reached Hopetoun I drove down the unsealed roads, navigating between weatherboard houses by the side-glow from my headlights. I pulled in round the back of our family house, beneath the fig tree. Before I turned off the lights I saw that the tree was overladen with fruits, most of them ripe. That meant I was the first visitor in some time, because any other member of my family would have raided the tree by now. Cassie was the greatest enthusiast for free fruit. Wherever we walked as children, she'd take fruit from trees and bushes that hung over public footpaths: gooseberries, plums, feijoas. 'Fruit belongs to nature,' she'd say, 'and now it belongs to me.'

I switched off the headlights, went inside and dumped my bag in the back room. I preferred that room because it was cool, out of the way. It was also the room I'd always slept in, just one white sheet on a mattress. I walked through the kitchen, the floorboards making the fridge door rattle. In the front room I walked past the piano (trying not to picture Cassie playing for us) and went to the mantelpiece. It was lined with gatherings from the beach: dried weed, logs polished by water, shells and tags of rope. There was also the pink anemone shell that Cassie had found on our last visit here, when Ron had come with us. It appeared to be intact, but I knew that there was a hole facing the wall. She hadn't dropped it, but simply held it too tight, her fingers breaking through. 'I can't believe I did that,' she'd whispered to me later, when Ron was out of the room. 'I'm more gentle than that.'

Further up the shelf there were two fan-shaped shells, so bright orange they looked artificial. For years we'd joked that they looked like the cups of a mermaid's bikini. The year that Ron came with us, he'd taken a Polaroid of Cassie in the bath, wearing nothing but those shells, one thigh over the other to cover the hair between her legs. That night he'd shown it to the family, who'd laughed with approval, snatching the photo from Cassie's constant grasping, passing it from one person to the next. When everyone was in bed, I'd crept through the house, trying not to rattle the fridge, and picked the shells up. They smelt faintly of sunscreen lotion. Their insides felt tooth-smooth, which had made me wonder how that cold must have felt against her breasts.

Standing there alone, years later, I was tempted to touch the shells again, but was distracted, because next to them were the dried bodies of seven sea-dragons. They looked like large unwound sea-horses, long pipe snouts jutting from their horse-heads. Their bony bodies had turned to something like dry leaves, eyes crisped. We found at least one new body washed up each year, but only kept the best ones. They are only found in that part of the world, and it saddened me to know they were being harvested illegally for sale to tourists. Sprayed gold and silver, they are sold as trinkets.

I realized that upon seeing them I would usually make some comment about the cruelty of the harvest, but there was nobody to talk to. It was the first time I'd been alone in the house, but rather than ponder that I knew it would be best to run a bath and relax. There are no baths in European hostels, only showers, so it felt good to climb in and soak. On the plaster wall beside me, sheathed in steam, was a pencil sketch Cassie had drawn when she was twelve. It had never been regarded as an act of vandalism, only decoration. It was entitled *Beyond Grogan's Hole* and depicted our favourite part of the beach, a reef-pool where the water was calm, surrounded by diving rocks. In her drawing, the far side of the pool was surrounded by mysterious creatures: smiling snakes, sea-horses with legs and winged roos.

I felt light in the water, as though I was rising from it, and thought the fatigue from my journey must be getting to me. Then I breathed out and sank again. I realized that my breathing was making me buoyant. It's the same principle sea-dragons use for rising and falling through the water, inflating and draining their swim bladders. That's partly why they move so gracefully. Their tiny fins only give small directional movement; the real work is done by bleeding air to and from their bodies. This ability to float also makes them vulnerable; when they are dragged from the water, the change in pressure ruptures the bladder, killing them.

I thought back to Cassie's letter. I'd read it enough times to remember her exact words. 'Loving you is like learning to use a gift for levitation. At first, every time I started to float I became nervous and the sensation was spoilt. Now I'm getting better and better at floating. I haven't touched down for days.'

I breathed out and sank again.

On our last visit, years before, there was a day when Ron drove out to the Fitzgerald National Park on his own. 'We're right on the doorstep,' he'd complained, as though that obliged us to visit the tourist spots. We preferred the privacy of Hopetoun, where the white-sand beaches were uninhabited, miles of coast to ourselves. As soon as Ron had driven away, I announced that I was going for a swim at Grogan's Hole. 'I might come with you,' Cassie had said, immediately gathering her towel.

I remember standing behind her half an hour later, rubbing sunscreen into myself, the same smell that had been in the shells. I stood behind, watching her wipe it into her skin, the moisture making her flesh look browner. She edged the cream under the straps of her bikini, stroking it around her neck. When her skin was glistening, she went straight to the water and lowered herself into it without pausing or reacting to the cold. Her hair settled and spread on the surface, then sank around her. We spent most of the afternoon hiding in the shadows of the rocks, using the water to cool our faces and wet our hair. Later, we practised floating on the surface. At one point, her hair wrapped around my legs; we were so still that it didn't tangle, but tugged at my knees, until she floated further away, and the strands uncoiled from me.

We sat on our towels to dry off; I felt close to her, but knew that nothing could happen. Not because she was my cousin, but because now that Ron was around, it was simply too late. That afternoon together made me realize how many times we could have held each other in the past. I've wondered since if the reason we stayed apart so long was because we had the security of proximity. When you're in love with a family member, you have the joy of knowing you'll see them all the time. You relish the build-up, believing it can last for ever.

The morning after my journey to Hopetoun I woke late, so I collected my snorkelling gear and a towel, picked a handful of figs and headed to the beach. The chalky-green skin of the figs split apart easily because they were so ripe; they taste at their best when they are a day from going rotten. I parted the skin with my thumbs, sucking out the red, wet seeds.

The walk to the beach took only two minutes, and although the sand was burning with heat, I was amazed at its softness. It's a habit to think of sand as granular and coarse, but this felt like hot silk. The beach was deserted, so I walked down its length looking into the turquoise shallows, trying to locate a kelp bed. I found one just past the rocks around Grogan's Hole, a scab-coloured mass beneath the waves. I put my flippers on and waded out backwards, then fastened on my face mask and snorkel, trying to swallow the rubbery taste as I swam out.

My lung capacity isn't what it used to be, but I took in as much air as I could, and dived to the level of the kelp. Spotting sea-horses and sea-dragons takes practice. Sea-horses are smaller, but easier to see; they change colour to match the background of kelp, but the swirls in their tails give them away. Sea-dragons are more difficult to spot because their bodies sprout weed-like appendages. Unless you knew to look for them, you'd think you were looking at seaweed. It took me several dives to find one; it was about thirty centimetres long, its body covered with stems and flat, green leaves. Nested among its foliage, I could see its long snout and the black dots of its eyes. The bulge of its cheeks squashed as it took in water, then fattened again.

My lungs were regaining the habit of air-holding, so after sucking in a good breath I dived to the floor, beneath the kelp. It took a while to get that low, but in the sparse bed of sea-grass I could make out twirls of sandy-coloured sea-horses. Their tails were wrapped around fronds of grass. Sea-horses are faithful to an individual piece of grass throughout their lives, making it their home, returning each night to curl around it.

I remembered my legs wrapped in Cassie's wet hair, beneath the water. At that moment I found myself sinking and had to swim up. By the time I reached the surface, fighting through the kelp, I was starting to panic. I tore off the mask and snorkel to gasp at the air, splashing my way back to the shallows. From there I threw my mask and snorkel on to the beach, flippers following them. When I reached the shore I lay in the sand, ignoring the burn of the sun, and let the tiredness come over me.

I opened my eyes under water, the crests of waves painting rainbow-edged lines of light on the sand. I felt Cassie's hand on my ankle, reached for hers, and we drew each other to the surface. She lay on her back, breathing in so that her lungs expanded, the shadows of ribs deepening, lifting her further out of the water. As she exhaled, her body and face sank, leaving her breasts exposed for a moment, before water closed over them. I reached under again, let her draw me down. Her body and eyes were luminous in the under-water sunlight. We held each other again by ankles, then feet and knees, moving to wrists. I trusted her to know when to release her hold each time and she did the same with me. Then we held each other close and breathed in, the weight of water in my lungs helping me to sink. The shimmered light looked like a liquid scar across her cheek, and over the wide pink blur of her smile.

She sank, kissing my chest, my solar plexus, pushing bubbles out of her mouth around the dip by my hip bone. The cupped movements of her hands stroked water over my groin. She sank lower, keeping a grip on my hand and took my testicles in her mouth; then she pushed me back, so that they slid free, cool water washing the spit away. Swimming between my legs, her wet hair stroked my thighs. She turned on her back, arms behind her head, eyes closed, and sank away from me.

Back at the house, I saw the ground surrounding my car was covered with emptied fig shells. Each one had been sucked clean, only the white pith remaining. I went into the house and stopped to listen. The fridge door rattled three times, then stopped.

In the bedroom, Cassie was sitting with her bare back to me, curled forward, arms wrapping the sheet over her legs.

She turned round, her smile fading.

'Don't look so worried,' she said. 'I'm still here.'

There was a dusting of sand on her shoulder. I moved to stroke it away, expecting grains, but it smoothed like talc over the soft warm of her skin.

ALICE
RON BUTLIN

With the approach of the thunderstorm Alice was becoming more and more restless. As the air became clammier and heavier the afternoon itself seemed to be slowing down and every breath stuck in her lungs like sweat. Outside, the sky had darkened to blue-black. She dragged herself up from her chair once more to wander around the sitting room. The window was open but no draught came in, and she sensed the same weighted calm had settled like a threat over the front garden and the street beyond.

She crossed to the mantelpiece where she stood watching her fingers pick up the glass sweet-jar. Plenty of the red-wrapped nougats, her least favourites. Her hand scrabbled among them for a last green one, then abruptly lost interest. The jar was replaced. She sat down again. Four in the afternoon, midsummer almost, and dark enough indoors to have to switch on the light. But she wouldn't.

Instead, she had soon struggled to her feet again. In the stillness of the room she could hear her own short breathless gasps. Having straightened the antimacassar on the couch she paused for a moment's rest – even with the top button of her blouse loosened she still felt choked. Off again, only to stumble against the small side-table, steadying both it and herself just in time. Who'd want to have Mrs MacDonald rushing across to find out if she'd keeled over at last. Sometimes it felt as if the whole street was waiting for her to go. All these phone calls first thing in the morning or doorstep visits about nothing in particular except to check she'd not died in her sleep.

They were being kind, and she supposed she was grateful, but there was always the unspoken pause, the split-second's refocusing of a glance that betrayed the real question: 'Not dead yet?' Well, she appreciated their concern, but fuck them.

Yes, that was the language to use. Only in the last few weeks had she discovered the relish of bad language. One morning she'd been woken by Mrs Miller asking, after the 'not-dead-yet?' pause, if she wanted something from the shop. She'd replied, there were a few words on the weather and then they'd hung up. Now for breakfast, she'd thought, and heard herself saying, 'Breakfast, bloody breakfast'. As she pulled on her dressing gown she'd been repeating to herself: 'Bloody breakfast, bloody, bloody, bloody, bloody breakfast.' It felt good, stimulating. Like a vigorous marching tune in her head. There she'd stood in front of the mirror: a kindly-looking, elderly, white-haired woman, vulnerable, frail but dignified – the word they no doubt used when talking about her to each other – and all the time behind the benevolent smile she was hammering out full-force 'Bloody, bloody, bloody, bloody, bloody breakfast'. She grinned to herself – and she'd not done that in months. In a short time the 'bloodies' had given way to 'hells', and the 'hells' to 'damns'; getting into 'fucks' had been her big breakthrough. It was after the postman went by a couple of days ago: 'No letters, well fuck him!' she'd thought, then announced, 'Fuck him! Fuck him! Fuck him!' to the clock, the empty armchair and to a whole clutch of photographs. Stopping herself in time from getting too loud. Not because it would shock the MacDonalds and Millers or whoever might be passing, she didn't care about them. It was simply because she didn't really want to share these words with anyone: coming from her they were hers, and hers alone.

But her words weren't working today. 'Fucking storm, fucking storm,' she kept repeating as she stood in the kitchen, letting the tap run for coolness, but she didn't feel any better. The water tasted heavy and tepid and there was nothing indoors for a person to breath even. She would go into the garden.

The sky was even blacker than before, with everything beneath gripped in sharp, shadowless light; and the air so sluggish she almost had to push her way through it. Nothing seemed to move out here. As she lifted back her damp hair she could see the MacDonalds, a group of stuffed figures crouched in a family circle around their umbrella table. Who were the MacDonalds, and the Millers? Where had they come from? Where had any of the people in the street come from? They looked different and were even dressed differently from the way she'd ever been: those track suits, yellow shorts, those plastic rucksacks they took with them wherever they went, like a company of oversized and witless children. This was not the world she'd been born into.

Had the green bush by the path been transfixed into complete rigidity? No, it did shake a little when her hand gave one of the branches a tug — but shook, she could sense, unwillingly. Her neighbour's spade was propped within reach; without thinking what she was doing, she leaned over the fence and picked it up. Its metal edge clanged against the stone path, a clang that seemed to fill the street. Too bad. She clanged it once more and her reward was five MacDonald faces panned in her direction. As she leaned towards the bush, its perfume stuck to her face and, in its sultriness, the scent seemed a solid thing. Perhaps, the air being so still, if she removed the plant and its scent, she could fit herself into the gap left behind and so withdraw from a world filled with strangers who had come along, long after her, bringing their strange ways.

She started spading out the earth. Not so hard really, but with every thrust and lift she had to stop to catch her breath. There was sweat trickling down her face and back. She paused for a moment to wipe her eyes clear and there, up on their hind legs, were a couple of MacDonalds staring over at her. The bigger of them, a wobble of pink flesh, baldness and glasses, was already starting in her direction. She carried on digging. Not that she could remember what the plant was called, nor what anything much was called these days — just that some things were living and some weren't. Still, who cared? One good tug and she'd have it free.

The wobbly MacDonald was standing at her gate: 'Mrs Williams! Hello there, Mrs Williams!'

Should she pretend to have gone deaf?

Yes.

Taking a good grip of the stem with both hands, feet braced for the effort, she closed her eyes for the Big Tug.

'Hello there, Mrs Williams! That's a lovely lilac you've got there: can I help you at all?'

The bush came out more easily than she'd expected, almost first pull, making her stagger a couple of steps backwards on to the path. She threw it to one side then picked up the spade to carry on digging.

'You really should be resting in weather like this, Mrs Williams. What are you doing?'

Before she could stop herself she replied, 'Digging my fucking grave. What the fuck else would I be doing?'

When she next looked up he had gone. She put the spade back; she didn't need it any more. Indoors, it was dark. She went through to the kitchen to wash her hands, then sat down as the first rumble of thunder sounded. Heavy drops of rain began spattering the window. She smiled to herself: in a few hours she would go to bed, but for the moment she felt rested after all that digging and might just have a short nap while she was in the mood.

THRESHOLD
COLM O'GAORA

Moonlight catches the riffled surface of the lake so that it looks like chainmail stretched out before us in the darkness. A breeze pulls at my shirt when we go to sit on the low wall that scoops up to the narrowest of bridges to watch the lake changing shape. We talk over the night that is behind us, the half-hour with the girls that might be before us, and the house we will return to where our father sleeps.

'The band were good, weren't they?' Carmel offers.

'They're always the same, always good,' Michael replies.

He hates the old standards they played but will do anything to agree with her now that the evening is beginning to close on them.

'I prefer a disc jockey myself, there's more choice and variation.' Isobel is small and the lime-green jacket she wears pulls the light towards it, leaving a soft and strange glow on her skin and in her frizzy tied-back blonde hair.

'You know, but I think I agree with you there,' I say, and she turns to smile. I wonder how old she is. Her face has no lines that I can see and barely creases with her smile, but her eyes light up anyway and that is enough for me.

'Good,' she says, pulling her jacket across against the breeze, which is stiffening into a wind.

'We'll agree to differ on that point then,' Carmel says.

Her voice is hard and the breeze has pinched her face into a knot. She has thin lips and her eyes have neither colour nor light. Michael had picked her out within seconds of arriving in the dance hall. We are brothers, twins, but I see different things than he does, and that is where it ends.

The talk turns to others in the hall, the young and the old, the farmers who came in taxis only they can afford to have wait outside in the hope of taking away a lonely widow or spinster who would be offered marriage within weeks, rescued from the dance halls for ever. A few came by car, gangs of lads squeezed into Toyotas and Nissans, handbrake turns made on the broken tarmac in front of the hall. Mostly they arrived by bus, rusting diesels whose seats smelled always of the sweat and boots of the GAA teams who used them on Sundays.

Michael and Carmel are discussing the couples in the hall, where they're from and who they used to go steady with. I know that Michael is making most of it up to tease Carmel. If she laughs when she realizes what he is up to, then he has her; if not, we will be on our way too soon.

A coot is moving through the reeds at the edge of the lake. The dab of white on its forehead nods to and fro, the ripples it makes beat out into the lake until other waves flatten them. Isobel has seen the coot also, but not Michael and Carmel. She says nothing, leaving it be. She has her own thoughts, and they also are enough for me.

Michael and Carmel are arguing now, their voices raised, the wind barely whipping the words into the distance where all the fields begin to look like water, dressed in the flat grey of midnight. Their faces are so close now that they might be touching. That first hour of melancholy is passing, when the glow of the dance hall and the being amongst others begin to fade then die until we are left with only ourselves. Michael senses also that it is passing, that there is so little time, knows that by seeming to push Carmel away from him he can capture her.

'Would you get away out of that, you filthy thing!' Carmel yells at him. She turns to Isobel.

'What?' Isobel enquires quietly.

'Did you ever hear the like of him? Did you?' Carmel cups her hands over her face as if it will stop her hearing what Michael is saying, or suggesting, to her.

'She's a one,' Isobel says into the darkness.

I know perfectly what she means. Michael is one too. His hand seizes Carmel's arm in the fashion of a predatory bird and he leans his mouth in towards hers. I turn away when she lifts her lips to his and his arms gather her towards him. The silence is sudden. Isobel has not seen them but I can tell that she knows what is going on. They kiss noisily, Carmel breaking away to slap him or remove a furrowing hand.

I am looking out at the lake again where nothing has changed except that the coot is gone. Small waves replace each other in careful sequence.

After our mother left there were only a few short months before our father began to invite each unmarried woman in the parish to the house for dinner. Young and old they came at half-past four on a Sunday, a box of chocolates or a Dundee cake under their arms, smelling of powder, the front door left ajar so they could come inside without being seen waiting. We waited in the hall, stiff in our collars, ties, and V-necks, to take their jackets and whatever they had brought with them. We delayed them there so that Da could move away from the net-curtained window and settle into the armchair from which he would rise to greet them.

None stayed, none even returned, and in a short time the supply was exhausted and he began for a while to talk of our mother again. She also has not returned, but Michael seeks her still in every face he meets.

'The night is getting on,' Isobel says.

'It is,' I say but can think of nothing more. Behind us Michael and Carmel are silent now, their mouths feeding on each other.

'At least it's a fine night,' she continues, 'there'd be none of this otherwise.' She glances over at Michael and Carmel. 'Well, even a thunderstorm wouldn't stop Carmel when she has a man at her...' She stops to check herself but the words are said already. I know that there will have been many other times, other men, of whom Michael is but a reflection.

She looks away, out across the lake whose surface is hammered down now by the wind.

'Who's waiting for you at home?' I ask, ready to heal what has been opened between us.

'Oh, nobody really. My mother's long since given up on the waiting. They leave the television on when one of us is out.' She shudders in the wind that is picking cold from the lake. 'And you?'

'There's only the two of us and the Da. He'll be sound asleep after a few jars in Doyle's.'

Michael and Carmel begin to laugh quietly.

'Did your mother die, is that it?' Isobel asks.

I catch my breath when she asks me this. I am so surprised that I begin to laugh, an uncertain laugh that rises from deep inside me. I look at her face to see what she wants. Even in the light of the moon I notice freckles across her nose and beneath her eyes. I wonder why I have not seen them before.

'I'm sorry, I shouldn't have asked,' her hand folds across my wrist.

It is not the question that has struck me but that she should ask it. Strange how the reality of another person can change, hinged on a few words or the smallest of actions, and become entirely different, another character unfolding.

'She went out one day, years ago, and has not come back since,' I offer as an explanation. 'A short while later the Da packed some of her things into a tea-chest and an estate car came to collect it, but he has never told us where it went to.'

'You've never asked?'

'No.'

'Isn't it strange?'

'What?'

'That you'd never ask?'

'No. If we asked, how would we know that any answer was the truth?'

It would be too easy to repeat what Michael and I have clung to for so long, a lie that becomes legend, then truth, yet is only what we want to believe in the end. 'For a while we thought she might be in London – she nursed there for a year before she was married – but when we saw the city on television it didn't look like a place she'd live in at all. To be honest, we don't know where she is. There's only the Da now anyway.'

I notice that Isobel's hand is still across my wrist. Michael and Carmel are talking again, their fingers entwined, hands swinging between them like a pendulum marking out the time that is left. I reach out and touch the lobe of Isobel's ear. She blinks when I press the softly whorled flesh against my palm.

Her mouth tastes of something and it takes me a few seconds to realize what it is. A dairy taste. The taste that grabbed your tongue in the milking parlour of O'Dwyer's farm, or the kitchen in the convent where the sisters made ice-cream for the orphans and us too because they considered us the same way. The taste is chocolate. But there is something else here too.

I place my hand at the back of her neck and can feel the narrow muscles tighten there, like cord beneath her skin, her shoulder-blades drawn together like wings. She does not know me, after all, and now I do not know her either.

Only now do I remember the dark chocolate melted in a glass bowl over a boiling pan, the water bubbling away to nothing as the block turned to liquid. Ice-cream left to soften on the sideboard, our fingers prised away as we sought the tub above our heads. Her skirt at the sink.

I lift my mouth from Isobel's and look out across the lake towards the trees that rise against the starred night, dark and strange, a strip of silver gravel hidden at their feet. It is no distance from here, but as children it was a challenge to race to the bridge and return to where she waited with our reward: chocolate turned into the ice-cream, livid brown seams in the burred white.

We swam then, thin-limbed machines driving through water inked with peat, as once we had been swimmers lost to the world in her belly, then slapped out like fish upon the delivery-room table. She waited with towels stretched between her hands. We thrashed back to her through foam and black water.

Isobel presses her mouth harder on mine as if she senses that I am detaching myself. Her perfume rises to my nose, a wild-flower scent, of foxglove, fuchsia, white-thorn, gorse, the same scent that summer breezes threshed from the roadsides we once walked along, ice-cream melting in our hands, towels damp on our shoulders, stones cutting the soles of our feet.

Isobel draws away, a thread of saliva snaps upon our lips, and I look into her eyes. She has the eyes of those women who hide a secret world that is closed to men. There is nothing for me to see there.

'Carmel,' she calls.

'Would you like us to walk...' I offer.

'We can make our own way, thanks,' she says.

The night is almost lost to us now. Everything seems broken and still I wonder why.

Suddenly, out on the lake a bird breaks from cover and moves blindly into the night, a slow clattering of its wings as it rises into the air and then it is gone, leaving only the imagined path of its flight away from us.

Isobel grabs my arm and just as quickly lets it go.

'What's that?'

'Only a swan, or a mallard maybe,' I say. 'A fox might have disturbed it.'

'Jesus, it scared the wits out of me.'

She calls to Carmel again but there is no answer.

I look up and Michael is standing on the edge of the bridge.

'Are you crazy or what?' Carmel yells at him, her hand spread across her mouth, but she is laughing. 'Are you crazy or what?' she yells again.

Michael is swinging his arms back and forth, threatening to jump into the water below. He bends and straightens his knees and keeps his hands pressed together in a point like the comedians in the black and white films we once watched together on Saturday afternoons. He won't jump. It is a last attempt to win Carmel over, and we all know this as we watch him on the parapet.

The wind tugs at his shirt, snapping it across his shoulders. His hair is pressed into a vane behind his head. He leans into the wind, eyes closed, balanced against the air. He jumps.

There is a white plume of water as the lake receives him. Carmel is shrieking with laughter, a shrieking that is close to the noise of sudden, racking grief. I lean out and stare into the black water where my brother has disappeared. The waves of his entry have already broken against the bridge supports, the reed beds swell and subside with them. I gaze into the water until I see the whiteness of his shirt billowing like a flag wrapped around his body. It hangs there for what can only be a moment before it descends, slowly and interminably.

My lungs fill with cold air as the water hits me. Isobel's scent is lost and there is only the sourness of the lake for me now. I can hear the girls for a moment, yelling and shouting, calling our names. The water shuts them out, shuts everything out. There is nothing to see. The water numbs every sense. As if they are wrapped in rags, my fingers feel nothing. I turn and kick downwards with my legs, arms sweeping.

Saxophone, snare, double bass; the sounds of the night's music return as I sink towards my brother. A mirror ball breaks the light into innumerable stars. Isobel's face is clearer now than ever before: grey eyes that are slow to move, slow to smile, strange as another race.

My heart beats slowly in its chamber, as if the blood has nowhere left to go.

I find his collar first but his shirt comes away in my hands, floats past me. I open my eyes and he is there; Michael, white skin shoaled with bubbles of phosphorescence, hair floating like weed, limbs moving back and forth, his eyelids shut and smooth as shells.

The music is more distant now, only the tin rasp of the snare drum can be heard. The stars have faded to nothing. Isobel is lost as though she has never been.

I put my arms around his chest and haul him upright before pushing upwards with my feet. The water clears and above our heads the surface is bright. I feel his chest pushing against the brace of my arms and let go. His face turns to mine and we both laugh as we break the surface.

In the still water his shoulders are smooth and clear as milk, beaded with water. He pulls his hair back across his forehead.

'Race you back!' he shouts and we both strike out for the shore where our mother waits on a strip of silver sand at the foot of the pine trees, ice-cream seamed with chocolate that is our reward, her face alive with laughter, towels held between her hands, swollen with air, generous as sails.

LESSONS IN PLEASURE
HILAIRE

Today, as every day, George is up early. He does not believe in wasting the day. He feels lucky that it is here, another day shining ahead of him, sweet with expectation. As soon as he wakes he goes through the house and draws back the curtains, opens the windows and props the back door ajar. George likes a breeze through the house; fresh air invigorates him. Even in the winter he opens up the house first thing.

George's house is small, just three rooms, but it gets the sun. He keeps his house spotless. It is a matter of pride. He is not like the other bachelors and widowers in the village, who let beer bottles pile up by the doorstep, who never open their tattered curtains, whose houses are held together by grease and cakings of dust. Three years ago George made the mistake of accepting an invitation to play cards at Shoemaker's. Parting the sticky plastic strips over the doorway to the kitchen had been a revelation. The light switches and power points were ringed with grey smudges. Hard yellow spots of fat spattered the walls. The worktop was buried in foil containers, empty packets, tins whose original contents were now uniformly green and mossy. He perched reluctantly on the edge of a filthy wicker chair and held the frayed cards delicately with his fingertips. It was the worst game of poker he'd played in his life.

Back in the bedroom he kneels down on the thin rug beside his bed. Slowly, his biceps quivering and his lungs puffing out, he performs ten push-ups. Unlike Shoemaker and the others, George is still in good trim. On the sideboard there's a framed photo of him in his sailor's uniform, thirty years old, tanned, and revelling in his good looks. Once a year, on his birthday, George weighs himself on the village scales. He keeps all the slips in a tobacco tin, testament to his unwavering weight over the last forty years.

In the bathroom he scrubs himself with cold water. He yawns and grimaces at his reflection in the mirror to wake his face, then he lathers up and shaves with studied care. On Fridays he gets his hair cut at the barber's, and then he treats himself to a hot shave. Pelicanos, who is not much younger than George, sharpens up the cutthroat on the leather strop, and then with a flourish poises the razor above George's foamy cheeks before slicing perilously through the bristles. Each time it's a thrill. Pelicanos's hands are infested with a continual tremble, from years of fine cutting with scissors, and yet when the cutthroat touches flesh his hand miraculously steadies. Afterwards, George's skin tingles; it's as smooth as his surprisingly hairless backside. Pelicanos's shave is a small, indulgent luxury, and George lives for such pleasures.

The shave he gets at home isn't perfect, but it's better than the scruffy standard of most of the village men. George reckons he could grate hard cheese quite easily on Porter's stubble. He splashes a little cologne around his neck and armpits, then neatly combs his hair into place.

After his ablutions it is time for breakfast. From a square tin he takes out two plain crackers and places them on a china plate. Sitting at the gleaming laminex table in the kitchen, he eats the crackers with a glass of tap water. As he's got older he's learned to delay his first coffee until later in the day. Already though he is planning it, deciding which café he will go to, which table he will sit at, anticipating the first taste of the coffee slipping through him and his old ticker doing a little tap dance in his chest. George smiles; what pleasures lie ahead of him today.

Before going out he washes the plate and glass from his breakfast, dries them carefully and places them back on the shelf above the sink. A place for everything and everything in its place, George thinks, and is glad that he is not burdened with too many possessions. His career as a sailor taught him that. A quick sweep through the house with the broom, and then George has to make one of the most important decisions of the day. He opens the wardrobe and studies the neat row of shirts: tropical prints, pastel cotton shirts with flamboyant ruffles, rayon paisley designs with drooping collars. He is known for his shirts in the village. Today he opts for a subtle number, a short-sleeved white shirt with pale green embroidery on the tips of the collar and scrolling down the front. The sort of shirt a cowboy might wear to his wedding.

Once he is satisfied that he looks presentable George ventures out into the village for his morning stroll. Sometimes he climbs the steep steps to the top of the hill, behind the village, for a view of the clock tower and the church spire and his fellow villagers busying themselves in the square, hurrying back and forth like frantic ants swarming over a sugar cube.

Or he makes his way in a semicircle along the back lanes, stopping to tickle the chins of the local cats sunning themselves on doorsteps. Or he weaves randomly through the higgledy-piggledy cobbled streets, past open kitchen windows and wafts of stewing beans or baked lemon pudding. But always his final destination is the market, the quadrangle of verandaed buildings which is the commercial hub of the village.

Today, after some quality time with his favourite felines, he approaches the market from the north corner. Peter the fishmonger calls out: *Morning, George*, and he nods briskly in reply. Hands clasped behind his back, he saunters past the glittering display of fish, all neatly sunbathing in rows on their beach of crushed ice. The next stall is stacked with hands of bananas, like yellow baseball mitts. It's only occasionally he has a taste for bananas; they're not what he desires today.

Kittens dart in and out beneath the stalls. Cardboard boxes and wooden crates lie discarded on the edges of the market. George enjoys the bustle of it all, the cries and banter, Peter the fishmonger's leather apron and huge rubber boots, the bruised fruit rotting in the gutters. A stall-holder building a pyramid of lemons glances up as George passes and comments appreciatively: *Nice shirt, mate*. George tips his head in gracious acceptance of the compliment.

Up ahead, at the end of the row of stalls, is Mado. George does most of his business with Mado. He is the best supplier. Theirs is a simple mateship. Mado understands what George wants and, more to the point, he delivers the goods. – *George, George*, Mado beckons, drawing him in behind the trestle tables. – *I've got some juicy ones today, nice and plump*. He speaks as one connoisseur to another. George savours the hint of complicity, as if their business is under the counter, cloak and dagger stuff. And Mado does in fact keep his best specimens back, out of the public eye, until George has made his selection. He knows how to make George feel that he is a valued customer.

From under the trestle table Mado drags out a wooden crate. He lifts the protective cardboard from the top, and there, nestled on scrunches of green tissue paper, are more than a dozen tomatoes. George catches his breath and sucks in his bottom lip. They give off a faint, warm glow, lusciously red. Tentatively, tenderly, George prods at them, testing for firmness, for just-ripe-ness. – *Take your time*, Mado encourages, as he bags up two bunches of purple grapes for old Theresa.

This one, George decides, and he drops the tomato into the palm of his left hand, reckoning its density. Yes, this is the one. He bounces it in his hand like a baseball. The soft slap as it hits his palm: it *sounds* right. He sniffs it, just as he's seen Marcel run his nostrils above a glass of claret, and it has the right combination of ploughed fields and heat and plummy juiciness.

A nod to Mado, and George slips him a crumpled note. Mado stuffs the note in his apron pocket, and reaches out to shake George's hand. – *Tomorrow, George*, he says, pumping his hand. – *Mind how you go*.

George is buzzing. There is a lightness to his step, as if his feet have been injected with helium. Mission accomplished. He leaves the market and sets off down a side street. Bushes and vines overhang the path and brush against him as he passes, the leaves stroking him affirmatively, whispering: *Life is good, George*. The tomato lends its small weight to the pendulum swing of his right arm.

Rita's café is on a corner, with a good view along the three streets which converge here. The table he had picked out in his mind this morning is, fortuitously, free. George likes to believe that it is the power of his thoughts which has secured him this table next to the whitewashed wall. He sits facing out and places the tomato lovingly in front of him. The sun pours down on to both of them. Later he will move into the shade, but for now they could both do with a top-up.

– *Short black?* Rita's son Ray asks, giving a desultory wipe to the table, deftly avoiding the tomato. George inclines his head to indicate yes, and Ray turns on his heel, flicking the tea towel out and sneering to himself. *And the tomato?* he'd wanted to ask, but there's no point. He'll just be back tomorrow, with another corker.

While waiting for his coffee George fondles the tomato. Its skin is taut, like stretched clingfilm. He imagines biting into the tomato, as you'd bite an apple, his teeth puncturing the skin, pink juice dribbling down his chin, and then sucking out the pulpy sac of seeds.

Ray slides a stainless-steel tray on to the table, tucking the bill underneath. Arranged on the oval tray are a little coffee cup and saucer, two double cubes of sugar wrapped in paper, and a tall thin glass of water. The composition is pleasing to George; if he had artistic inclinations he would paint a still life of it. He positions the tomato in the centre of the table.

George studies Ray's contemptuous back. He's young, George reasons, he doesn't appreciate life's small pleasures. No doubt Ray has previewed his life on fast-forward, pausing at the fabulous and glamorous successes which await him. All the youngsters want to escape the village. George understands, he ran away to sea after all, but at a certain point you begin to long for home, for the familiar. Domestic ritual, George continues, addressing his thoughts to the tomato, domestic ritual is a rich enough seam, milking each day for its subtle differences.

George draws the coffee out over an hour. In that time the sun shifts several degrees. Beneath a rhododendron bush a mottled cat supervises while her kitten pats and paws at a fish with puzzlement, tantalized by its smell but unsure what to do with it. Young men speed past on buzzing mopeds. Inside the café Ray leans across the counter to whisper something to Delia, the village beauty, who has done something very strange to her blonde hair: *Shirley Temple gone mad*, George muses. She tilts forward on her stool and as she laughs she tosses her bouncy ringlets over her shoulder.

Porter shuffles round the corner, clutching a cereal packet, his shirt unbuttoned and untucked, his hangover throbbing in the heat of the day, pulsing out from his worried forehead. George raises a hand in greeting, but Porter can't see beyond the oily colours swarming around him like a malignant ectoplasm. Over-indulgence; George shakes his head pitifully. The trick is to learn under-indulgence, to extract maximum enjoyment from the most minimal of circumstances, to stretch out and delay each moment and keep yourself on tippytoes with anticipation.

The shadow cast by the whitewashed wall lengthens, bathing George in a brief coolness. He drinks the glass of water in one long slow gulp, deposits a few coins on the table and picks up his tomato. Time to stretch the legs and see where the action is.

George walks upright, not stooped like Shoemaker and the others, with his hands behind his back cradling the tomato. Their tour takes in most of the village's hot spots. Pelicanos is hanging out faded pink and blue towels on a plastic clothes-horse in front of his shop. A few doors down, in the grocery, Maria is dusting the shelves of tinned and bottled food, George notes approvingly. Diagonally opposite is old Theresa's startling house, encrusted from top to bottom with bottle caps, glinting in the sunlight.

He turns down the next street, heading towards the square. Shoemaker and Porter are sitting in deckchairs outside Shoemaker's house, airing their pot-bellies. They have a bottle of beer apiece, and alternate swigs of beer with handfuls of cereal from the packet on the ground between them. Porter has shed his ectoplasmic hangover, and, briefly, the world is sparkling and clear. – *George*, he roars, brandishing his beer bottle. – *George, join us for breakfast, mate!*

George declines with a wistful shake of his head, an amused, child-tolerant smile. He squeezes the tomato reassuringly. Hours yet before he will succumb to its succulent temptations.

The narrow street opens on to a square which is lined with cafés. George strides slowly around the piazza, completing a full circuit before deciding which café warrants his custom. They all have long awnings sheltering clusters of tables and chairs. Most of the cafés have been here for years, owned and run by the same six families.

Quinn's, on the eastern corner, changed hands recently, the subject of much discussion and speculation in the village. Now, instead of the familiar wooden tables and rush-bottom chairs, there are angular metal tables and purple chrome stools. The name has changed too. The jagged lettering above the awning reads QUINCUNX. George is vaguely scandalized by the name, more so by the look of the place. During the day it is deserted, but at night the youngsters flock here. He toys with the idea of invading this adolescent zone but knows it is not the sort of place he would want to linger, despite the satisfaction it would give him of causing a stir among his fellow villagers.

Instead he chooses a table at Fraser's Bar. Here the seats are low and cushioned, just right for whiling away an afternoon. He rests the tomato in the seat next to him. A couple of tables to the right, Marcel is playing chess with an invisible opponent. For George, this is all the company he needs, the presence nearby of other people without any pressure to interact, and a ripening tomato by his side. When Lauren places a glass of chilled rosé in front of him, anticipating his usual order, George reflects again how lucky he is to have woken up to a day such as this.

For a while he watches the activity in the centre of the square. By the old stone well carts piled with flagons of wine are being unloaded. Patient donkeys flick flies away with their tails and hope for the lumps of sugar which children no longer proffer, brainwashed from an early age in the stringencies of dental hygiene. George feels an affinity with the animals' near-silent passage through the world.

The rosé melts inside him. He rotates the tomato between his fingers; this increases his sense of well-being. Surveying the village square, George wonders exactly how many chairs are set out in the surrounding cafés. They must far outnumber the village population. For years a tourism boom has been predicted, but the only tourists are the handful, admittedly increasing fractionally each year, who come to marvel at old Theresa's bottle-cap house. Ginny, who owns the newsagent's on the south of the square, has started selling black and white postcards of Theresa's house, alongside the carousel of incongruous pink plastic buckets and spades. The village is more than a day's drive from the coast, but Ginny still manages to sell several sets each summer.

These are the sorts of mysteries George ponders on his afternoons by the square, rolling a tomato in the palm of his hand as if it were a meditative aid. Perhaps Marcel, under guise of his chess game, is contemplating George's fruit fixation, but in George's estimation his fellow villagers are a superficial bunch unconcerned with the niceties of daily life.

Towards sunset the café owners wind in the awnings and switch on the strings of yellow, red and blue lights. Pelicanos arrives for his first beer. At the neighbouring café the market stall-holders congregate, shouting out their orders and noisily rearranging the tables.

This is George's cue to be on his way. Waves of heat still rise out of the cobblestones as he heads homewards, towards the moment he has been waiting for all day. But he knows not to hurry. He can wring out his anticipation a little longer; he relishes the discipline.

His route today takes him along Poacher's Alley, and the sight of The Cavern suggests to George that another coffee may be in order. It's a cosy café, set down a couple of steps from the alley, with only four stools at the counter. On the walls are dozens of framed black and white photos of film stars and pop celebrities, all apparently autographed to the owner. *For Arthur, You make a great cup of coffee, Sly.* As far as George knows, no one has ever spotted any of these personalities in the village, but it lends an aura of mystique to Arthur's establishment.

In Arthur's hands the making of an espresso is a sublime piece of choreography, a series of twirls and flourishes and precise movements. The cup and saucer twist to a halt in front of George and as a final gesture Arthur flicks up the lid of the sugar dispenser. Ray could learn a thing or two from Arthur, George considers.

The tomato gleams at George, contrasting nicely with the polished zinc counter. The ways to devour a tomato are numerous and George has been running through the possibilities over the course of the day. He has almost decided the fate which will befall today's chosen one. Nothing complex: the method should simply intensify his enjoyment.

A rustle of plastic bags distracts George from his musings. Old Theresa has balanced herself on the stool next to him. At her feet are the bags she collects her bottle caps in. They're bulging, so George guesses it's been a busy day for her. Arthur raises his eyebrows in query. Theresa nods wearily, and Arthur spins into his espresso routine.

But it doesn't end there. Next to the espresso Arthur uncaps a Coke, pours it from shoulder height into a glass and slips the cap across the counter towards Theresa, who pockets it quickly before anyone else (*who?* George wonders) gets to it. Then Arthur shakes up a can of artificial cream, creating figure-of-eight shapes in the air, and extrudes coil upon coil of shiny synthetic cream into a bowl held at an angle in his left hand. He tops this confection with a swirl of chocolate cream and presents it to Theresa with a long-handled spoon.

George sips his coffee, fascinated and slightly appalled. Old Theresa stirs some of the cream into her coffee. She drains the cup in one go, then sets about the dish of cream, scraping at the sides to get every last lick of aerated froth. No sooner has she finished than she downs the Coke as a chaser. George harbours a secret admiration, even though his insides feel clogged and queasy merely witnessing Theresa's gluttonous consumption. He sneaks a sly look at her. She is swaying slightly on her stool and her eyes are glazed over. A quiet burp jolts her body and she grips the counter briefly to steady herself. Arthur catches George staring at her. – *She'll sit there like that for an hour now*, Arthur informs him. – *Takes all sorts, I guess*, and Arthur resumes obsessively straightening the sugar dishes and ashtrays on the counter.

George slips off his stool and leaves Theresa to her post-cream hallucinations. He walks purposefully back to his house. The evening is cool. A light, jasmine-scented breeze ruffles his hair. The sensations remind him of the days before he ran away from the village, his bubbling sense of excitement, and the way every shy girl was suddenly intensely alluring. If George had a strong faith he would pray for such days as these in heaven.

The house retains the heat of the day. George opens the windows and invites the evening breeze inside. He places his shoes by the front door and eases his feet into the soft Chinese slippers he acquired years ago in Hong Kong.

In the kitchen he sets a place for himself at the table. In the middle he arranges the breadboard and knife, having cut two thick slices from the village loaf. He takes a bottle of beer from the fridge, uncaps it and puts it on the coaster to the right of the table mat. The salt cellar stands to attention between the table mat and the breadboard.

When everything is ready, he rinses the tomato and places it on his plate. He flicks out a blade on his Swiss Army knife and reverentially introduces it into the centre of the tomato.

George divides the tomato into eight wedges. His mouth waters at the sight of the tomato's glistening interior and the little pool of rosy juice forming on the plate. But he is not going to gobble; George knows how to prolong his pleasure. He taps a few grains of salt on to the first slice and observes closely as the white crystals are absorbed into the firm flesh. Only then does he spear the tomato wedge with his fork and allow it to dissolve in his mouth. Eyes closed, he savours the piquant and paradoxically sweet morsel. Now he is in that golden place old Theresa rushed herself off to, pure self-indulgence. And there are seven more pieces to eat. George has a long evening ahead of him.

eta
CONRAD WILLIAMS

I met my wife shortly after a nervous breakdown. Mine, not hers. She had been visiting her grandmother in Winwick Hospital, where I had been convalescing. I no longer really needed to be there, but I enjoyed the relaxed surroundings and there wasn't anything to hurry back to. I was walking the grounds, enjoying the cold air on my grey arms and the spring of the grass beneath my slippers. I stopped for a while by the pavilion to watch swallows describing invisible patterns across the scorched flat of the cricket pitch. The only sounds were the drone of a distant heavy-duty lawnmower and the concussions of a tennis match. It was a cloudy day, but I noticed a sudden break in the cover. Sunlight sprayed through the rent and picked out a door on the east wing. To my delight, it opened and a wheelchair containing a broken figure, an autumn leaf of a woman, emerged, pushed by another woman whose long brown hair trapped the sun in thick bands of copper. The core of sunlight followed them, like a tractor beam in a cheap SF film. But then the cloud healed and the trick was over. I felt invigorated by the fluke, however, and walked across the cricket pitch on a line that would cut the couple off as they reached the path into the woods. My cheeks were aching from a smile.

They stopped for a moment by a large swathe of buddleia, mauve flowers depending like sore, tired teats. I caught the last few words she was saying to the old woman, something about travelling to the sun.

'Hello there,' I said, raising a hand.

The old woman remained mashed into her wheelchair, a silver thread of drool connecting her lip to her knee, light snarling on a golden, bird-shaped clasp in her hair. Her companion lifted a blade of hair from her own face and, looking up at me from beneath it, said: 'Hello there yourself. Are you lost?'

'No,' I said. 'I own all this. You happen to be trespassing.'

'Oh really,' she replied, a really quite beautiful smile moving across her mouth, like a ripple. She must have known I was a patient but she was indulging me. I liked that. I liked her. 'I do apologize, only my mother wanted to get a breath of air.'

'What's your name?' I asked, pulling out the notepad in which I write down descriptions of the aircraft I see. I frowned and poised my pen above the surface. 'This is very serious.'

'Emma,' she replied. 'Emma Elderfield.'

'I'd best walk with you a while,' I said, indicating the path. 'I wouldn't want any of my guard dogs to find you.'

'How kind,' she asked. 'Am I allowed to know your name?'

'I'm James De Haas,' I said, bowing slightly.

'Well, this is my mum, Helen.'

The three of us walked down to the woods, where we picked up a track that ribboned the pond. A few boys were fishing there. Three hundred yards away the M62 was a grey strip, moaning with traffic.

We talked about where she'd grown up and what she was now doing. An only child, she'd spent her formative years in Knutsford, going with her father to Tabley Mere, where he would spend long hours painting watercolours. Since his death, she had been caring for her mother, who had suffered a stroke fifteen years previously. A look told me that her care was no longer enough, that there wouldn't be a lot of time left.

'What about you? Why are you here?'

'I worry too much,' I said. 'I get a lot of panic attacks when I think about dying, or rather, other people dying. I needed to relax or it was likely my hinges were going to come off for good.'

'You worry about other people dying? That doesn't seem like a reason to be here.'

'No, well, people say my fears are irrational. What bothers me, I mean more than starving kids in Mogadishu or bus bombs in

Jerusalem, what bothers me is air travel.'

'Air travel?'

'Yeah. Or rather, not so much the travelling as the coming out of the sky.'

'What? Landing? Or do you mean incidents?'

'Air crashes. The people who tell me I'm being irrational call them incidents. "Isolated incidents," they say. "Rare occurrences." Oh really.'

She bowed her lips and nodded her head. One hand had moved unbidden to her mother's hair and stroked it tenderly. In that moment, I knew I wanted to be with her more than with anyone I had ever known. 'They've got a point though. It's much safer to fly than to walk down the street.'

'They say that to me too. Usually with a pitying little smile on their features. I bet you're one of them. I bet, instead of saying "An aeroplane ploughed into a mountain" you'd come out with "There was an occurrence of controlled flight into terrain". It's much safer not to get on an aeroplane in the first place. Sheer madness. I'd like to talk about it but I'd probably relapse.'

'How are you now?' she asked.

'I'm not tuppence short of thre'pence ha'penny, if that's what you mean.'

She smiled. 'You seem fine.'

Her hand stroked. Her mother's face dipped and the line of spinning saliva turned red. I managed to reach her before she slipped from her chair. I held her, gurgling and spasming into my shoulder. Emma backed off, the same hand that had been loving her mother now a stricken bird flapping against her mouth. I guessed it wasn't a good time to ask her out.

Helen had suffered another stroke, a bad one. The next time I saw Emma, she seemed disoriented. She was sitting on a wooden bench in a hospital corridor I had never visited before. Having shaved and showered, put on some fresh clothes, I wasn't surprised that she didn't recognize me. I sat next to her and took her hand. She favoured me with a weak smile that somehow managed to transform her face. I lost myself in the cast of her features for ten or fifteen minutes; traced the journey of her veins on the back of her hand.

When the doctor emerged from the room, hours later, to tell her that Helen had died, we moved against each other like a mirror image; neither of us having to initiate, no awkward clashes of limbs. She left me for a little while, went in to see her mother and talk to the doctors.

'I'll take you home, shall I?' I suggested, when she returned. She was dazed; it took a little time for her to register what I'd said.

'What about your treatment?'

'I discharged myself this afternoon. I'm taking up space here. Dr Jessop said I could leave ages ago – no, really. I've just got to – what is it the Americans say? Get a grip on to my shit. Man. Or something like that.'

She rallied a little, allowed herself to be steered towards the door.

'Is there someone at home?' I asked. She shook her head.

'Just me now,' she said.

I got her home, which proved to be an unassuming little house in a terrace in Appleton. I hesitated on her doorstep but she wasn't going to faff around with formalities; I followed her in and shut the door. And then she started crying, hunched over a box of chocolates on the drop-leaf table.

'I'd forgotten. They were meant for her. I should have taken them this morning.'

I reached for her and she turned, moved into my shape like the interconnecting leaves of a Chinese puzzle. I stared at the bowl of oranges on the table and the shelf of dog-eared paperbacks above the television. I smelled apples in her hair.

Before the night was out, I'd asked her to marry me.

My father took me to Manchester Airport on a drizzly morning in 1979 to welcome my mother back from her native Amsterdam, where she had been signing books (she was a moderately successful author of children's novels) and giving talks in schools. We were early, so we walked up to the public gallery and watched the jets as they came in to land. They were stacked like pearl studs in a grey shirt, assuming form as they lowered, rearing as their wheels sought the runway. I clapped at every touchdown, squealing with delight at the clouds of spray powering up from the tyres, the roar of the thrusters as the engines reversed power.

'Here she comes,' said my father, checking his watch and squinting into the louring heights. 'Yes, look, you can see the logo on the tailfin. See, James?'

The sounds the plane was making were different from those that had approached before it. I looked at my father for reassurance but he just licked his lips. There was a high-pitched grinding noise; the plane was coming in too steeply and it was skating around on its horizontal axis as though it were appraising the sights to port and starboard.

The touchdown was all wrong. One of the sets of landing gear collapsed and the plane went into a roll.

Even when the fuselage split and liquid flame sprinted from the ruptured tanks, consuming the disintegration, the jet retained an almost balletic grace, folding and crumpling like a tragic figure. I watched from the tightening crook of my father's arm, my hand still waving, waving.

Try as I might to conjure my mother's face in the following years, all I invoked was a plume of fire webbed with black oil-smoke. Her features had been subsumed by that delicate moment on the runway when a jet had forgotten how to fly and suffered gravity's punishment. I recorded crashes from TV dramas and documentaries, replaying them in the whispering dark of my flat at night when the boom and crackle of fire helped me regress to a state of fascination I'd known at the airport's public gallery. In these moments, drenched in the special TV colour of explosions – that swollen blood orange – I felt close to the phantom that was Anna, my mother.

Soon after, I dreamed for the first time of a black matt aircraft with pendulous engines and no windows. It was lumbering along a blasted airstrip, taxiing to the end of a runway that was littered with naked, wrenched corpses with astonished expressions. Severed limbs made a grotesque flotsam on this still sea. The jet straightened up and the engines cleared their voices.

The fuselage was as broad as twenty 747s. There were six rows of wings; twenty-four engines and boosters at the tail. The empennage appeared too big, as though at take-off it would simply drag along the floor until the inevitable happened: the fin might have passed for a clipper's mainsail. Humours of fuel hazed the black hulk, making its shape uncertain, molten.

Gathering pace, the plane moved along the runway as smoothly as alcohol rising in a thermometer. Skulls and ribcages were pulverized beneath the massive wheels; tiny clouds of bone dust rose in their wake. Engines screaming, the nose lifted and the plane arched into the night, wings flung out like a bizarre multi-mirror reflection of Christ. There were no lights to follow as it diminished, only its troubled, monotonous banshee call. And then, after a short while, even that was gone.

The sky was coming to after a close, balmy night. I watched thin light paring away from the rind of dark, separating more swiftly as the sun worked its muscles. I didn't feel tired. Something far off breathed in the blue limit that stretched from the view I had from Canary Wharf to Battersea Power Station. I waited like a butterfly collector, eyes stationary, fixed on a point above the centre of the city, waiting for the miracle to stain my peripheral vision. As always, the sound tricked me, even as it gained in depth and impetus. In my dreams, this was the sound the sky made when it was screaming. In my dreams, the sky was racked with guilt, turning these great white sharks of the clouds away like a finger flicking scraps from the arm of a chair.

All of these horrific disasters are trapped in my mind; the fuselages pinned to a black velvet board, shattered wings splayed, the colour of catastrophe spilling in blood red and petroleum blue. Bodies recovered from a Brazilian jungle, all of them naked. Their aircraft spiralling out of control (calm yourself with a glance at the smiling stewardess, reassure your jangling nerves in the knowledge that this airline's safety record is second to none, the confidence of the captain's announcements, another drink, stretch out in the remarkable leg-space, watch a film), breaking apart at ten thousand feet when the stresses become too great. The forces at work tear off everybody's clothes. Half-buried by the impacts, flesh sheened with fuel rain. I've tried to convince myself that they were dead before they knew what was happening. Yeah, sure. One of the photographs I have filed from that crash, tucked away in a black folder on my Apple Mac, is of the head of an immaculately goateed man. Well, half a head. His mouth is partly open as if he were in the process of kissing someone. Or saying, 'What the fu– '

Or how about the poor souls on a JAL flight, August 1985. The 747 went awry shortly after take-off. Heading directly for a collision with Mount Osutaka half an hour away, the controls not responding; the passengers had plenty of time to write messages for their loved ones back home. Five hundred and twenty people died. What went through their minds? Did they smell death? Did they see some sign of their imminent passing? Were they calm enough to do so, or was it just blind panic? An ecstasy of screaming. What about the Easyjet flight that went down in the Everglades of Florida? They recovered scorched dollar bills that pointed to a cabin fire before impact. People were burning, melting, screaming, choking even before the crash smashed the life from them. The people on board these craft know their number is up and they know it for some time. It takes a while for a big jet to come out of the sky. What do we think as the ground rushes up to consume us? What is the extent of our terror?

There it was. Landing gear down, beginning to bank into the airspace above the city. I picked up my binoculars and confirmed that it was a 747-400 Combi. Passengers in the front section, cargo aft. Korean Air (they'd dropped the 'Lines' from their name after KAL 007 was shot down by a Soviet fighter in 1982...as if that would reassure people it wouldn't happen again). Twin swirls of vapour twisted away from the upturned wing tips. I heard the engines powering down as the Jumbo readjusted for its trajectory in to Heathrow. The pilots ought to be concentrating on the job now; a directive forbade casual chatter below ten thousand feet.

My fear of these monsters was offset by a fascination with their beauty too, and the sheer force of the miracle. I have to look up when they go over. And I have to restrain myself from shouting at the people in the street who walk blithely by. Do you not see what is happening? Does this madness not bother you?

I went back to bed, having watched the jet move out of sight. Emma rolled over and planted a sleepy kiss on my shoulder.

I said, 'By 2025, if these accidents go unchecked and the volume of flights continues to rise, we can expect a dramatic increase in air disasters. Bank on it.'

'Go to sleep, Statto,' Emma pleaded.

'A double-decker aircraft. Imagine it. Over six hundred people slamming down on the centre of London. The world would shake with the impact. With the weight of all the screaming.'

'They're not going to make a double-decker jet. That's daft.'

'Oh, is it? Tell that to the design team at Airbus who have blueprints for the A-3XX. Ready by 2003. There are going to be bigger Jumbos. Stretch Jumbos. Double-decker Jumbos. Fucking Triple Supreme Jumbo bastards with extra fucking mayo. Strap enough engines on the UK, find a big enough airstrip and you could fly that cunt too.'

'James. Please, calm down.'

I crashed into sleep and the black jet was there to greet me.

It flew low, clouds sliced into vortices by the wings, a matt coating of frost stubbling its skin. I wasn't in so much control of my dream that I could get inside the fuselage to see what its cargo was. I harboured a strong doubt that there was any cargo at all: freight, passengers, even crew. As if to mock me, the plane banked to the left, flashing me its underbelly. No livery. No windows. No doors that I could discern. It seemed fashioned from the very stuff it flew through. Occasionally, through patches in the cloud, I could see an ocean like a sheet of hammered tin. I didn't know the name of the sea. The jet could be a couple of thousand, or just a couple of hundred miles away from me. Same as ever, tracking me through the dreamtime of my growing years, dogging the trajectory of my fear, slowly gravitating towards the here and now. Catching me up.

Sleep miles.

I knew that when the plane crashed, I would die.

I had been working for a chemist since leaving Winwick; gentle work, the most taxing aspect of which was trying to keep up with the welter of products that appeared on the shelves. I had to pretend I knew what customers were after when they asked for a packet of Zubes or Hacks or raspberry-flavoured Phlegms. The chemist, Lucas, never bothered coming into the shop. He lurked in the rear, behind his counter, behind his off-white overalls. Behind his copies of *Readers' Wives*, *Beaver Fever* and *C***S!*. He would make up prescriptions hastily and with much resentment that he had been distracted from his glossy procession of butcher's-shop-window shots.

There was a large noticeboard upon which photographs of local drug addicts had been fixed. If they weren't getting sorted out with drugs at the dependency clinics or the bent GPs, they came to the chemists. We were sanctioned by the hospitals to prepare their fixes for them and we provided a needle-exchange service. I had to mark their names on a sheet and make sure notification, signed by Lucas, was faxed over to the right people at hospital. I don't know what happened then. Maybe they were filed away in the wastepaper basket and forgotten about. I never saw any of these users cleaned out, that's for sure. We were supposed to regulate the amounts so that users were unable to overdose, which meant we saw them quite a few times each week, when they expected to be topped up. The addicts we got were the addicts every chemist got. You couldn't blame the junkies for milking what they could from every sweet-shop owner in the area. That they kept coming back to us in particular wasn't because we kept the doses small but because Lucas didn't give a shit who was served or what was served to them. On one of the few occasions he deigned to talk to me, it was to offer one of his cod philosophies of life, no doubt lifted from the screaming leader pages of the tabloids he worked through during lunchtimes.

'They're going to die eventually. Let them die smiling. Better that than seeing them shot to pieces by the police as they rob your granny's handbag, hey?'

I ended up measuring out the doses and I was scrupulous in my work. At first. Various blasted figures would come in for their civilized fixes. All of them had the nous to hover by the Milton Sterilising Fluid or the whistlepops while the clean customers bought condoms and coal-tar soap or queued up for worming tablets and warfarin. Once the coast was clear, they'd shuffle over, brandishing a piece of paper, and I'd try my hardest to assimilate the pickled ruin of this or that imploring face with this or that obscured Polaroid. Get you, sir? What'll it be, madam? Uppers and downers for people who wanted to opt into or out of life's daily drudge.

Some of them graduated to a bizarre level of abuse; I once saw a breathtakingly wasted character called Varley slumped against the toilets in Bank Park. He was injecting what looked like Chicken Bisto into a vein while a stooge poured Special Brew into his mouth at the same time.

'Flyin',' he gentled as I walked past. 'Am fog'n' flyin' an' thez fog all youze can do about it.'

With that he took out his landing gear and pissed all over the stooge, who then set about him with the can, which he'd torn into a weapon. Varley never felt a thing. He was blissed out, cruising at forty thousand feet. I crossed his name off our list the following week, when it transpired he'd thrown himself off the multi-storey car park. He'd made an indentation in the rime of snow covering the tarmac on Sankey Street, a childish posture of flight: arms outstretched. I can hear him launching himself into the nicotine yellow of Warrington's skyline.

'Varley one to tower. Am ah cleared for fog'n' take-off or fog'n' what?'

Or Jenny, who dressed in a pink, waxy mackintosh, tightly belted over grey pyjamas and a towelling bathrobe no matter the weather. Along crypt-cold avenues or with the tarmac melting on the roads, she'd journey to town, traipsing into the shop, her flip-flops slapping out a tattoo of need. I often dreamed of her once I'd forced myself into thin slumber with mugs of tea laced with rum. She came to me naked, barefoot, but still making that wet, slapping sound. It was her breasts, her flip-flop boobs, like two wet fish beached and breathless. She'd reach out for me, her stinking mouth wide open, to offer up the collapsed ruin of her black veins, slumped beneath the flesh like feedlines in peeled prawns. I always woke from those dreams with a hard-on and, whenever she came into the shop, I'd blush, and if she wasn't too wired, she might notice and tease me a little. When she hadn't been into the chemist's for three weeks I called the hospital and they sent someone round to see her. Nobody got back to me, so I walked to her address after work. I got there in time to see her mattress being carried out. A hank of hair was glued to one end, where her head had started to rot into the sponge. Jenny had been dead for a fortnight, among the hottest weeks on record. She'd been so desperate for a lift, she'd injected cleaning fluid along with her usual shot of methadone.

Jon Sconn was another of our regulars. Sconny to his mates. I once caught him behind the counter when I'd gone to give his weekly request for methadone to Lucas.

'What are you doing?' I asked.

'Serving myself,' he hissed. 'The shit you give me is piss weak and does nothing for me *when taken orally*. I want something in these hungry fuckers.' He exposed the wastelands of his forearms. His small, brown eyes were trying to rage but they were too soft for that. He'd always be a little boy, no matter what age he achieved. He looked like Robert Carlyle but without the jut, without the angles.

'Mr Lucas?' I called, but Lucas flipped his middle finger at me. He was leaning back on his chair, his face obscured by a glossy magazine. A woman on the cover was bent over a shopping trolley, a cucumber crammed deep into her mouth. A cauliflower obscured her crotch. *Veg-inas*, the magazine was called. Lucas was branching out. And in more ways than one: his trousers were tented spectacularly.

'Well, what do you need?' I asked, nervous now. I didn't want some old giffer coming in for her Ventolin and aniseed twists to be confronted by this maniac rifling through the cupboards.

'I don't know. What's this?' He asked the question but he was too unstrung to even notice what he'd picked up. He stuffed it in his jacket and looked at me with what I'm sure he hoped was menace but was really quite endearing. Sweat was lashing off him; his skin leached of colour in the wash of the strip lighting. 'Follow me,' he said, 'and you're fuckin' dead.'

I had to follow him; he'd left his methadone and needles. And his duffel bag. I chased him up Museum Street and across the road into the gardens by Bridge Foot. Then he seemed to realize his mistake and he swore. He looked at what he'd thieved from the chemist and swore again. Then he swore one more time, inventively. He threw the jar away. Vick's VapoRub. He couldn't even steal properly.

When he saw me he thrust his hands in his pockets and set his baby jaw. 'What did I tell you? Fucking dead you are.' But he didn't make any move to carry out the threat. He kicked at an imaginary stone and wandered off down to the footbridge, where he stared at the Mersey, grey, fat and tired as it slurped between its banks.

'You forgot your bag.' I offered it to him.

'I'm not really a drug addict,' he said, taking it from me. 'I'm an actor. The druggie is my new character. I'm in a play opening in Manchester next month. I'm getting into character. What do you think?'

'You forgot your methadone too.'

He took the pills and needles from me, shrugging as if it didn't bother him, as if he'd just as much launch the fix into the Mersey than go home and take it.

'Do you live around here?' I asked. A jet's engine rose, a measured scream above the burr of traffic. I looked up, licking my lips. Hello there. Swissair 737-600. Wingspan 112 feet seven inches. Length 102 feet six inches. Forty-one feet three inches high. Range 3,720 miles. One hundred and eight passengers. Cute little coffin with wings. Suspected of having rudder problems in 'extreme' conditions.

'Yeah, I live around here. You interested in planes?'

'You could say that,' I said, watching the jet bank severely and knowing there'd be quite a few poor bastards up there who were laying a turtle's head into their M&S underwear.

'Me too. I could sit and watch them all day. I wouldn't get on one of the cunts though.'

I returned my attention to him. 'No?'

'You must be joking. Potential toasties, the lot of 'em. And you know,' he leaned into me, conspiratorially. I smelled beetroot and stale B&H. 'I'm not even convinced that it's real. I mean, look at it. Fucking madness. Trains and cars and boats get totalled too, I know, but at least you've got a chance to step out of the wreckage in one piece. You hit a mountain in one of those things and you are soup, boy. I have this dream, see, where I'm on a downed plane, smeared against some mountain, my spine burst out of my back. And as I die, I'm watching a wolverine gnawing on my leg. Twenty fucking feet away. Nah, it's all a con. Them skies, see. Sponsored by Disney. Monster blue screens with CGI cleverness all over them. Capricorn fucking Five, mate. I can't get it into my head how those big buggers can get off the floor. Jumbos. Shit. They say that a full load, passengers and cargo, weighs – '

'Around 800,000 pounds,' I said, thrilled and frightened to death that I had made contact with someone who was as sane as me. 'How many elephants is that, hey? I'm with you on this. Sheer bloody madness.'

'Blue screens,' he said again. 'Walt bloody Disney. A big fake.' We both turned to watch another jet slide across the sky. So unspeakably awesome, so unutterably horrifying. And beautiful too.

'It's real, I'm afraid,' I said.

*

I went home that afternoon with a real sense of hope and purpose. Sconny had proposed a meeting in a pub that night to discuss further the collective insanity displayed by people when they boarded a plane and how best we might combat it. I was to take him a goodly-sized supply of methadone and in return he would let me in on his dossiers. He kept dossiers!

We met often over the following weeks. Sometimes I would have him round to my place, where we would mumble over endless cups of dark coffee about the tragedies that seemed to happen with frightening regularity. He was charming to Emma, who abided him with admirable charity. Sometimes, for a break, we would talk about drugs and I would tell him about new drugs that were being developed, or the stash that Lucas had at our chemist for a lucky few. I told him about Harmonyl and Loozyt, but he was most interested in a persuasive drug that was being tested called Influence. He pumped me for information about these jujubes, these tantalizing dips into a narcosis far removed from the mundane drudgery of methadone or smack.

'Can you get some for me?' he'd whine and I'd say sorry, no. Lucas, although he doesn't appear to give a shit, would string me up worse than an object of lust in *Rope 'n' Grope*.

One night, after he'd gone, I took a bath, then came down to find Emma sitting with a cup of tea in front of the television, wrapped in a huge woollen cardigan that made her seem too small and vulnerable. I kissed the top of her head and sat beside her. On the screen, a body covered with a red blanket and belted securely across the middle was thrust into a black van with the force of a missile loaded into a silo.

She reached for the remote and I let her change channels, careful not to let my hands turn to claws on the armrest of the chair. She was watching me.

'Good day?' she asked. I couldn't let my attention waver from the screen: a game-show host bantering with his plasticized assistant, fringe and a broad white smile. Her green dress glistened like the skin of a wet reptile.

'OK,' I said. I was tired but I was afraid of going to sleep; I was dreaming too frequently of the aeroplane.

'I went to see Dr Jessop today,' she said, looking away from me now, back to the screen. The game-show host was mock-enduring some joke at his own expense, mopping up the laughs with a raised eyebrow. His skin was orange. His assistant stepped back, shaking with mirth, a manicured hand covering her mouth. I wondered if he was fucking her. They usually did.

'At Winwick?'

'Of course at Winwick. That's where he works – you know that.' Perhaps realizing her voice was too angular, she paused a while. Then, softer: 'I'm worried about you. In your sleep you... you're saying names. Alphabetically ordered lists of names. *Crash victims*, for Christ's sake!'

'I'm concerned.'

'You're *obsessed*.'

'The other channel just now,' I said, trying a smile that felt as solid as a wafer in a dog's mouth. 'What was that?'

Emma sat up and leaned over her knees, eyes boring into my own. 'A Garuda Airlines passenger jet went down in northern Sumatra. Two hundred and thirty-four people are feared dead.'

She was daring me to react, I could tell. She'd reached the maximum cruising altitude for our relationship and, strapped into her seat, was suddenly at the mercy of a mechanical problem. She wanted to bail out but she couldn't. She wasn't like that. In my head, while she waited for me to do something other than grin like an idiot and mash my hands together, I heard the absurd politeness of a pilot *in extremis*: – Excuse me, ladies and gentlemen, this is your captain speaking. Thank you for flying with Coffin Air. We're currently at thirty thousand... no, twenty thousand... no, ten thousand... oh shit –

'If you were Sioux City,' I said, losing it badly now, 'I'd be the DC-10 with no hydraulic power. Attempting to land on you.'

She frowned and then, slowly, her face cleared. She couldn't give a fuck what I meant by that (thank God, really, because I'm buggered if I knew).

'You're bloody nuts,' she said, her voice rising. 'You are FUCKING MAD.'

Yeah, I thought, tensing myself for the slam of the door. Oh yeah. And I suppose you reckon the earth is flat. I'll tell you what's mad. Those people who got on Korean Air flights to Guam when they heard of the disaster there that took the lives of their relatives.

What they needed, these planes, I thought, flicking on the scenes of smoke and sorrow, what they needed was some kind of massive airbag that was triggered at the moment one went arse over tit into the ground. Something to suspend animation, other than death, of course. Gel-filled cabins with user-friendly oxygen masks. Runways made out of marshmallow...It bothered me that, with so many design faults at large – the tendency to crash in Apple Macs, the fan belts in Vauxhall Astras, Jesus, even the dumb proximity of the oesophagus to the trachea – we could give ourselves to machines that swept us up into the sky. Cars break down. Trains break down...You fill in the gap.

I took a deep breath. Let her have her prettified view of smiling pilots lifting hundreds of smiling passengers into happy clouds to the strains of Holst. I needed a drink.

The walk into town refreshed me; there was a fine mesh of rain to move through – its whisper against my face was Emma's lace body as she hitched it over her breasts on our wedding night.

One beer at the pub and I had the phone in my hand. He answered on the first ring.

'Did you see?' I asked.

'I saw. Oh yes.'

'How do we stop them from doing it, putting our lives at risk like this?'

'Come over,' he said. 'I'll show you something.'

'I'll be five minutes.'

'Not if you go to your chemist shop first, you won't.' An edge to his voice. A hunger.

'Fifteen, then,' I said.

I got him a dose and locked up after clearing Lucas's jazz mags from his desk and wondering which of the glossies he was spending his time and seed over this evening.

Sconny lived in a flat across from the railway station. I rang the bell just as a late evening train loosed an asthmatic gasp of relief pulling into the station. When he didn't answer the door, I stepped back on to the road and called up to his window. A drab curtain shifted in the breeze, in front of a weak bulb.

'Sconny?' I called.

I went round to the alleyway behind the terrace where, by counting houses, I worked out which was the rear of Sconny's flat. I was getting a little worried now, thinking that he might have become desperate enough to overdose on something dumb such as K-Y or Anusol. Jenny flip-flopped into my thoughts.

Climbing up on to the brick wall that separated the building containing Sconny's flat from its mate, I edged along until I could haul myself on to the fire escape. There was a wobbly moment when I was working his bathroom window, clinging to one of the rusting balustrades, when an El Al Boeing 767 chuntered overhead, its pale belly like the underside of a shark oozing through black water. Heart keen, I bundled through as the window finally popped and I listened as the engines slowed, the jet banking for Manchester. Standing in his bath in the dark, I was struck by a bout of dizziness so I crouched and closed my eyes. Immediately I was greeted by the vision of another plane: the giant black jet of my nightmares. It was sinking into great drifts of silver cloud and as I watched, its landing gear engaged, jettisoning bones from their housings. All these years of its flight, through the uneasy sleep of my motherless upbringing, and now it was making its final approach. I didn't feel any different, however, and I firmly believed that it marked the natural end to just one of the strange cycles – albeit an exceedingly long one – of the follies of the human mind. There was no longer the adolescent conviction that its landing would herald the moment of my death.

'Sconny?' More strident now. There was no answer but I could hear the buzz of a television and, as I approached what must have been his living room, its strange clout created an uncertain wash against the walls.

It wasn't what I was expecting.

There were no filing cabinets, no stacks of documents, no charts or ranks of video cassettes pointing to the fascination he had confided in me. It was an ordinary room with a few unexceptional knick-knacks and pictures. A small shelf supported two rotting Jeffrey Archer novels, a Madhur Jaffrey cookbook and an unfinished glass of wine.

When I looked at the television, I had to sit down.

A home movie, of Sconny, naked from the chest up. He's holding the camera and he alternates POV between his face – red, perspiring

– and the area below the frame. He licks his lips and blows into the lens, clouding the picture a little. When it clears, he's swapped perspectives and I'm looking at the head of a woman slowly bobbing up and down over the top of his thighs. A compelling vision but a distracting one when I realize he must have set the video to play for me. What was he doing?

And then the woman made a noise. The same kind of noise she made whenever she went down on me. A kind of moan-gasp through her nose. Jesus.

I kicked the TV over and slammed out of the flat. Caught a cab back home and she was gone too. No note. I thrashed around from room to room, looking for signs, but there was nothing. Then, just as I was calming down and about to cane a bottle of Teacher's, I saw an envelope in the bin with a British Airways logo on it. It was date-stamped yesterday.

I dropped the bottle, scooped up the car keys and ran. Driving, windows closed, nothing on the radio, I watched Warrington's pallid halo of sodium lights diminish in my rear-view mirror. What was she doing with him? I couldn't think properly, beyond the fact that she had been mildly in favour of decriminalizing drug use and thought that uptight suits dropping soundbites about zero tolerance ought to wake up and smell the toast. I never believed that her liberal streak would extend to having affairs with junkies.

He must have abducted her. But why? To get at me? I wondered just how long Sconny had planned his careful currying of my favour. How was he going to get Emma through security at the airport against her will?

Oh yeah... how?

'Influence,' I said. The word was suddenly empty, poisonous. My Emma. My God.

I let my gaze fall into the interstices between the cones of light spilling across the tarmac. I saw her there, as the road's dividing lines stabbed into the dark beneath the windscreen, folded around Sconny in some grotesque mutation of their physicalities: Emma's haunted eyes swimming out of the frangible curve of his face; the powdersoft swells of her breasts deflating on the malnourished hobbles of his chest. Her centre liquefying on the flaccid comma of his sex.

There was precious little traffic on the motorway. I wished I had a mobile phone so that I might call the airport and alert security. I was scanning the hard shoulder for a yellow SOS call box when a dark shape behind my eyes blotted out every source of light. Its engines groaning, the black jet fell into the meaty loam of my head and disintegrated, spraying life in every conceivable permutation of body part from kneecap to breastbone to – in one quite beautiful arc of pink froth – a whole human brain.

Lashed beneath this criss-cross of carnage, trapped beneath the flayed skeleton of the fuselage, straining through a lattice of steaming metal, I saw a queue of traffic up ahead and the spatter of blue light against concrete. We funnelled through the filter lane the emergency services had created, rubberneckers slowing the procession even further, until I drew level with a vehicle that had been sheared in two, having gouged a route through the embankment before coming to rest on what remained of its roof. I didn't recognize the car, but as a blanket fell on a lumpen pool of black liquid, I almost yelled with relief when I noticed the glitter of Helen's, of Emma's, golden bird hairclasp sprawled in the wreckage. The irony thrilled me to such an extent that, when I was voided from the filter's constraints, I stood on the accelerator, took my hands from the wheel and closed my eyes. Let it come...

A young man wakes from a terrible, thick unsleep of shattered transport and splintered bone to find the smile of the woman he loves fall upon him like a shaving of moon dropping into the night.

'You're safe,' he slurs, having to force the words through a mouth as spongy as the seat he is reclined upon.

'Of course, silly,' she chides. 'And so are you.'

'I feel dreadful. I thought you were dead. God. My *head*.'

Her hand, a cool glove for his own. 'Bad dreams, my love. My fault. Influence. I had to.'

'Influence?'

Somehow, despite the torpor of his limbs, he manages to lever himself upright. The bitter blue flood sweeping away beyond the window has him keening. Looking away from the four miles of nothing separating his backside from the Pacific, he manages to find some measure of calm in the darker hue of the sky, of universe curve.

'We needed a holiday, honey,' she soothes. 'I was going mental, cooped up at home while you wittered on about freak accidents. I tell you, if you were born on an aeroplane, you could spend two lifetimes in the air before you were involved in a fatal accident.'

'That cod philosophy comforts you, does it, Biggles? All those cosy facts made up by airline companies who want you to feel snug and secure. Tell it to my mother.'

'Don't shout at me.' The hand retreats. 'You'll thank me for this.'

Do the cabin crew have those smiles impacted on to their faces when they join the airline, he wonders, gritting his teeth against the panic that piles up inside him. Do the tinkickers pull their Joker faces from the disaster sites?

He remembers the black jet and finds a cautious moment of optimism. It might not be too bad after all. The black jet's crashing must surely signify the termination of his lifelong mistrust of flying that had begun all those years ago with the death of his mother. Maybe he had arrived.

'Emma – ' he begins, ready to apologize. Damn it, he'd even have a G&T to celebrate. Learn to relax. 'It landed. It came down. I didn't die. *You* didn't die. It's all – '

Something like the shriek of a claw upon a blackboard travels the length of the fuselage. James sees the face of a stewardess fold. In the moment before the plane judders into an impossible pitch and yaw, he wonders why the static won't resolve itself into a voice and then he realizes the pilot is screaming too.

The final seconds of his life, before the plane succumbs to the gross pressures inflicted upon it, are filled not with desperate, grandiose pleas of a religious bent or even of screamed utterances of love – which Emma has chosen to make – but with the fear that one of these flailing passengers might notice that he has pissed his pants.

A DESIGNATED SPACE
TREZZA AZZOPARDI

Peter almost drove into them as he pulled out of Tesco one Friday night. It was very dark, but he had no excuse: the man and woman were dressed completely in white, right down to their shoes.

'I'm terribly sorry,' he said, racing round to the front of the car, 'I just didn't see you. Are you all right?'

'We're fine,' said the woman, in a quaking voice, 'but our child needs help.' She pointed to the ground with her glove. Peter followed to where the little white figure lay. Its lower half was obscured by a shopping trolley. As he wheeled it away, Peter noticed the boy's enormous, round head and two-dimensional body. The child slid to his feet, filling out in the headlights.

'Is he hurt? Can I do anything?' Peter watched as the family joined hands. The parents exchanged looks.

'It would be very good of you to take us away from here.' The father gestured to the rows of parked cars with his free mitten. 'You see, we don't have transport.'

Peter tried to concentrate on the traffic, but kept catching sight of their pearly faces in his rear-view mirror. They were the palest people he had ever seen. In the darkness of the back seat, they shared a luminous glow which hurt his eyes. Peter introduced himself. There was a whispered discussion and then the father spoke.

'I'm Derek,' he said, patting Peter's shoulder. 'This is Linda, and our boy, Jeff. We need you to help us. We've got to find the Embassy before they notice we've gone.'

'We're refugees,' Linda offered.

Peter didn't know where the Embassy was either, so he took them home. He would look it up in his *A–Z*.

They stood in a line along his galley kitchen, holding hands. They looked like a paper cutout. Peter surreptitiously studied the family as he made tea. He noticed they shared the same stumpy physique, and a lack of definition on their faces, as if they had no worries. They were dense and chalky all over. They even wore their hair in identical Artex whirls. Maybe it's a disguise, he thought. He had a feeling that he knew them. Perhaps they'd been on the news.

'So, you've escaped from...?'

'Tesco's,' said Derek.

'But before then. Have you been staying round here?' Peter tried to speak casually. 'Only you look very familiar.'

Linda let out a little scraping laugh. 'Of course we do, you've seen us in the car park. You've driven on us,' she said.

Peter was alarmed. 'I have not!'

'We're the Parent With Child Symbol,' Derek boasted, gesturing to the others with his free arm. 'You always park on us.'

'But never on Disabled,' added Linda, with a tilt of her dazzling head. Her eyes locked on to Peter's in the silence.

Derek shuffled his family out of the kitchen. 'Look, we'll show you. You'll have to use your imagination a bit,' he said, easing himself down on the living-room carpet, 'we work best on tarmac.' They lay down in a row, and assumed an air of indifference.

The realization thumped in Peter's chest. They were the archetypal family. He saw them every Friday when he did his shop. Too lazy to look for another space, he'd park on them. It infuriated him that supermarkets made such a big deal about people with kids. He'd even imagined petitioning Tesco's for a single person's parking space. They would probably put it at the far side of the store. And they'd make it extra narrow. A wave of indignation hit him, but then Derek popped his head up off the floor. It resumed its spherical shape. The broad face beamed.

'Come on down, Pete. It's surprisingly comfy.'

Peter grasped the offered hand. It felt massive and sure, like his dad's used to. He lay with them, staring at the light bulb in the centre of the ceiling. Heat seeped from Derek's palm to his own, warming his fingertips. Peter felt connected. He floated for a while on this strange sense of community.

As they rose, their bodies filled out. Derek's face shone like the moon.

'Nice, isn't it? But you see, Pete, it won't be like that for much longer.'

'They want to change us,' cried Linda, 'they want to make us less human.'

Peter didn't think they looked very human to start with, but refrained from pointing this out.

'They've done it already at Sainsbury's,' Linda's voice broke into a sob, 'they've got rid of the baby and replaced it with a buggy!'

Peter watched as a milky tear rolled down her cheek. He leaned into his pocket and pulled out a folded handkerchief. She bent forward shyly for him to dab her face.

'We've got to make a stand, Pete. We'll lose our Jeff, you see. We just can't let them do it.' Derek raised a thick right arm in salute, and baby Jeff copied with his little left one. Linda stood trapped in the middle, holding their other hands. Her eyes cracked Peter's heart.

He had never heard of the Allegorical Embassy, but Paradigm Place was just across the Common. He thought they ought to drive there to avoid attracting attention. When he pulled up, he couldn't park.

'They're all bloody Disabled spaces,' he shouted through his teeth.

'That's PR for you,' muttered Derek from behind.

'I'd like to meet their agent,' said Peter.

'I meant proportional representation.' Derek slid the family off the back seat. 'There are so many of them in the symbolic world. And not many of us. It's not a bit like real life. I think you ought to prepare yourself.'

Peter followed them through the door marked 'Door'. Just inside, he saw a man struggling with an umbrella.

'I wouldn't worry, mate,' he said, 'it's not raining out there.'

The man glared at him from his bending position. 'Are you taking the piss?'

Derek whispered into Peter's ear, 'That's Reg from Road Works. Moody sod. I'd keep out of his way if I were you.'

The hall was large and gloomy, full of smoke. It looked more like a nightclub than an embassy. Peter followed the family as they wound their way through the fuddle of signs. Leaning against the far wall was an obstruction of exclamation marks, holding a silent protest.

There was a general air of disgruntlement. Roundabouts contended with Crossroads, while a pair of Two-way Traffic arrows argued with each other about who had priority.

'I've got the exits covered!' shouted a dashing young man, to no one in particular. A gang of Disabled Drivers screeched about on mean yellow circles.

'Get back in the bloody car park where you belong!' someone yelled. It was Reg from Road Works.

There were people everywhere, dressed in black, with black skins, black hair. Peter stepped into the path of two ebony children holding hands.

'Oy,' said the girl, 'watch where you're going.' Her little brother clung on, his back leg flung out in a permanent skip.

'I know you,' said Peter, 'you're the School Crossing kids.'

'Patrol, actually,' sniffed the girl. She tugged at her brother's hand. 'He needs the toilet,' she confided. And then, over her shoulder, 'He always needs the toilet. Can't you tell?'

Derek sidled up with Linda and Jeff in tow. He looked uncomfortable.

'I feel a bit conspicuous, Pete. We're the only white people here.'

'And I'm the only real person here,' grinned Peter.

The three big heads radiated hurt. Linda's shoulders sagged. 'Oh Pete, don't say that. We thought you were our friend.'

Peter felt the same stab that he'd got when he wiped her cheek.

'I think we're stuck in Traffic,' he said, to cover his feelings. 'Let's split up and see what's in the other rooms.'

Peter wandered around the hall. I'm falling in love with another man's wife, he thought, narrowly avoiding a Dangerous Bend. A Sharp Deviation took him to a door marked 'No Smoking'. As he opened it, a plume of smog bellowed out. In the fug he could make out a crowd of symbolic women leaning against the washbasins. Some of them were bending close to the mirrors, arranging their hair into feminine representations.

'Can't you read?' said a Victorian cutout, primping her bustle. 'This is the Powder Room.'

'Ladies' Toilet,' corrected Little Bo Peep, sucking on a cigarette. Two stumpy Italian widows barged past him.

'Take no notice of them. They're just angry because they've been made to look so FAT AND UGLY!' she shouted at their backs.

'Do you think I could steal a fag?' whimpered Peter from the depths of craving, 'only there seem to be so many in here.' He trailed his arm along the shelf of burning cigarettes. Bo Peep offered him a fresh one.

'Go ahead, but only take three drags, and then put it there.' She indicated a scarlet circle with a diagonal bar across it. 'Otherwise they can't use them. It's got to be regulation size.'

Further down the ledge sat a curly black wig with a single stiletto shoe dangling from it.

'Turkish toilets,' shrugged Bo Peep, by way of explanation. 'You should see what they put on the doors of the men's.' Peter held in his smoke.

'A mirror,' she said.

Back in the main hall, the mood had lightened. Signs were dancing. No Pedestrians cut the rug with his twin, Pedestrian Crossing. Reg scooted his shovel across the floor, while the chap from Elderly People shuffled back and forth on his stick, not daring to cross. His wife bent close behind him, picking his pocket.

Peter cast around in the semi-darkness and decided to head for the bar. There were lots of mad people working behind it, which apparently helped. He saw Derek and Linda and little Jeff next to the jukebox, looking glum.

'We've just been talking to Vaughan and Fiona, and they say we haven't got much of a case. There aren't enough of us yet.'

Vaughan was standing next to them, sinking a pint. Fiona gripped a baby buggy with her left hand and stared sadly into the distance. They had the same bobble-white bodies, but no clinging child.

'They're from Sainsbury's,' confided Linda, 'see, their baby's been turned into a push-chair.'

Derek was cuffing his head in a figurative gesture of despair. 'If only people would leave us alone. All we want is analytical asylum.'

Linda raised her hands, forever glued to her family's, and stared once more into Peter's eyes. 'And a chance of freedom,' she said, almost too quietly.

They said their goodbyes to Vaughan and Fiona, and followed Peter to the car park. All the Disabled spaces had gone.

'...a bit stuck up, though, don't you think? And that paint job – ' Peter heard Linda stripping the sheen off her friends from Sainsbury's.

They were suddenly brought up short by a squat of black mongrels crouching in the gutter. Peter made to move round them, but Derek stuck out his arm and stopped him. After a few seconds, a deer leapt into their path and skidded up the steps.

'We left just in time,' said Derek, 'it'll be bedlam when Heavy Plant Crossing gets here.'

Peter drove them back to Tesco. 'Are you sure about this?' he said, missing them already. 'Perhaps you could seek emblematic immunity or something.' He offered Derek his hand. 'Would you like me to join you in the struggle?'

They looked pale, tender.

'Thanks, Pete, but someone might notice. We'll just have to wait for the revolution. It's best this way,' sighed Derek, flattening himself on to the tarmac. Linda began to fold. She leaned over, put a kiss on Peter's nose.

'You've been lovely, Pete. Take care. And don't worry, there'll soon be enough of us,' her voice levelled into two dimensions. Jeff lay down obediently beside them.

Peter stood in the darkness for a moment and looked at the thick white figures on the ground at his feet. They were his best friends.

The Friday shop at Tesco was hectic as usual. Peter drove up to the front of the store and, with his car perched on the Taxi point, got out to look at the Parent With Child spaces. Freshly painted people sunbathed on the tarmac. He searched for Derek and Linda, swinging his head under the parked cars. The figures beneath looked starched and clean. The women's hands gripped a buggy. Baby Jeff had been erased. Peter wandered among them, looking for his family, but he couldn't tell one from another.

He turned his car into a Disabled space and switched off the engine.

GRACELAND
JOHN BURNSIDE

You'd remember Wendy if you saw her. She was one of the daughters in *The Best Years of Your Life*, the one with the short black bob who dressed like a boy and was always getting into trouble. I imagine the show is still running somewhere, on some cable channel in the middle of the afternoon, and Wendy is still coming home, the twenty-five-year-old who's supposed to be somewhere between twelve and fifteen, pretty and confident and self-contained in a way that leaves her immune to everything. She was the one who played tricks on people, putting frogs in the bath, or spreading trails of trick blood across the floor. Whatever she did, she got away with it, and because she was on television, I was never altogether convinced that she was real — or at least, real in the ordinary sense, the way my mother was, or Miss Chandler, who lived next door and taught English at my school. Maybe that was why I had a crush on her, when I was the age she was supposed to be in the programme. Naturally I never expected us to meet — we lived in such different dimensions. I certainly never thought she would find me by the side of a country road, where I'd been dumped by a lorry driver who'd picked me up two streets from home then decided he didn't like the sound of my voice. Or maybe he thought it would be better to have nothing to do with me, after I told him I was running away. I had run away five or six times in as many months, and each time I'd got a little further. If I hadn't met Wendy, I probably would have made it altogether that July afternoon, and who knows where I would be now.

It was a shock, seeing her. It was the kind of afternoon where anything can happen: a faint haze hung over the fields after the long warmth of the day, and I felt as if I was the last person in the world, standing alone on the lush verge, between an orchard and a wheat field. I had been there for around half an hour when the open-top car pulled up, and this beautiful woman asked me with a smile where I was going. I once fell through the ice on Bircomb Pond, and the shock was just like that, my whole body gloved in cold, my head emptying, an almost electrical sensation in the very marrow of my bones. If someone had told me, a few minutes before, that I would meet Wendy, I would have resolved to play it cool, and I probably would have managed a neutrality of sorts, the kind of gruff, awkward self-containedness that I usually assumed in such circumstances. As it was, my whole system was confounded. I had resolved, in the long half-hour before she arrived, that I wouldn't say anything about my plans to the next driver: I wouldn't be running away from home, I'd be headed for London, where my older brother was at college. Or my sister, maybe – that might sound better. I wouldn't say anything about Graceland, either: that only made people feel uncomfortable. As it was, though, I couldn't say a thing. I just stood there, in the afternoon heat, and stared at her till she laughed quietly and told me to hop in. It was odd, that, when she said it, as if she were still the Wendy from the old days, in her white jeans and that black and white striped T-shirt, too young to drive, really, but capable of anything, and bound to get away with it, because that was how it had to be, for someone like her.

Looking back, I see that any story I might have told her would have made no impression whatsoever. It wasn't just that she would have seen right through me, standing by the road, so obviously fifteen in my cheap nylon jacket and faded jeans. Everybody I'd ever hitched a lift from had seen through me, whether I'd told them I was on the run from home or not, but most of them still gave me a lift, and only one had ever dumped me at the roadside and told me to go back to my parents. It might have made a difference if I'd told her about Graceland, but I doubt it. Looking back, I see now that she really did think of me as someone her own age; that was why she had stopped. I have to work hard to see her as she really looked that day – most of the time, I imagine her as she was on television, suspended in that magical light where, if you have the gift, you can be anyone you want to be – but with some effort I remember that she looked about thirty, and I can still see the wrinkles around her mouth and eyes, which would have been barely noticeable, if she hadn't been wearing so much make-up. It made me think of my mother, who always did that on the odd occasions when Dad took her out: she would sit down at the mirror as a forty-year-old woman and rise, about an hour later, looking ten years older. Still, magic has a long, possibly infinite, half-life, and the only thing that really mattered was that *this woman* was Wendy. Even when I saw her as she was, I still saw her as she could be, as television, and the attention of millions, had made her.

She seemed happy, and I let myself imagine that she was glad to have met me on the road, that there was some instant bond between us that cancelled out any difference in age or status. She did most of the talking, to begin with, but she didn't introduce herself, or say anything about television, or the show. I suppose you get to be that way, once you've been famous. You don't talk about yourself, you show an interest in the other person – and that was what she did. She wanted to know where I lived and where I was going and, when I'd dutifully stumbled through my older-brother story, she asked if I went to London often. When I said I did, she wanted to know about my favourite places. The car sped along the country road, while I did some hard thinking.

'I like the National Gallery,' I said, at last.

Wendy laughed. It obviously wasn't the answer she'd been expecting.

'Really?' She sounded incredulous. 'What else?'

'I went to Madame Tussaud's once,' I said. 'That was pretty interesting.'

As soon as the car had pulled up, I had wanted to tell her my idea about Graceland, and how I'd started thinking about it when I saw the waxwork of Elvis at Madame Tussaud's, and then, a few weeks later, a picture of the house, looking much smaller than I had expected, in one of my mother's magazines. I thought she would like the idea, the fact that Graceland didn't have to be in one place or another, how it existed in people's minds, and everyone could have a Graceland, if they wanted. Maybe that house in *The Best Years of Your*

Life had been Graceland for some people: it was just an idea of what you most desired, of the magical, of everything you didn't have, all the places and moments you had missed, through no fault of your own. I wanted to tell her that — because it would have been a way of telling her something else — but I couldn't; as soon as I mentioned Madame Tussaud's she laughed again, and I was too embarrassed.

'Sorry,' she said. 'I didn't mean to laugh at you. Actually, I like Madame Tussaud's too. I go there quite a lot.'

I didn't believe her, but I was glad she was making the effort to be nice and, after that, the conversation was a little easier. I began to relax, and now it was my turn to do most of the talking. I didn't tell her about running away, though, and before I could say anything about Graceland, she interrupted.

'Listen,' she said. 'I'm not going all the way to London. Well, not right away. But I'll be going there later. There's just one thing I have to do first.'

She paused and glanced over at me, as if she expected some reaction, so I nodded.

'I have to drop in and see some friends,' she continued. 'It's a bit of a party, in fact, and I just want to say hello. You can come too, if you like — and then we'll go on to London. I'll drop you off at your brother's. What do you think?'

She didn't look at me this time. She kept her eyes on the road, with that air of someone who expects to be looked at and doesn't want to wait too obviously for a reply.

'That'd be great,' I said.

'Sure?'

'Definitely.'

'Your brother won't mind? If we're a bit late, say?'

'No,' I said, quickly. I almost added that he was a big fan of hers, but then I remembered that I didn't have a brother and, besides, I suddenly realized that I wasn't supposed to know who she was. It wasn't just good manners on her part that had made her ask about me and say nothing about herself. For some reason, she wanted to forget about *The Best Years of Your Life*, and I wasn't going to be the one to remind her.

We got to the house around eight o'clock. The first thing I noticed was the sign on the gate. It was standing wide open, and Wendy drove in quickly, straight past the trees at the entranceway and along the drive, but I still caught a glimpse of the black and white lettering in the half-light among the shrubs. *Graceland*. It startled me for a moment, then the house appeared, much larger than I had expected, and lit up from end to end with brightly coloured lights.

'Is this it?' I asked.

Wendy nodded. I looked at her face and noticed that, as she parked the car and unlocked the door on her side, she looked a little nervous. Then, with a surreptitious flutter, she opened her bag and, under cover of powdering her nose, slipped something out of a cellophane wrapper and into her mouth. She swallowed carefully.

'There,' she said.

I looked away. The big main door at the front of the house was closed, but there was another to one side of the car park, a set of old-fashioned French doors that someone had left open, with a big bunch of balloons pinned to the lintel. As I opened my door, a girl of around sixteen, in a bright-red ballerina's dress, ran out squealing, followed by a much older man dressed as a clown. Wendy watched them disappear into the garden.

'Looks like fancy-dress,' she said.

I glanced at her.

'Didn't you know?'

'No,' she said. 'There are parties here all the time. I can't keep track of them.'

She crossed the car park to the French doors, her feet crunching on the gravel.

'Come on,' she called. 'Let's get a drink.'

Inside, there were at least forty, maybe fifty, people, all standing in one huge glass-roofed space, lit here and there with candles and brightly coloured bulbs. They were all in fancy-dress. The nearest group — a harlequin, a fairy, another clown and a man in a red devil suit — turned to look at us as we came in, but they didn't seem to recognize Wendy and they quickly went back to their conversation. Further on, a whole gang of fairies was standing by a long table covered with drinks and food, talking loudly and laughing; some were even waving sparklers around. Wendy stopped just inside the doorway and looked into the crowd. I wasn't sure if she was looking for somebody in particular, or just pretending to look, and I had begun to feel nervous, what with the party being fancy-dress, and her not seeming to know about it. I was relieved when a tall, thickset man with slicked-back hair and a white suit stepped up out of the crowd – though it took me a few moments to realize who he was supposed to be.

'Wendy!' he called loudly, taking her by the arm. Wendy flinched, almost imperceptibly. 'What a surprise!'

He glanced at me, then turned back to her.

'Who's your little friend?' he asked in the same loud, mock-friendly voice.

'He's on his way to London,' Wendy said, quietly. 'I'm giving him a lift.'

The man laughed.

'Really,' he said. 'Well, bring him over and we'll see if we can't corrupt him.' Then he leaned down into Wendy's face and murmured, ' – or are we too late for that – ' before resuming in the loud, party voice, with just a hint of Elvis twang, 'What's your poison, son?'

He led the way to the table and the fairies dispersed in a flurry of laughter and sparklers. Wendy picked up a glass of red wine, and the man in the Elvis suit waved his hand generously over the massed bottles and glasses.

'Help yourself,' he said. He turned back to Wendy and assumed his quiet voice.

'Stewart isn't here,' he said.

I kept glancing at the table. I couldn't decide what to have, but I didn't want them to think I was listening. Not that I could avoid it. They weren't making any effort to keep their conversation from me.

'Really?' Wendy smiled softly. 'I suspect he'll be here, though. Eventually.'

Elvis grinned. Looking at him then, the thought came to me that I had never seen anyone who looked less like the King.

'Well, sure, honey,' he said. 'You know Stewart. Just promise me – I don't want any fuss. You remember what happened last time.'

Wendy nodded.

'I just want a word,' she said, handing me a glass of wine. 'Then we'll be on our way.'

Elvis grinned, but he didn't say anything. He just kept his eyes fixed on Wendy a moment longer, then turned to me.

'Enjoy yourself,' he said, making it sound like a warning. Before either of us could say anything more, he turned and walked off into the crowd, and I heard his big, party voice behind us, greeting another gang of arrivals. Wendy looked round eagerly, then turned back to me.

'Come on,' she said, grabbing a bottle of red wine and a couple of fresh glasses. 'Let's get some air.'

It was much cooler, now. The air was fresh, with a slight breeze blowing across a perfectly manicured lawn, to where Wendy had sat us down, in two old-fashioned wooden deck-chairs on the patio. It felt oddly criminal to me, to be sitting there, enjoying a stranger's wine, in a garden he must have taken a great deal of care over – especially when the stranger was someone who obviously disliked our presence in his home. Wendy didn't seem to mind, though; all of a sudden, she was bright and happy again, confident and invulnerable, the way she had always been on television. I suppose that was what I most liked about her, in *The Best Years*: no matter what happened, even when she was trouble, she looked at home wherever she was, as if she could always tell that things would work out in the end. That's probably the real art in that kind of acting: where other characters would mug it up, looking worried and anxious, or trying to make the audience think there was some kind of danger, Wendy never took anything seriously, she just kept on being Wendy. That was the reason we loved her. Now, suddenly, in the half-light, I could see that Wendy again, and I was happy.

I've wondered, sometimes, what it means to be happy. I used to think it was a state of being, a semi-permanent condition, and I suppose I felt cheated because I didn't have what other people call a happy childhood, or a happy home, or any of the big, happy occasions in my life that people always take such trouble to record. Yet, if I stop and think, I know I have been happy, in an odd, detached way, for moments or even hours at a time. I wasn't leaping up and down, or going around singing – it wasn't that kind of happiness, the kind you see on television, *happy* in the way Wendy's sister Grace always was, because she was pretty, and popular in school, and always had something to do. My happy times have been so quiet as to be almost imperceptible. They usually came when I was alone, walking by the side of a road, or sitting under a tree between rides. Sometimes, when I was running away from home, I would think of myself as being on the road, just travelling, always between places, like the men in the old country songs. I would have stopped somewhere, and it would feel as if time had stopped all around me, as if the whole world of other people had moved off somewhere – just a few feet from where I was standing, maybe, so I could still see and hear it, but it was muffled and removed, so that it didn't matter any more. There would be a happiness, then, which I couldn't really describe; all I can say is, it was a kind of detachment, a settled feeling, a new rhythm in the world that included me. It was simply a matter of stopping, of being wholly physical and isolated, sitting in the sun and letting the warmth seep into my skin, or realizing I was thirsty and going into a corner shop to buy a cold drink. Sometimes I could be happy beyond belief just sitting down by the side of a country road and feeling the wind on my face.

We must have sat out there for an hour or more, drinking the wine, listening to the music in the background and the occasional soft flutter of birds in the shrubbery. I wasn't used to wine and I hadn't eaten much that day, but I didn't think I was drunk. Now and then, a couple in fancy-dress would erupt noisily around the corner of the house, catch sight of us, then disappear into the garden and, once, the door behind us opened, hung ajar for a moment or so, then closed quietly before I could see who it was. After a while, the wine ran out, and Wendy said she was going to get another bottle. She stood over me, smiling, as she said it, and I remember how she looked then: fifteen years old, in her black and white T-shirt, with the blue from the garden lamp on her face.

I waited a long time. For a while, I didn't even notice that she had been gone too long. My body felt loose and warm, like something new that I had just found, something well-tuned and easy to use. I thought about Graceland again, about how visitors always expected it to be much larger than it was. They would travel from all over the world to stand outside and gaze at the house, and they would come away every time with a sense of wanting more, with that same sense of frustration you get when you hear a story and you don't understand it. Somebody should have told them that they had come to the wrong place, that they should have gone on living with just the word, and the house they imagined, because everyone had a different Graceland, and it wasn't fair on Elvis, to try to steal his dreams. My mind was wandering, I suppose, and I don't actually remember falling asleep. I only recall the moment of fright and cold when I started awake, thinking I'd heard Wendy's voice, her fifteen-year-old's voice from *The Best Years*, calling to me for help.

Inside, the glass-roofed space was empty. Most of the candles had burnt out, and the room was almost dark. There was litter everywhere – empty bottles, streamers, dead sparklers and cigarette butts, scattered across the floor – and the air smelt of stale smoke and spilt wine. I had expected to see Wendy, but there was no one there and, in a moment of panic, I thought she might have left without me. I was about to rush out, to find the car, when the voice came again, a soft, hurt cry from the far end of the glass-covered room. I started across the floor, then, towards the narrow doorway, I could only just see beyond the shadows. I was almost half-way when I realized that I wasn't alone after all. A man in a light-coloured suit was sitting alone, just off to one side, smoking a cigarette. It was only when he spoke that I realized who he was.

'Where do you think *you're* going?' he said.

I stopped dead. The man stood slowly and moved out of the shadows. It was the same man who had greeted us when we arrived, and he was wearing the same white suit, but now his face was covered with a full-size Elvis mask.

'Oh,' he said. 'It's you.' He came a few steps closer.

'Don't you know, sonny,' he said, in the Elvis drawl, 'that this is way past your bedtime?'

Before I could say anything, the voice came again from the room behind him – a sharp cry this time, a cry of sudden and unnecessary pain. Involuntarily, I moved towards the door, but my muscles felt slack, all of a sudden, and I felt I would lose control of my body entirely and fall in a heap on the floor, or jerk away, like a puppet on strings. In the pit of my stomach I felt a sickening lightness, as if any centre of gravity I had ever had was dissolving. For his part, Elvis moved as easily and deliberately as before, unhurriedly blocking my way, so I stopped dead in my tracks again, frozen with indecision and fear. Beyond him, the room fell silent again, which frightened me as much as, or even more than, the cry I had heard a moment before.

Elvis stood in my path, watching me, waiting to see what I would do next. He made it obvious that, no matter what I did, he was more than capable of handling it – and that was when I knew I would do nothing. Even if Wendy began to scream blue murder, or cry for help, I was incapable of passing the masked figure who stood between us. At the same time, I understood that *he* knew I was helpless. There was something in the way his body relaxed, in the sense I had that he was smiling behind the mask, smiling softly with triumph and contempt; there was something in his whole ease of being that inscribed helplessness into my very soul. And now, when there was no need, when he knew for sure that I was incapable of action, he stepped forward. He moved slowly and, if I had run, he probably would have made no effort to pursue me. Yet I couldn't run. Some remnant of pride held me there, I suppose, or perhaps it was just the shame I felt, at abandoning Wendy, or at my own helplessness. Even now, I feel a swell of anger when I think that I did nothing, even to protect myself. When he moved closer I could smell the cigarettes on his breath, and the sheer bulk of his man's body was like a gravity field, pulling me into his orbit. He reached out slowly; then, with a quick, easy movement, he took hold of my neck and raised his cigarette to my face.

'I don't like you, sonny.' He spoke slowly, in the same Elvis drawl. 'I don't like people who come where they're not wanted. I don't like people who drink other people's drinks and poke their noses into other people's business.'

All the while, he was tightening his grip, with a sickening, measured power. At the same time, the cigarette ember moved closer, till I felt it against my cheek. My mind blanked. I have no idea, to this day, how far he intended to go, but at the time I knew there were no limits to the pleasure he would take in damaging me. I didn't even see the ballerina – she was standing behind me, I suppose – but when she called out, Elvis loosened his grip and let me fall. I felt sick and giddy, but there was something in my mind, now that it was too late, that found its bearings and got me out of there. I lay still a moment; I could hear the woman's voice, from an impossible distance, asking him what was going on, then I heard Elvis move away. I think he was trying to reassure her, to get her to go back to bed, and if she had given in sooner, he might have returned to me, to finish what he'd started. As it was, she kept talking and, though I couldn't hear what it was she was saying to him, I knew she was trying to help me. The delay gave me the chance to escape, but it was nothing other than complete and utter panic that got me to my feet and out of there, staggering to the door and then running, while his laughter rang out behind me, through the still house.

I ran as far as the gate, then along the road in the dark, away from the house, stumbling as I went, but too scared to stop. It was a long time before I slowed down – from fatigue, rather than the understanding that I was out of danger, that no one was coming after me. I had no idea where I was. I stopped and looked around: it was an ordinary country road, among fields; I could see a pale orange glow on the sky, some distance away, but no sign of traffic, or other houses. Nearby, some animals were standing together by a fence; a dim, ruminant presence in the summer darkness. I hadn't paid much attention to the road on the way to the party; now, I saw that my only option was to keep walking till I came to a main road and found out where I was.

I must have gone three or four miles before I came to the lay-by. I kept thinking of Wendy, and wondering what had happened in that room, and I felt sick with shame that I had done nothing to help her. At the same time, I was angry with her, too, for she must have known what could happen at the party and she should never have gone or, if she really had to go, she shouldn't have taken me with her. I remembered what Elvis had said, about me going where I wasn't wanted, and I told myself that everything was her fault.

Then I saw the lay-by. I had no idea what time it was, but it must have been late – after midnight, at least. The cars were parked side by side, with their headlights on full-beam – three of them, with a middle-aged couple in each, sitting upright in the front seats, gazing out at nothing. They were all around the same age: the men were dressed identically in dark-coloured suits; the women had their hair done up as if they were going out somewhere special, and they were wearing print dresses, with thin crocheted cardigans over their shoulders. Two of the women were wearing glasses, the kind secretaries were supposed to always wear. I'm not sure when, or even if, they saw me – if they did, they took no notice. They sat stock-still, their eyes fixed on some distant point. I turned around to see what they were looking at, but there was nothing except the white beam of their combined headlamps, reaching away into the darkness. I waited. I suppose I expected them to notice me, maybe even to help in some way, but they didn't move. After a while, I walked on. For a few miles more, I half expected Wendy to appear, to drive up suddenly and apologize, and take me to London. She didn't, of course. Finally, I stopped walking and climbed over a stile into an empty field. I must have slept for some of the time, because I remember having dreams, though I have no idea what they were about. All I know is, when I came to myself again, there was something I had seen and forgotten, a clue that would have explained everything, nothing more than a detail, but something essential that was lodged in my mind for ever, even though I couldn't find it.

Eventually I made it all the way to London and, though it wasn't easy, with no money, and nowhere to stay, I managed to spin it out for almost a fortnight. Still, nothing lasts for long. My parents had called the police – just as they had done on all the other occasions I had run away – and by a series of accidents, and mistakes on my part, I was picked up and taken home. I never saw Wendy again. I haven't even seen her on television, though someone told me recently that there had been repeats. I was in hospital for a while, after that trip – I suppose the party had given me a bit of a fright – but eventually I wandered away and, though it's been almost twenty years, I still disappear, every now and then. Naturally, I haven't found Graceland yet. Once, as a holiday, I went to Memphis, like all those other pilgrims, just to see what it was like – but I knew it wasn't the place I was looking for. Sometimes I tell myself I should stop searching, that Graceland doesn't exist, except in the word itself and in my imagination. That's easy to say, of course, but it turns out that life is much longer than I had ever expected, and I have to do something, to stay occupied. Most of the time, I understand that, like the others, I'm probably looking in all the wrong places, but so far all I know is that Memphis, or anywhere else, is an illusion. I've thought about it long enough to know, sitting up late in rented rooms and describing the journey to myself, looking out at dark gardens in the suburbs and imagining an endless highway of gas stations and cheap motels, and mile-deep woods just beyond the edges of the light. I know it's an illusion, because I played that game every night in the hospital: every night I'd choose a place on the half-formed map of America that I carry in my head, from years of old B movies and rock and roll songs. It's probably there, somewhere, in Illinois, or Colorado: an ordinary house in the suburbs, with a neat lawn and a Coup de Ville in the drive. It's the kind of place where Wendy would live for ever, and it's probably as much as Elvis was really looking for – an idea of home, something in black and white, the smell of cheap lilac soap and the radio playing in the kitchen. Breakfast in the morning dusk and midnight feasts of beer and fudge cake with a girl like Wendy; and maybe, from time to time, as a kind of joke, a Hallowe'en night of horror films in a darkened room, and a mouthful of trick blood on the bathroom floor, to keep the night at bay.

BLACK AND WHITE
DEREK MARLOWE

The prologue and first two chapters of the author's last, unfinished novel.

Prologue

At the funeral, she wore her bridal veil. It was no longer white. Nor was it exactly black, but a deep Prussian blue, the colour of school ink. This was not by design. The dye she had used had appeared darker in the bottle than when it dried on the lace. When she realized the mistake, seeing it in the light of day, it made no difference. Besides, she rather liked the colour.

As the coffin was lowered into the grave, she noticed a man standing behind the mourners, standing alone in the shadow of an elm tree. Lifting the veil, she saw that he was tall, dark-haired, not handsome but attractive in the way that men who like women are attractive. Later, when the mourners had left, he approached her and offered his condolences. She looked at him but couldn't see his eyes.

'Did you know my husband?' she asked.

'I killed him.'

He waited, didn't walk away.

And then she said:

'Thank you.'

One

In the town of Grasse, in southern France, there is a house dedicated to the memory of the Comte de Mirabeau. According to the guidebook, Mirabeau was born in Bignon, grew up disenchanted with life, married an heiress for love or money or both, abandoned her and went to Paris to appear centre-stage, during the French Revolution, with Robespierre and Saint-Just. He died before the curtain call. There is, of course, more than his thumbnail in the sketch, but I, myself, am not concerned with the man but with the house. It is where this story begins, eight months ago, after the ex-wife of Walter Kemble mislaid her beauty and ran off with a man blinded by love.

'He needs me,' she had written to him from Kailau-Kona. 'He has lived alone all his life. He has no friends. When I buy picture postcards, he waits for me at the corner café.'

After that, Kemble left England and rented a house in the south of France, as he had done the year before, and the year before that. It was never the same house, but was always in the same area, between Provence and the Alpes Maritimes. Usually, it was a converted mill with granite walls and small windows. Not luxurious, but pleasant, if the weather is fine and one can sit under a tree and not get too bored. Anyway, this year he was recommended a house in Bar-sur-Loup, about thirty miles north of Nice. It belonged to an English widow who collected Agatha Christie in those green and white Penguins that unhappily no longer exist.

It was a small house, on the bank of a valley and as comfortable as a cushion, where Kemble would spend the days walking, reading, or, preferably, doing nothing whatsoever. One evening, he decided to write a letter to his ex-wife (Amy), but couldn't think of a single thing to say. When the marriage ended, someone had asked him what had gone wrong. 'I don't know,' he had replied, but later he had told someone else that he had felt betrayed. He never elaborated on that statement, but in my brief acquaintance with the man, I would say that Kemble saw women with the desires of an alchemist and that Amy had proved to be false metal.

On the first Sunday in Bar-sur-Loup, Kemble drove to Grasse in a green Peugeot in order to visit the cathedral. He was not a religious man; rather he was what one might call 'a holiday Catholic', taking the opportunity of idleness to remind him of childhood prayers. He left during the sermon and began to walk back towards the main square and, almost immediately, he realized he was lost. At first, he was not too concerned, since he spoke enough French to ask directions, and besides, it was a warm, dry day and he was in no hurry to get anywhere.

After fifteen minutes, he discovered he was alone and the streets had become alleyways, some so narrow that he could touch the opposing walls with his outstretched hands. He passed a steel-shuttered silversmith's, and then, ten minutes later, found himself standing before another, identical in every respect to the former, including the Georgian pepperpot on the right-hand corner of the top shelf. He immediately became anxious, then dismissed the reaction, saying to himself that he was being absurd. He would just walk in one direction and stay with it and eventually he would reach a park or a statue that he recognized from previous visits. He could then find his green Peugeot and drive home. Instead, after walking two blocks on cobbled stone, he found the silversmith's once more.

Surprisingly, Kemble now felt more irritated than concerned; he convinced himself that he had not been concentrating, that he had been walking in circles because the streets in the old part of the town had been designed that way. There were no other people around because it was Sunday and the shops were closed, although earlier he had seen a flea market that had attracted the curious. He told himself to relax, and remembered the old adage: that the best way to find a missing sock was to look for a missing shoe. And so he forgot about his car (the green Peugeot) and decided to retrace his steps to see if the cathedral was still there. It was in this manner that Kemble finally arrived before an open door, above which was a plaque, a coat of arms, and the single word: Mirabeau.

The name meant nothing to him. But despite the anonymity of the building, Kemble could see that it was some kind of museum that offered not only a diversion from his wandering, but also a blessed coolness from the increasing heat. And so he entered, bought a ticket and a guidebook, and began to walk around. He was the only visitor.

His immediate impression was that there was something surreal about the building. The floor in each room was identical, black-and-white chequerboard. And each wall was the same colour blue, a darkish blue, similar to the shade one used to see on the back of certain matchboxes. But more importantly, all the doors had been removed, so that if one stood in one room and looked back, the adjacent room seemed to mirror its neighbour, and that one echoed the room beyond, like a series of looking glasses. Whether this was intentional or by accident, it was unclear.

Taking his time, Kemble walked around, looking at this and that, when suddenly he heard footsteps. At this point, he was standing in the far salon, next to a portrait of a dandy, with his back to the heart of the building. And he heard footsteps. Of course, he told himself that this shouldn't be unusual, but he had got used to being the only one there, and, moreover, he suspected that this was not just another curious passer-by like himself. The sound was hurried, urgent, as if the visitor was escaping from something outside and didn't give a damn about Mirabeau. There was also something sinister about the tap-tapping of those high heels and he couldn't really explain why he thought that.

After a moment, the footsteps stopped and there was silence. At first, Kemble wasn't sure whether to turn around, but he could see in a mirror that he was hidden from the other rooms by a large Buhl cabinet. So he slowly turned and saw a woman standing about twenty feet away on a black square, framed by four Baroque arches. She was in profile, her eyes in shadow, and she seemed unsure what to do. Kemble watched her glance back towards the street, then move to the window, then retreat. As if she were trapped.

In appearance, she was tall, about five foot eight, with straight blonde hair, a wide mouth, and the nose of a Gibson Girl. She was wearing a white straw hat, with a white ribbon, and a white dress. Kemble was not very knowledgeable about fashion, but the dress didn't seem very modern in design, more Victorian, or even earlier. He recalled a painting by Whistler of a woman in a dress that was similar.

The woman had now stopped pacing up and down (black square, white square) and was standing very still. It was then that Kemble noticed her eyes. Not the colour (he was too far away) but the expression: it was a mixture of hatred, anger and despair, all of it focused on the object she held in her right hand.

It was a book.

It was a book that she kept opening at the flyleaf, reading whatever was written there, then slamming it shut. Then opening it again, more slowly each time, as if hoping the words would disappear. Obviously they didn't, because she suddenly tried to tear the page out, then changed her mind and seized the handle of a window, presumably to throw the book into the garden. Then, when she heard the scream, she dropped the book and disappeared back towards the street. After a moment, someone obviously switched off the alarm, because there was silence. Kemble didn't move for about a minute in case she returned, then he walked slowly over to the window, picked up the book and held it in his hand.

In appearance, it was a plain blue, leather-bound hardback, without a jacket and with a bent spine, as if it had been read by someone who cared more about the content than the book itself. Opening it, Kemble saw that it was an English novel, or at least that it was written in English. It was also second-hand, since someone had pencilled '12 frs' at the top of the flyleaf. Kemble assumed the woman had just bought it at a local bookstall, possibly in the flea market he had seen near the cathedral. Beneath the price, was an inscription in ink. It is this:

> *To my darling Leonora, this book could not have been written without you. Please remember that no matter what happens to us, I will love you always.*
>
> *Christopher*

Kemble read the inscription twice and assumed that Christopher was the author, Christopher Gersh, as stated on the title-page. He had heard of the name and even recalled reading one of his earlier novels, although he had forgotten its plot or even whether he liked it or not.

Later, while sitting on the terrace of his house, overlooking the valley, the book beside him, Kemble telephoned his friend Hoddle, who had worked in publishing until his father died, and asked him about Gersh.

'Don't know much about him,' Hoddle replied. 'He hasn't given an interview in years as far as I know. He's not a recluse like Salinger or Pynchon, because everyone knows where he is. In the south of France somewhere. Or is it Spain? Anyway, he's not a hermit, just elusive. Damn good writer if you like that sort of thing.'

'Is he married?'

'Married? Yes, I think so. Can't be sure.'

'Could you *be* sure and let me know?'

'Why? Is this some kind of quiz?'

'No. I'm just curious.'

That evening, Kemble began to read the novel, but put it aside. He kept thinking about the woman in the museum, about the look in her eyes as she tried to destroy the book, as if she were trying to kill it.

The next morning, Hoddle telephoned while Kemble was away from the house, swimming in a pool set amid pines and bougainvillaea.

At lunchtime, he telephoned again:

'Found out a few scraps about Gersh. Not much but I'll fax them to you.'

'Don't have a fax.'

'Then I'll send them to you. But I was right about the wife. She's American. Frightfully rich apparently, from one of those New England families. Old money, is that what they call it?'

'What's her name?'

'Delacourt.'

'No, her first name?'

'Helen.'

Helen. It wasn't Leonora, but then he never expected it to be.

'Is there any mention, among the stuff you've got, of someone called Leonora?'

'No. No one called Leonora. Why?'

In the afternoon, Kemble walked to the village to buy some bread and fruit. The bread had sold out early that morning, so he bought peaches and two bottles of Merlot.

Walking back, he began to think about the book. Why did this particular copy, which was obviously so precious to the owner – or at least Gersh believed it to be – end up in a backstreet junkshop in Grasse? On the surface, it represented, at the very least, an extraordinary passion between the writer and Leonora – and yet it had been discarded to be sold for twelve francs to any passer-by. Except that the passer-by had been Gersh's wife. A photograph of Helen, that accompanied the mail from Hoddle, confirmed that.

A blue leather-bound book.

No matter what happens to us, I will love you always.

A blue leather-bound book entitled *A Woman of His Acquaintance*.

That night, Kemble read the novel in bed and didn't finish it until seven in the morning. It was not a remarkable book, and the style reminded Kemble too much of Ford Madox Ford's *The Good Soldier*. As Ford's story was a tale of an adulterous affair, so was Gersh's; a husband's obsession with a younger woman and the madness of that obsession. At one point, Gersh says of the husband that if he could orchestrate his life, he'd cut out everything except the second movement. Just the andante. Kemble liked that analogy. He could sympathize with it.

He also found himself fascinated by the description of the younger woman, her cries, her enthusiasms. He wanted to know more about her. Undoubtedly, she was Leonora.

And Leonora, unlike her fictional counterpart (Antonella), existed. She was walking, sitting, breathing, somewhere out there. Maybe not too far away. She was dressing, undressing, smiling, combing her hair, undressing, removing her clothes. She was naked.

During the rest of his stay in Bar-sur-Loup, Kemble discovered that he was thinking more of Leonora until he was thinking of nothing else. She entered his garden, his house, his room. She sat next to him in the car when he drove to the market. She sat in the shade of an oleander while he swam.

And when he returned to London, she, of course, went with him.

All this took place in September.

In that same month, a tall, middle-aged man in his mid-fifties walked the three hundred yards from his villa to his usual table on the terrace of a restaurant and waited for his midday meal. He didn't order it, didn't even glance at the menu, since the waiter knew that the man would eat the same course he ate every Monday: tomato salad followed by pasta, accompanied by two glasses of dry white wine. No conversation took place between waiter and customer, since it had been long understood that the man preferred to be left alone while he smoked a Senior Service and stared at the Mediterranean, a spiral notebook placed beside him but rarely opened.

Once, it had been his custom to read the London *Times* (a day old), folding the newspaper to the crossword puzzle, after glancing at the obituaries. But that practice had been abandoned as the man grew more disenchanted with his own country, and even more with that country's cricket team. Instead, he would day-dream, allowing nothing to disturb him, and fearing only the sound of an English voice. If it was female, the accent pinpointing Bourton-on-the-Water or Tonbridge, he knew that he would be approached by a middle-aged, red-faced woman, slightly overweight, who would ask him if he was who he was, then beg him to autograph something or other, before retreating to a nearby table. Sometimes, on more fortunate days, this ritual would be followed by the click of a camera as he was photographed scooping a coil of linguine into his mouth. Mercifully, these occurrences were rare now, as his popularity faded and his novels remained on the shelves just a little longer each year.

It was while Gersh was finishing his salad, on this particular day, that the waiter approached the table, apologized, and told him, almost as a warning, that he had a visitor. Turning his head, Gersh saw his wife standing at the door of the restaurant, presenting him with a smile that he knew was the closing parenthesis to a tranquil day.

As she sat opposite him, refusing a glass of wine, Gersh observed Helen's pose as she perched at an angle to him on the chair, the straight back beneath a dove-grey suit that he'd never seen before, the angle of her neck, the fine cleft in her chin that he used to kiss, a tanned knee, smooth as stone, the thinness of her wrists (he'd never seen that watch before either), her teeth, her eyes behind the dark glasses. He attempted to listen politely as she told him how she had driven down from Paris, after flying in from New York (or was it Boston?), but his attention was drawn to a man on the beach who was carrying a child on his right shoulder as if it were an earthenware urn he was taking to the sea to fill with water. And then he heard Helen's voice suddenly shift from major to minor, as she asked him questions that made him feel weak, helpless, as if he were sinking into a quagmire. He heard her repeat a name, biting out the syllables, her tongue finding right angles in the softest of consonants, and he knew he could not lie to her. She knew that too. She once said it was her insurance.

And then Helen was no longer there, the chair empty, her image replaced by a rectangle of sky bisected by the darker blue of the sea.

Gersh didn't move, couldn't move. He was aware of silence, of faces staring at the back of his head. In his mind, he repeated the words his wife quoted, repeating them as if they were a mantra. She had talked of Fate guiding her, of a star rising here, of another in retrograde, and other such nonsense. If she hadn't stopped in Grasse, if she hadn't chanced upon an antique market – it was all madness and he was deaf to most of it. Except those words that he had written on that winter evening, when he knew all was lost: *My darling Leonora... no matter what happens to us, I will love you always.*

Sadly, it was still true.

Two

The man, in the apartment in Rome, sat on the bed, cleaning a gun, listening to *Belkis* by Respighi. The room was in shadow, even though it was almost noon, since the shutters were closed, as they were always closed, both day and night. Outside, the view would have added nothing to the austerity of the white walls and the bare boards, since it consisted solely of the traditonal tide of terracotta tiles and the banks of television aerials perched like storks on the rooftops.

However, at the rear of the apartment there was a small terrace containing table, chairs and greenery, from which one could see the dome of a church and a rather pretty garden inhabited by statues. At dusk, the man would sit there alone, in the darkness, for an hour or so, thinking of this and that, before retiring to bed. If it rained, the man would do the same, his chair pulled back beneath an eave.

He received no visitors, nor did he expect any. The name on the doorbell in the courtyard was not his own. It belonged to a Swiss called Victor Melnikov who rented the apartment to strangers. Now and again, letters addressed to Melnikov arrived and were placed unopened on a side-table, beneath a watercolour of Ravenna. They were never collected and they were never thrown away, even though some dated back two years, long before the man rented the apartment.

He had arrived in Rome in June from Panama, and, for the first three weeks, had stayed in a hotel near the Spanish Steps. He rarely left his room except to take a brief exercise, walking the city, visiting the usual tourist sights, remaining anonymous. In the hotel register, he had signed his name Jack Keats, not only because it amused him to do so, but also because it was a precaution to keep himself alive.

His name, in fact, was Gabriel Jesus Hoyt, born of a Bolivian mother and an American father. The parents were both dead, one of cancer, the other of grief. I myself met him for the first time on a train between Cologne and Düsseldorf. We were sharing the same compartment and he was sitting opposite me, staring through the window at the night, enabling me to see both his faces, left and right. At one point, he gestured to an illuminated cross in the sky, set in a circle, and asked me if I knew what it was.

'It's Bayer. The pharmaceutical company,' I replied. 'This must be Leverkusen.'

He nodded, looked at me. And that was it. We never spoke another word and, at Düsseldorf, when I left the train, he was asleep. This was five years ago and Hoyt must have been about thirty-five years of age. He had blond hair then and I have never been sure whether he dyed it black later, or if his natural hair was dark, and he had chosen to be blond at that time for his own reason. I suspect the latter.

Hoyt placed the gun (a Smith and Wesson 745) on the top shelf of the stove, selected a black and chalk pin-stripe suit from the wardrobe and dressed as the church bells sounded noon. He considered taking a Burberry, since it was now December, then decided against it.

At ten minutes past twelve, he left the apartment and walked slowly along the narrow street towards the Campo de' Fiori. He took his time; the encounter was not for an hour. At a bookshop, he bought an American paperback by Kaminsky; on a corner, he watched a man sitting on the flagstones, recaning the seat of a chair. Entering the square, he walked past the market stalls, past a fountain, a statue of Bruno, until he reached the Carbonara, a popular but inexpensive restaurant where the waiters knew his face but not, since he always paid in cash, his name. It was the only restaurant Hoyt visited, having discovered many years previously that it was far safer to be known in one place than to be seen in many.

He sat at a table to the left of the door, facing the square, the book face down by the side plate, ordered a coffee and waited. Though Rome was not his favourite city, he felt comfortable there; comfortable because he was ignored. In truth, he was not distinctive in appearance, not the kind of man one would see a second time and say: 'Ah yes, didn't we meet at that dreadful party in Gstaad?' He was not memorable in any way, partly because his image was unremarkable by nature (average height, average build, a second-billing face), and partly out of deliberate choice. He did not wish to be remembered, and there were women, beautiful women, exciting women, who never wanted to forget him. It is said that the wife of a high-profile American senator adored him to distraction and that when she woke up and he was gone (the key to her apartment folded within a hundred-dollar bill), she took to madness.

'Hello, Gabriel.'

Hoyt finished the coffee, set the cup in its saucer and looked up. The man, standing at the table, was sweating but it didn't bother him. In his left lapel was a white rose.

'Sit down, Arthur,' Hoyt said.

He was Arthur Siegel, British by passport, Viennese by birth, who collected butterflies and liked little girls. Being a bibliophile, he was not unaware of these Nabokovian desires; indeed, he owned one of the finest libraries in England, most of them modern first editions, of which he had read each and every one. A signed copy of *Lolita*, however, was not his most prized possession. But a signed copy of *The Big Sleep* was. He was a man of taste.

'You're looking well,' Siegel said, pulling a chair closer to the table.

'I'm looking well?'

'You're looking well. You've lost a bit of weight but you're looking fine.'

'I'll tell you what I'm looking,' Hoyt said quietly. 'I'm looking at six months I've been doing nothing. I'm looking at what I could have been doing and I'm looking at you, Arthur.'

'I'm here now.'

'You're here now. Yes. I can see that.'

'You were paid. You had a retainer.'

'That's not what I'm saying.'

'I know what you're saying.'

'What I'm saying is, I've been bored.'
'I realize that – '
'Let me finish. I don't like silence.'
'There was a reason.'
'You could have kept me informed.'
'I had to be sure.'
'Of what? Of me?'
'No. Of course not.'
'What then?'
'What then? Of the client, of course. I had to be certain. I don't want what happened last time.'
'Don't blame me for that, Arthur.'
'I'm not blaming you. Do I look as though I'm blaming you?'
'You look – forget how you look.'
'I'd like to know.'
'Why?'
'Because I'd like to know. I'm vain.'
'Who's the client?'
'Gabriel – you know I never tell you that.'
'Until now.'
Hoyt turned slowly, raising his head and looking at Siegel.
'Until now, Arthur,' he repeated.
A waiter approached, adjusting his bow-tie, placed two menus on the table, then stood back, two paces, and stared across the Campo de' Fiori. A group of men had appeared, in blue singlets and blue trousers, and were dismantling the stalls, folding up the trestles and stacking the boards on to a cart. Other men were sweeping the discarded vegetables and fruit into a gutter to await the garbage truck. A girl with a Botticelli face was standing very still, eyes lowered, head on an angle, playing a violin.
'Antipasti,' Hoyt said. 'Followed by spaghetti carbonara.'
'For two?' the waiter asked.
'For two.'
'Wine?'
'I hate your wine. Minerale.'
'Minerale.'
Siegel watched the waiter enter the interior of the restaurant, then said:

'I like wine with lunch.'
'Not here you wouldn't.'
'I'll risk it.'
'You're paying, Arthur. It's your money.'

Siegel smiled, a strobe smile, aware that he didn't want to offend Hoyt. He needed him. He considered changing the subject, telling him a joke he had heard the previous evening. The one about the Italian hell. But he couldn't tell jokes, didn't know how to.

So, instead, he said:

'Gabriel – maybe we should discuss this later. It's rather public here, isn't it?'

Hoyt shook his head.

'We could talk in your apartment,' Siegel continued. 'Don't you like your apartment? Let's talk there.'

'No.'
'Why not?'
'Who's the client, Arthur?'
'I can't tell you. You know that.'
'I want to know.'
'Why?'
'Because I want to be sure.'
'About what?'
'About the risks. I was almost killed in New York – '
'I couldn't predict that.'
'Yes, you could have done. Yes, Arthur. Now don't fuck with me or I walk away now.'
'Look – oh, shit, we can't talk here. There are people at the next table. They can hear.'
'So let them hear.'
'Are you serious?'
'Believe it.'

Siegel didn't move. A beggar approached. He gave him two thousand lire. He listened to the girl playing the violin. He ordered a carafe of white wine. He never looked at Hoyt. Finally:

'It's a woman.'
'The client?'
'Yes.'
'Husband or lover?'

'Husband.'

'Where is she now?'

'I think she's in Paris.'

'What do you mean – you think?'

'She's in Paris. All right? Paris. France.'

'And where is the husband?'

'She's not sure.'

'She's not sure?'

'No.'

'Jesus Christ, Arthur – '

'I said she's not sure. But I am. At least, as of last month. That's why I kept you waiting.'

'So where?'

'The south of France.'

'Where in the south of France?'

'Near Nice.'

Hoyt considered this, studying Siegel's face, then suddenly stood up and began to walk away.

'Let's go.'

'What about the meal? We've just ordered lunch.'

But Hoyt was already walking out of the Campo de' Fiori, returning to his apartment, without looking back.

'Her name is Helen Gersh,' Siegel said, standing with his back to the shutters, a ladder of light moving diagonally across the floor. 'Her husband's name is Christopher Gersh. He's a writer.'

'Do you have a photograph?'

Siegel placed a book on the bed beside Hoyt. It was a mint copy of *A Woman of His Acquaintance*, the jacket covered in a protective seal. On the back was the face of Gersh, looking directly into camera, unsmiling.

'Do I need to read this?' Hoyt asked.

'You don't have to. But it's not bad. He's written better.'

'I'll give it back when I've finished.'

'Keep it.'

'It's a first edition.'

'There isn't a second.'

Hoyt looked at the photograph again then threw the book aside.

'Tell me about Helen Gersh.'

'Why do you insist on knowing about her?'

'Tell me about her, Arthur.'

Later, the two men sat on the terrace, in the darkness, drinking wine. They talked of indifferent matters, merely to pass the time. For example, Siegel described a recent visit to Greece, seeking out the beaches that encouraged nudity. He had befriended a German girl of thirteen with a bottom that he had wanted to frame and hang on a wall. When Siegel was drunk, he used phrases like that. He would also quote from his favourite novels, proud of the fact that he knew the opening sentences of at least forty books by heart. *Thirty years ago, Marseilles lay burning in the sun, one day* is the first line of *Little Dorrit*.

'The placing of *one day* just there,' Siegel said, 'is enough to convert anyone to Dickens.'

Later still, as it grew colder, Hoyt lit the fire in the drawing room, and they listened to Blue Note jazz, sitting in leather armchairs, keeping a space between each other.

Finally, Siegel left, saying goodbye. Hoyt gave him the gun, since he couldn't travel with it, didn't need it any more, and, besides, he could buy another in France. If need be. He then remained awake until the light appeared, reading Gersh's novel. Then he slept until mid-morning.

At noon, he left the apartment with all his possessions, few as they were. He left no trace of his existence, except the door key, placed in an envelope, addressed to the landlord, Victor Melnikov.

By evening, Gabriel Jesus Hoyt was no longer in Rome, no longer in Italy. He was on board a plane that had taken off from Leonardo da Vinci, at fifteen hundred hours, and was now flying north-west towards Nice.

FRAMEWORK OF LOSS
ART CORRIVEAU

For Carin, Claire and Michele

1. The Ides of Mark

I'm Simona. Twenty-nine years old, a decent enough graphic designer and mother of a three-year-old named Phoebe. Everyone thinks I'm much too young to have lost my husband (Mark, thirty-one, also a graphic designer). I am. But that doesn't change anything, does it? Mark was broad-sided in his vintage Beetle by a drunken Bronco driver. Six months ago this weekend – 15 March – the Ides of Mark. I don't even have the luxury of wishing the other driver dead. He is. Everyone thinks I look like hell, but they're always telling me how *good* I look. I look like hell, trust me. And I hope it goes without saying: I wish I were dead too.

Last week I got a warning at work, my first one ever. My boss assured me he understood what I was going through (everyone is always saying that too: *I understand*), but he had growing concerns about my commitment to the team. We're a small firm, he reminded me, we all rely on each other to get the job done. (This from the man who disappears for whole chunks of the day because he's cheating on his wife during business hours. Asshole.) I reminded him he owed me a week of vacation and two weeks of comp time, left over from our busy season. Maybe I should take it all now, I said, to get my head together. He thought this a very good idea. They'd somehow find a way to squeak by without me. Secretly, he doesn't want me to come back. Well, I can't lose this job, asshole; I have a daughter to raise. By myself.

So anyway, here I am, at my mother-in-law's beach house in Wellfleet. Day one: getting my head together, getting over Mark. I've brought a three-week supply of Dorothy L. Sayers mysteries, a full prescription of antidepressants and my watercolours. I've left Phoebe with Phyllis, the mother-in-law, in Boston.

I'm not getting over anything. I'm getting drunk.

Phyllis just left. She hired a sitter and followed me down here in her own car, to settle me in. We stopped at the supermarket in Orleans to cram my trunk full of groceries. You should have seen Phyllis in that Stop-N-Shop, racing up and down the aisles, throwing toilet paper and peppermint tea into the shopping cart; bubblebath and sandwich meat, tanning lotion and fresh peaches. I just loped along behind her. (Here's what I put in that shopping cart, my contributions to my salvation: a case of beer – Mark's brand – and an embarrassingly large bottle of cheap cabernet. Screw top. Screw it.) Phyllis paid for everything. Then she put it all away when we got to her house. She made up my bed, took all the slip covers off the living-room furniture, did a little dusting. Back on the road within the hour. Phyllis lost *her* husband years ago. She sent out all her thank-you-for-the-flowers within a week of Mark's funeral. I haven't sent mine yet. I think I get up to a year. Or am I confusing that with wedding gifts?

2. Independent Dining

Night is falling and I haven't eaten a single peach. But I am on my second six-pack. I've spent the afternoon staring out across the harbour. I've made friends with a wooden rocking chair on the screen porch. The green paint is chipping off its arms. I'm whale-watching, helping the chipping process along. I've only gotten up to get another beer or to pee. (Where did Phyllis put that goddamn toilet paper?) I haven't seen a single whale yet. But I'm not that worried, I've got three weeks. Imagine: three whole weeks of this. The phone rings; it's Phyllis, of course. She's back in Boston – (already?) – and just checking in with me. Would I like to speak with

Phoebe before she puts her to bed?

Hi baby, Mommy misses you. No, darling; I'm not with Daddy. I'll explain it all when I get back, OK? Be a good girl. Now put Granny back on the phone, OK? Nighty-night.

Right, dinner, getting myself together. I open the fridge and bask in the cool yellow light. When did Phyllis sneak that jar of dill chips into the cart? I hate pickles. I slam the door shut. She doesn't know me at all, not the first goddamn thing about me. How can I possibly cope with cooking a meal right now? I grab my car keys.

I turn left on to Route 6. Yes, I'm driving drunk. I've decided to eat at the first place with more than three cars in the parking lot. But it's mid-September and everything's boarded up for the season. Before I know it I'm cresting Pilgrim Heights. The Truro tidal flats lie before me. Off to my right I can see the murky outline of Provincetown's monument. I'm frankly running out of Cape. Screw it. There's bound to be something open in P-Town.

I end up at this hopelessly romantic guest house with a restaurant on the main floor. Ten minutes till the kitchen closes. The waiter is not happy to see me. *Table for the independent diner this evening?* He seats me near the fireplace, which is too hot. I order a Stoli Martini with extra olives. Phyllis should have bought olives, not pickles. Or those little cocktail onions. Something useful.

I'm going to drink up and leave. The restaurant is emptying out; the older couple next to me have just asked for their cheque. A sad-looking, middle-aged man is sipping coffee and reading a German guidebook on Cape Cod. When the waiter brings my Martini, he suggests I order right away. The kitchen. Never mind, I tell him, I don't feel like dining independently after all; he can just bring my cheque too. A slightly awkward moment. He apologizes. He hasn't meant to rush me, it's really no trouble. It's just that the staff are all going out tonight. There's a bonfire at Herring Cove Beach. But it'll keep till they get there. What would I like?

I burst into tears. Uh-oh. The alcohol, I guess. Phyllis's fucking emotional efficiency. My asshole boss. The vagrant wish for a pressing, after-dinner engagement.

The couple next to me arch their eyebrows and stand up. The German signals for his cheque. My waiter, a study in dismay, tells me he'll be right back. Just what he needs: crazy crying woman at closing time. He bids the old geezers good night, attends to the German who wants to pay in cash. I blow my nose on the cloth napkin in my lap – it's an emergency. I also take a good slug of my Martini. Then another. I'm fully expecting the waiter to slap my cheque in front of me. But he doesn't. He escorts the German to the door and flips the 'open' sign to 'closed'. He makes his way over to the bar and pours himself a Jack Daniel's. Then he takes a seat at my table.

– I'm Michael.
– Simona. Sorry about that.
– Bad day?
– My first time alone in a restaurant, Michael. Some jerk killed my husband a couple of months ago in a car crash. This is how well I'm dealing with it.
– We're just about to have our dinner in the kitchen, Simona. Grab your Martini. You can eat with us.

This, Simona, is where you should scrape together what's left of your dignity. This is where you should thank him for his random act of kindness, pay him for the drink, leave him a big tip. This is where you should get yourself a cup of strong black coffee and drink every drop of it in the 7-Eleven parking lot before creeping back to Wellfleet at about twenty miles an hour. But you can't. You're much too young to have lost your husband. You grab your Martini, just like you're told. And you follow Michael into the kitchen.

3. Girl Talk

– Boys, this is an old college friend, Simona. She just got into town, like, five minutes ago, and her cupboards are bare. We're taking pity on her. Simona, the one in chef's drag is Gabriel. The other one, over at the sink, is Peter, a.k.a. the Best Little Busboy in P-Town.
– Formerly, darling. *Formerly*. Tonight's my last night of slavery in this godforsaken *hell hole*. Free at last, free at last...
– Hi, Simona, have a seat. I was just about to serve up the salad. Michael, why don't you open a bottle of that Pinot Grigio? And Peter, get Simona a plate.
– Yassuh, Massuh Gabriel. Right away, suh.
– I don't know nuthin' 'bout birthin' no Pinot Grigio.

Too many names. I say a general hello and take the nearest chair.

Soon I am absorbed by the din of getting dinner on the table. Just what the doctor ordered. I drain my Martini and wonder, not for the first time, whose brilliant idea it was to shuffle me off to the Cape. I'm pretty sure it wasn't mine. I'd sort of planned on sitting around my apartment in my sweatpants for three weeks, eating Ben & Jerry's out of the container until I exploded. *Simona's always loved her watercolours. What she needs is to get back into her painting. It'll take her mind off things.* As if I don't already spend enough time alone.

The chef, Gabriel, sets a large bowl of mixed greens in the centre of the table and begins tossing them with balsamic vinegar, olive oil and a little dry mustard. He's an astonishing-looking man in his mid-thirties: green eyes the colour of Chinese silk, closely cropped salt-and-pepper hair, a swimmer's body under those chef's whites. Why don't straight men ever look like this?

Peter, the busboy, brings me a plate and some cutlery and seats himself at my left. Michael sets four goblets on the table and splashes a little wine into Gabriel's glass. After Gabriel tastes it and nods, Michael pours it out and sits at my right. He squeezes my arm and nods in Gabriel's direction. Gabriel is holding up his glass. We all follow suit. He thanks Michael and Peter for a wonderful summer; he hopes they'll return next May. He welcomes me to P-Town. Ching-ching. *Bon appetit.*

I realize, as soon as I have my first bite of salad, that I'm starving. I want to stuff this arugula and frisée and radicchio into my mouth with both hands. I've been skipping a lot of meals lately. Not much of an independent diner, I'm afraid. A meal, by my definition, requires at least two willing participants. (Sorry, three-year-olds don't count.) I can't think of anything more ill-advised than the elaborate preparation and consumption of food by just one person. Not when there's Oreos. I look around the table. Everyone is eating industriously, no one is talking. Should I say something? Meals also require conversation. But I'm not sure I can manage that right now.

Screw it. Help yourself to more salad, Simona. These men are used to strangers turning up at mealtime. It's their *lifestyle*. Look at them. They'd much rather gossip about tonight's customers: the unruly lesbian birthday party, the regular couples, the anniversary dinners, that weird German guy. When Peter asks you what brought you to the Cape, you tell him 'late vacation'. He'll nod and top up your wine glass. And when Gabriel asks you again how you know Michael, you just say 'college'. Follow Michael's lead on that one. Gabriel will only nod and tell Peter to gather up the salad plates.

For our main, we're having what's left of tonight's special: roasted duck in a blueberry sauce. Apparently the birthday lesbian didn't like it and sent it back. I think it's delicious. Michael opens a nice little Napa Valley merlot. Conversation veers to the evening ahead. Turns out, it's not just any bonfire. It's the End-of-the-Season-Townies-Only bonfire with special drag appearances. Turns out, Peter is one of these: Princess Panoply from the Planet Love. Clever, I say. Lost on the gay boys, he sighs. Philistines in tight white Calvin Klein underwear. They're always getting it wrong and calling him Penelope. I try to imagine Peter in drag. I just can't see it. He's young and athletic-looking and hip. Gorgeous teeth.

– Why don't you come along, Simona? Should be a trip.

– But it's 'townies only' you said.

– Honey, you're eating in the kitchen. Let's not split hairs.

– Fangs in, Penelope. She didn't mean it like that.

– I'm just dishin' her 'cause I like her. I, Princess Panoply, dub thee, Simona, honorary townie with all the honours and privileges bestowed upon that order. What's for dessert?

– I should be getting home. I've already imposed enough on your hospitality.

– Sit yourself back down. You're coming with us; it's all settled. Who knows, you might meet the girl of your dreams.

– She's not a dyke, Pot-O-Pee.

– Honey, they all look like dykes to me.

We decide to skip dessert; we're watching our figures. Instead, Gabriel cuts up a few Mackintosh apples while Michael makes us cappuccinos laced with Kaluà. Peter and I are rinsing plates and putting them in the dishwasher. He tells me he and Gabe are having an affair. He swears me to secrecy; Michael doesn't know this. Gabe owns a house in Truro with his boyfriend of eleven years. Boyfriend is away this week, visiting his parents in New Jersey. Tonight will be one of their last together. Tomorrow Gabe has promised to take Peter to Nantucket for the day, before escorting him to the Greyhound station in Hyannis. Peter has never been on a real island before. Then it's back to Boston. He's starting the graduate architecture programme at Harvard. He and Gabe may never see each other again.

Michael wants to know what we're whispering about. Girl talk, Peter says, don't be jealous. Michael says he is jealous; after all, he hasn't seen me since college. Good, Peter says, then he won't mind taking me up to the attic (where he and Michael have been living all summer) to lend me a pretty sweater, just like in college. It'll get chilly out on the beach.

I start to laugh. I can't help it. My day-to-day life is never this weird. Usually I wake up, drop my daughter off at day care, design mutual fund prospectuses for eight hours and pick her up again on my way home. I make Phoebe's supper, I skip mine. I watch a little TV, then go to bed having no idea what I've just watched. Sometimes I sleep, sometimes I don't.

Today, though. Today I woke up and moved to Wellfleet. I drank a six-pack of beer and whale-watched. I drove drunk to a restaurant twenty miles away. I burst into tears in front of the waiter and he invited me to dinner. Now I'm going to a party on the beach. It's all just happening to me and I'm letting it. I feel alive right now. I tingle. Provincetown. I've never been this far out there before.

4. Bonfire of the Vanities

We all pile into Gabe's 1967 Cadillac convertible. Tomato red, of course. The top's down, but it sort of *has* to be. Princess Panoply's wig is too high. Good thing there's not much wind. It's sort of a Marie-Antoinette number made out of Christmas tree tinsel. The rest of Peter's outfit makes him look like a majorette from outer space. I don't tell him this. I'm not sure it'll come out as a compliment.

We've brought along more wine from the restaurant, plastic cups, one of the guest house's retired Laura Ashley bedspreads, Peter's automatic-focus camera and a couple of extra sweatshirts. In the back seat, I advise Michael to choose the college we were supposed to have attended together. He shrugs. He's never quite made it to college. I decide on Villanova because I've always liked the sound of it.

The party is in full swing by the time we pull into the Herring Cove parking lot. A drag policewoman brandishing a flashlight greets us at the edge of the sand. We all know the rules, she says: no alcohol on the beach, no controlled substances, no public nudity, no defacement of public property. Does anyone want to buy pot? Michael asks for a couple of joints, pays her and leads us over the dune. We head in the direction of the orange glow, sand squeaking beneath our feet.

The bonfire itself is enormous. Its nucleus looks suspiciously like a picnic table. We're careful to spread our blanket upwind. Michael uncorks another bottle of merlot. Princess Panoply dashes off to join the back-up chorus of a drag duet lip-synching 'Enough is Enough'. Gabriel offers to make us some s'mores. Just me and Michael now. *I always dreamed I'd find the perfect lover.* I look up. The sky is drenched in stars. Michael encourages me to lean into him. He wraps his arms around me. We both look up. He tells me I shouldn't be surprised if Gabe and Peter disappear off into the dunes. They're having an affair. He swears me to secrecy; they don't know that he knows.

– There's something else I should tell you, Simona.

– Oh, for heaven's sake, Michael. I know you're gay. You're safe with me.

– Give me a break. Listen, I lost my lover last winter. After six years together. So I kind of understand what you're going through.

No more tears. Enough is enough.

– Did he suffer, Michael?

– We both did. And it isn't over. It was his house and his money. The family challenged the legality of the will and they won. They threw me out. That's why I'm waiting tables down here; Gabe's an old friend. But I've got a good lawyer now. And we're contesting it.

– Um, what about you? Are you OK?

– Do you mean: have I got it? Yes.

The drag queens end their number and begin a new one. It's something from the 1930s or 1940s. I don't know it. I flash back to Mark's funeral. There are my parents, trying to muster grief when all they can feel is relief that it was Mark and not me. And there's Phyllis, too wrapped up in the actual event – the music, the pall bearers, the speakers, the buffet luncheon, the flowers – to feel much of anything. And there's me, standing off to the side, holding my daughter on my hip, trying to explain to her what's going on, failing miserably at grief because all I can feel is hatred. The most terrible anger. Mind-numbing, all-consuming rage. At him, at Mark. How *dare* he do this to me?

I turn to face Michael directly. Thinning blond hair, little round glasses. Ordinary nose, a completely ordinary-looking guy. It's not fair, I tell him, what his lover's family has done to him. It's bigoted and cold-hearted and inhuman. He agrees. But he's had some good advice recently. With this sort of thing it's best to try and function within society's accepted framework of loss. That makes me snuffle a little. No more tears. He's right, I say, wiping my eyes on the sleeve of his sweatshirt. It's something I've got to get better at – understanding this framework of loss.

Laws, he says, not loss. Society's framework of laws.

It's Gloria Gaynor's 'I Will Survive' next. There's a general roar of approval. People are jumping up all over the place to dance. Thank goodness! Saved from utter weepiness by ridiculous coincidence. I grab Michael's hand and haul him to his feet. We are soon joined by Princess Panoply and Gabriel. The four of us are hugging each other and spinning around in the sand. Peter is insisting we all fly to Nantucket tomorrow morning. The plane leaves at ten-thirty. It'll only cost forty dollars each. We'll go shopping, have a little lunch, rent mopeds. We'll take the ferry back. Gabriel is trying to shut him up by jamming a white chocolate s'more into his face. We all take bites out of it while we're spinning. I imagine us with wings, taking flight, spiralling up into the stars. But the sensation is more like falling. We're definitely going to fall. We fall. We end up in a big messy, tinselly, sticky heap. We're fine though. We will survive.

5. The Secret Garden

It's only a matter of time, I suppose, before the real police raid the party. Good parties are like that. When somebody eventually notices the blue flashing lights over the dune, panic ensues. Next thing you know we're all dumping bottles like mad, burying nickel bags in the sand. We part company with Gabe and Peter in the mayhem. They've got the bedspread with them; they're seeking refuge in the dunes. Michael and I decide to take our chances in the general exodus back to town. Peter makes us swear we'll be on the front porch of the guest house at eight-thirty sharp. The two of us watch them slink off together, Peter with cha-cha heels in hand, his wig listing badly to starboard. God, is Gabe gorgeous – even from behind and in the dark.

Michael and I dash through the surf in our bare feet, pretending we're in a James Bond movie. We soon tire of this, though, and make a tack toward the silhouette of the first lifeguard chair we see. We're hoping there's an opening in the dune behind it; we're elated when we find out we're right. We put on our shoes and skirt the patrol cars by sticking to the outer edges of the parking lot until we reach the pay booth at the entrance. We don't have our thumbs out very long at all before a pickup truck stops for us. We climb into the back and ride into town with Josie and the Pussycats. I have no idea what time it is. I've lost my watch somewhere along the way.

We're let off several blocks from Michael's guest house. Everyone else is going on to the dance bar for last call. We find ourselves alone on Commercial Street. The fog has rolled in; everything's gone watercolour and soft: edges all feathery, light with too much liquid in it. Michael suddenly remembers the two joints in his breast pocket. We spark them both up and begin walking.

It starts spilling out of me. I know I've had a lot to drink, I know I'm a little bit stoned. But everything seems so clear. I tell Michael that Mark and I weren't getting along very well when he died – no one knows this – but we were barely speaking. We hadn't had sex in weeks. We'd begun to communicate with each other through our daughter: what she wanted, what she needed. Meals eaten in total silence. That night, the night I got the phone call to ID the body – 15 March – I didn't even know where the fuck Mark was at the time. He hadn't come home for dinner, he hadn't called to say he'd be late from work. I know these are ordinary problems, I tell Michael. I'm angry all over again. Most married couples go through them. Mark and I will just never get the chance, to work our way through them.

Michael hugs me. We're standing in front of a Victorian bed and breakfast. Its walkways are planted in a riot of red geraniums. They're everywhere, ferocious, defiant. He bends down and starts pulling up two of the plants by their roots. Don't just stand there, he whispers, dig! I manage to dislodge two plants of my own from the moist, salty ground. We continue down the street, clutching geraniums like puppies in our arms. There's a guest house farther along, he tells me, that doesn't have a single flower in front of it, just a fence with half the pickets missing. When we get there, we dig four evenly spaced holes along the sidewalk. We hum 'Enough is Enough' while we transplant our geraniums where they will be better appreciated.

Back at his guest house. He insists I stay over, it would be crazy for me to drive home at this hour. I follow him inside. He takes a key from a hook behind the desk. We don't go up to the attic though. He leads me to Room 6, lucky six. Six months later. We get undressed and climb into bed. And again I realize I'm starving. But I relax into it. I recognize this skin hunger for what it is. I snuggle my shoulder-blades into Michael's chest. He buries his nose in the nape of my neck. Soon he is sleeping, soon I am on Nantucket.

6. Whale-watching

The four of us drive to Hyannis in Gabe's Cadillac. The top's down and we're playing the AM radio full-blast. Gabe and Peter are in the front seat, holding hands. Michael and I are snuggled low in the back, out of the wind. We're running late, it's ten-twenty by the time we pull into the airport parking lot. We race up to the ticket counter, breathless. The plane hasn't left, there are exactly four seats left. Gabe throws it all on his credit card. We'll sort the money thing out at the end of the day, on the ferry back.

There are only eight seats so what we weigh matters. I'm instructed to sit next to the pilot because I'm the lightest. Gabe and Michael are told to take the next two seats. Peter, to his horror, has to sit with a nun. Two more nuns bring up the rear. Pretty unlikely we'll crash today, the pilot whispers, firing up the engines. We fly right through any of the puffy white clouds in our path. In twenty minutes we are at Nantucket airport. We jump into a taxi. It's driven by a little old lady. She takes us to the cobbled centre of town. She's completely deaf. The ride costs five dollars.

We find out about a moped rental place from the Information booth. Here we cut a deal with the owner: we'll only pay twenty-five dollars each, half his regular rate. He has no choice. It's probably the only hundred he'll make today. We promise to return the scooters before the four o'clock ferry. After our safety lesson, we head for the opposite end of the island, racing each other, attempting Shriner formations. Along the way we pass lighthouses and cornfields, weather-beaten old cottages. We wish we lived here. We hope this day will never end. Enormous sunflowers bow down to us as we careen by.

In Siasconset we stop at the package store and buy an embarrassingly large bottle of screw-top cabernet. We drive our mopeds right on to the beach. We take all sorts of photos of each other with Peter's camera, because we've forgotten to take any at the bonfire: Peter and Gabe, Michael and I, all four of us together with the automatic timer. All of us alone. We lie in a heap and whale-watch. Michael thinks he sees one, but he doesn't really. It's just the crest of an unusually large wave.

We're back in Nantucket village with barely enough time to board the ferry. We've sprung for first class – it only costs twenty-one dollars. There's a free platter of sweaty cheese cubes and a full bar. We order wine and gobble half the cheese while old ladies and men look on, sternly. We've been behaving badly for almost twenty-four hours. Why in hell should we stop now?

Stop now.

You're not going to Nantucket tomorrow, Simona. You're going to let Peter have his own private day with Gabriel. But you know exactly how it will go: the plane, the nuns, the taxi, the mopeds, the sunflowers, the beach. You can imagine every single detail of it because you've been there before. You honeymooned on Nantucket with Mark. It was Mark who thought he saw a whale at Siasconset beach.

Let Gabe and Peter stand at the bow of the ferry alone as it pulls into Hyannis harbour. Allow them a passionate goodbye kiss. Gabe is going to have to get into his Cadillac and drive home to Truro alone. Peter is going to have to take that long bus ride up to Boston. Gabe's lover is on his way back from New Jersey, Peter has school to think about now. They may never see each other again.

And you, Simona. Tomorrow *you* are going to head back to Wellfleet with an enormous hangover. You're packing everything back up into the trunk of your car – the peaches and sandwich meat, your watercolours and paperback mysteries – and you're driving straight up to Boston to claim your daughter. And tomorrow night, Simona, you and Phoebe are going to have a real dinner together. *No sweetie, your daddy loved us very much but he's not coming home. He can't. Ever. It's just you and me now, OK?*

But tonight, tonight you're going to lie here in Michael's arms. And the two of you are going to sleep the sleep of the dead.

BIOGRAPHICAL NOTES

Trezza Azzopardi is a recent graduate of the Creative Writing MA course at the University of East Anglia. 'A Designated Space' is her first published short story. An extract from her novel-in-progress appears in *Take 20*, the most recent UEA anthology.

Alan Beard's short stories have been broadcast on Radio 4 and have appeared in various magazines and anthologies, including *London Magazine*, *Panurge*, *Critical Quarterly* and *Best Short Stories 1991*. His début collection, *Taking Doreen Out of the Sky*, was published by the Tindal Street Fiction Group and the rights were bought by Picador. Married with two children, he lives and works in Birmingham.

Gabriel Brown. 'Not That Funny' forms part of Gabriel Brown's novel *The Erotic Adventures of B*, which is seeking a publisher. Born in London in 1970, he lives in Notting Hill and, apart from writing fiction, performing poetry and making short films, he is unemployed.

Christopher Burns, who lives in Whitehaven, Cumbria, is the author of five novels – *Snakewrist*, *The Flint Bed*, *The Condition of Ice*, *In the Houses of the West* and *Dust Raising* – and one short-story collection, *About the Body*.

John Burnside was born in 1955 and now lives in Fife. He is the author of several collections of poetry, including *Swimming in the Flood* and *A Normal Skin*, and one novel, *The Dumb House*. He has won a number of awards, including the Geoffrey Faber Memorial Prize, and was selected as one of the twenty Best of Young British Poets in 1994.

Ron Butlin was born in 1949 in Edinburgh and brought up in Hightae near Dumfries. A novelist, short-story writer and poet, he lives in Edinburgh with his wife and their dog. His books include a short-story collection, *The Tilting Room*, and two novels, *The Sound of My Voice* and *Night Visits*. His work has been translated into ten languages and broadcast in Britain, Europe and the USA.

Art Corriveau was raised in a small farm community in Vermont, graduated from Boston University and received an MFA in fiction writing from the University of Michigan. As a freelance consultant to the international travel industry he has worked in the USA, France, England and the Netherlands. He now lives in Boston, where he is working on his first novel; his shorter work was featured in *First Fictions 13* (Faber and Faber).

Emma Donoghue is a novelist, playwright, anthologist, biographer, screenwriter and broadcaster. Born in Dublin in 1969, she now lives in Cambridge. Her books include *Stir-Fry*, *Hood* and *Kissing the Witch*; her short stories have been published in anthologies in Ireland, Britain, the USA and Canada.

Louise Doughty is a novelist, critic and broadcaster. Her first novel was *Crazy Paving*, which was shortlisted for four awards, among them the John Llewellyn Rhys Prize. It was followed by *Dance with Me*. Her most recent novel is *Honey-Dew*, which she is adapting for film. She has also won awards for short stories and radio drama. She lives in north London.

Christopher Fowler is the author of eight novels – *Roofworld*, *Rune*, *Red Bride*, *Darkest Day*, *Spanky*, *Psychoville*, *Disturbia* and *Soho Black* – and five short-story collections – *City Jitters*, *The Bureau of Lost Souls*, *Sharper Knives*, *Flesh Wounds* and *Personal Demons*. He lives in north London and is the director of the Creative Partnership, a film promotion business based in Soho.

Jason Gould was born in 1971 in Hull, and works in local government. He has had fiction published in, or forthcoming from, *The Third Alternative*, *The Third Alternative's Guide to the Millennium* (edited by Allen Ashley), *Kimota*, *Nasty Piece of Work*, *Lateral Moves*, *Dreams from the Strangers' Café* and other magazines; and on the Internet, at *Gothic.Net*, *Infinity Plus* and *Masters of Terror*. He is currently at work on his first novel.

Bonnie Greer was born in Chicago in 1948. Married, she now lives in London. Her plays have been produced in Chicago, New York, Utrecht and London, and broadcast on Radio 4. Her first novel, *Hanging by Her Teeth*, was published by Serpent's Tail, who will publish her new novel in 2000. 'The Big Picture' will appear in her first collection, *Eating Grits with Princess Di and Other Tales of African-American Women Abroad*, due in 1999.

Hannah Griffiths was born in Pontypool in 1971 and brought up in Cardiff. She quit London to live on a ranch in the Rocky Mountains but returned to set up the Literary Consultancy in 1996. 'Umph' is her first published short story.

Hilaire grew up in Melbourne and has lived in London since 1986. Her stories have appeared in *Metropolitan*, *ABeSea*, *Writing Women*, *em one* and the anthologies *5 Uneasy Pieces* and *The Ex Files*. She is currently working on a novel, for which she has been awarded a grant by the Australia Council.

BIOGRAPHICAL NOTES   327

Brian Howell was born in London in 1961, and has been writing fiction since 1990, during which time he has taught English in England, Hungary, the Czech Republic and Japan. He has had stories published in anthologies, magazines and newspapers, including *Panurge*, *Critical Quarterly* and the *European*. In 1996 he completed the UEA creative writing course and he is currently working on a fictional biography of the painter Jan Vermeer. He is married with one son and lives near Tokyo.

Christopher Kenworthy was born in Preston in 1968, and has lived in Garstang, Ludlow, Bath, London and Western Australia. He ran the influential independent press Barrington Books and edited three anthologies of original short fiction by new writers, *The Sun Rises Red*, *Sugar Sleep* and *The Science of Sadness*. His own first collection, *Will You Hold Me?*, is published by the Do-Not Press. His first novel is forthcoming from Serpent's Tail.

Toby Litt was born in 1968 and grew up in Ampthill, Bedfordshire. His collection of short stories, *Adventures in Capitalism*, was published in 1996. He has recently adapted his first novel, *Beatniks*, for the screen.

Derek Marlowe, who was born just outside London in 1938 and died in Los Angeles in 1996, was the author of nine novels – *A Dandy in Aspic*, *The Memoirs of a Venus Lackey*, *A Single Summer with LB*, *Echoes of Celandine*, *Do You Remember England?*, *Somebody's Sister*, *Nightshade*, *The Rich Boy from Chicago*, *Nancy Astor* – published between 1966 and 1982. He adapted *A Dandy in Aspic* for the screen; *Echoes of Celandine* was also filmed, as *The Disappearance*, leading to a reissue of the novel under that title. Although he worked increasingly as a screenwriter, he had started a new novel that was left unfinished on his death. Its working title was *Black and White*.

China Miéville was born in 1972. He graduated from Cambridge in 1994, and is studying for a PhD in International Relations at the London School of Economics. He has written reviews and commentary for magazines and fanzines, and has worked as an illustrator and comic-strip artist. His first novel, *King Rat*, is published by Macmillan. He has always lived in London.

James Miller was born in London in 1976. His short stories have been published in *The Third Alternative*, *Violent Spectres*, *Time Out Net Books*, *Dreams from the Strangers' Café*, *Last Rites & Resurrections*, *A Book of Two Halves*, *Dark Terrors 2* and *The Ex Files*.

Tim Nickels was born in Torquay, Devon, in 1960, and has had numerous stories published in magazines and anthologies, including *BBR*, *The Third Alternative*, *The Science of Sadness* and *The Ex Files*. He runs a hotel in Salcombe, Devon.

Fred Normandale was born in 1948 in Scarborough. After twenty-seven years at sea, he came ashore in 1991 to concentrate on the administration side of running seven fishing boats and a fishing vessel agency. The chairman of Scarborough Inshore Fishermen's Society, president of Scarborough Sea Cadets and honorary secretary of

328 BIOGRAPHICAL NOTES

Scarborough Lifeboat, he began writing in an effort to record a way of life that is dying out. 'Fishy Tales', extracted from a longer project, is the first such work he has published.

John O'Connell was born in 1972 and grew up in Staffordshire. He now lives and works in London. 'Me and the Rest of the World' is his first published short story.

Mike O'Driscoll spent six years running a video store in Swansea and is currently completing the final year of an Open University arts degree. His stories have appeared in a number of anthologies, including *Off Limits*, *Lethal Kisses*, *Darklands 2*, *Noirotica 3*, *Cold Cuts* and *The Sun Rises Red*, and in magazines such as *The Third Alternative*, *BBR*, *Interzone*, *Fear*, *Far Point* and *Crime Wave*.

Colm O'Gaora was born in Dublin in 1966. His short stories have been widely published, anthologized and broadcast, and have appeared in *Cosmopolitan*, *Best Short Stories 1991* and elsewhere. *Giving Ground*, his first collection, was published in 1993. His first novel, *A Crooked Field*, will be published by Picador in January 1999. He lives in Blackrock, County Dublin.

Stephen O'Reilly was born in York in 1967. When he was five his family moved back to Ireland, where he lived in Donegal and Dublin. He has had a variety of jobs, ranging from fairground attendant to IT manager. Currently working on his first novel, he now lives in London. 'The Ball' is his first published short story.

G. A. Pickin was born in 1952 and lives in south-west Scotland with her partner and twin daughters. Her work has appeared in several anthologies, including two volumes of *New Scottish Writing*.

David Rose has published short stories and other pieces in *Main Street Journal*, *em two*, *Panurge*, *Literary Review*, *Iron*, *Odyssey* and *Northwords*. Born in 1949, he lives in Middlesex and works for the post office.

Cath Skinner was born in 1968, and has worked in New York, Guatemala City and London; she currently lives in Manchester. She has been writing for five years and 'Spaces' is her first published short story.

Conrad Williams's short stories have appeared in a wide variety of anthologies and magazines, including *Sunk Island Review*, *Panurge*, *A Book of Two Halves*, *Dark Terrors 2 & 3*, *Northern Stories 4*, *Darklands 2*, *Blue Motel* and *A BeSea*. His first novel, *Head Injuries*, was published in 1998 by the Do-Not Press in their new fiction imprint, Frontlines, and has since been optioned by Revolution Films for whom he is currently writing a script. Born in Warrington in 1969, he now lives in London.

APPENDIX

An incomplete list of literary magazines that publish short stories.

Ambit
(Martin Bax)
17 Priory Gardens
London N6
mainstream/literary

Back Brain Recluse
(Chris Reed)
PO Box 625
Sheffield S1 3GY
e-mail bbr@fdgroup.co.uk
website
http://www.syspace.co.uk/bbr/magazine
SF/fantasy

Billy Liar
New Writing North
7/8 Trinity Chare
Quayside
Newcastle upon Tyne NE1 3DF
tel 0191 232 9991
fax 0191 230 1883
mainstream/new writers/youth

The Devil
247 Gray's Inn Road
London WC1X 8JR
tel/fax 0181 994 7767
e-mail thedevil@play-333.demon.co.uk
website
http://www.play-333.demon.co.uk
mainstream/literary

The Edge
(Graham Evans)
111 Guinness Buildings
Fulham Palace Road
London W6 8BQ
tel 0181 741 7757
e-mail houghtong@globalnet.co.uk
website
http://www.users.globalnet.co.uk/~~houghtong/edge1.htm
Sinclair/Moorcock/horror/SF

em writing & music
(Karl Sinfield)
PO Box 10553
London N1 2GD
tel 0956 671138
fax 0171 704 8580
e-mail karl@em.sonnet.co.uk
website http://www.sonnet.co.uk/em
mainstream/weird/new writers

Entropy
(Gareth Evans and Ben Slater)
10B Narford Road
London
E5 8RD
tel 0181 806 6272
Sinclair/Erickson/cultish

Interzone
(David Pringle)
217 Preston Drove
Brighton BN1 6FL
tel 01273 504710

e-mail interzone@cix.compulink.co.uk
SF/fantasy

London Magazine
(Alan Ross)
30 Thurloe Place
London SW7
tel 0171 589 0618
mainstream/literary

Main Street Journal
(John Moser)
29 Princes Road
Ashford
Middx TW15 2LT
mainstream/beat

The Third Alternative
(Andy Cox)
5 Martins Lane
Witcham
Ely
Cambs CB6 2LB
tel 01353 777931
email TTAPress@aol.com
website
http://members.aol.com/ttaldyer/index
slipstream/literary/horror/SF

This Is
(Carol Cornish)
Writing Space Publications
PO Box 16185
London NW1 8ZH
tel 0171 586 0244
fax 0171 586 5666
email Writingspace@btinternet.com
website
http://www.btinternet.com/~writingspace/thisis
mainstream/literary

Most of the above rely on subscriptions to survive. Contact them for details. To purchase individual copies, try the following shops in London, or call the magazine and ask where they are distributed:

Dillons
82 Gower Street
London WC1E 6EQ
(0171 636 1577)

Dillons Arts Bookshop
8 Long Acre
London WC2E 9LH
(0171 836 1359)

ICA Bookshop
The Mall
London SW1Y 5AH
(0171 925 2434)

Compendium
234 Camden High Street
London NW1 8QS
(0171 485 8944)